the money book

Other books by Jasmine Birtles

A Bit on the Side
A Girl's Best Friend Is Her Money
A Woman's Little Instruction Book
A Man's Little Instruction Book
A Mother's Little Instruction Book
A Father's Little Instruction Book
A Sister's Little Instruction Book
A Brother's Little Instruction Book
A Grandparent's Little Instruction Book
A Cat-lover's Little Instruction Book
A Dieter's Little Instruction Book
A Student's Little Instruction Book
A Little Book of Abuse
A Little Book of More Abuse
A Little Book of Excuses
Bollox Detox
He Says Mars, She Says Venus
The Top Notch Nannies' Guide
The Top Notch Nannies' Guide for the Millennium

JASMINE BIRTLES

the mney book

Control Your Money, Control Your Life

PIATKUS

The moral right of the author has been asserted

A catalogue record for this book is available from the British Library

ISBN 0 7499 2677 5

This book has been printed on paper manufactured with respect for the environment using wood from managed sustainable resources

Edited by Andy
Text design by Paul Saunders

Typeset by
Action Publishing Technology Ltd, Gloucester
Printed and bound in Great Britain by
MPG Books, Bodmin, Cornwall

Contents

Acknowledgements

Big thanks to my researcher, Alison Tarleton, who helped a lot with many of the chapters and made a mean cup of tea. Also thanks for the help and information I received from financial journalist friends including Julian Knight (BBC website), Sam Dunn (*Independent on Sunday*), David Kuo (Motley Fool), Cliff D'Arcy (Motley Fool), Jane Mack (Motley Fool) and Maisha Frost (Daily Express). Thanks, as always, to my hugely supportive agent, Euan Thorneycroft, editor Alan Brooke and all the team at Piatkus. My love and gratitude go, again, to my mother for her inspiration and my friend Tom Johnsen for his continuous support.

Introduction

'Money can't buy you happiness but it can buy you the kind of misery you prefer.'

– Anon

'**Control your life by** controlling your money' – an over-confident statement? Perhaps. Certainly there are many aspects of life, other than money, that can affect our experience but if you're in control of your spending and saving on a day-to-day basis you will find yourself *much* more in control of your life and destiny than you ever were before.

That's the point of this book – it's to put *you* in control of your money rather than shops, financial institutions, the media or your relatives. You don't have to be a mathematical genius, or even good with numbers to do it. You just have to have common sense, an ability to read and count and a willingness to learn and change your thinking and habits. Once you change your attitude to money – and to life generally actually – the rest will follow.

How to use this book:

1. Read it – at least the sections relevant to you. Actually, you'd be surprised how many people just put books like this on their shelves assuming that they will gain the knowledge in them through a process of osmosis.

2. Pay most attention to the general principles in it rather than the specifics to start off with. You can always check up on the specific rules, percentages and contacts in the various websites mentioned later on. The most important thing is that you develop a new way of thinking about your finances.

3. Once you've read the book, keep yourself generally informed about money, new rules, new products, Budget changes, etc, by reading the money pages in the Sunday papers every now and then or looking at some of the general money websites.

4. Don't worry, don't panic and don't think it's all hopeless just because you've never saved and you don't know how you will get out of the mess you're in now. You can and you will. Just give yourself time.

The wonder of websites

You will notice throughout the book that I constantly refer to websites as the source of the most current information. The reason is that things change so frequently in the world of money – new products come on the market almost every day, new rules come into effect a few times a year and certainly new statistics come to light each week – that it's just not possible to give up-to-date, specific information in a book. It goes out of date far too quickly. Websites, on the other hand, can be changed within minutes so they are the best place to go for the very latest savings accounts, mortgages, government rules and legislation that has just come into effect.

If you don't have access to the Internet at home go to your local library. There are many Internet cafes about, of course, but they tend to charge while most libraries don't. The local library is also a wonderful place to borrow books for free and look up all kinds of useful reference works that could make you money (directories of grant-making bodies, books on how to run a business and directories of agents and businesses that could find you work, for example) so don't neglect the place. Why pay if you can get it for free?

Why bother learning about money?

I worked out, recently, that on average we are ripped off in a lifetime to the tune of about £500,000 each. Just add up the amount we're over-charged by shops, department stores, restaurants, travel companies, car showrooms and other retail outlets together with the huge amount we're swindled out of by mortgage and loans companies and advisers selling us badly performing pensions and investments, not to mention the outright criminal fraud that most of us fall prey to once or more in our lives, and you see how it can get to that level. Half a million is a lot of dosh and we would be better off with it in our own pockets. But so long as we remain as children in our financial knowledge, all of these organisations will continue to fleece us without our even knowing it.

It really is only our own knowledge and understanding that can protect us. Business is business and our economy rests on the profitability of our major companies, and, in the service culture that we have become, some of the biggest and most profitable companies are the financial firms. Look at the FTSE 100 (the index of Britain's top 100 companies) and you will see that the main financial companies are all up there. London is a world centre for finance, second only to New York, and the health of our economy largely rests on the profitability of what we call the City (the financial district in London). The problem is, much of that profitability depends on you and me giving our money to them.

Of course, no one in government wants to rock the boat within our financial services sector. Frankfurt with its sophisticated financial district is waiting in the wings to take over from London as Europe's main money centre. The City needs to be cosseted and cherished by the government in order to keep it strong, and indeed it is. Even the Financial Services Authority (FSA) has a dual role as both a regulator of the industry and a promoter of its services, which means that although it can and does impose rules on financial companies, it still allows the sector as much freedom as possible in order to keep business going.

In other words, we're on our own. If we want to make money, or at the very least stop losing it, we have to arm ourselves with financial knowledge so that we can spot bad and expensive products, stop ourselves being ripped off and wrest control of our money from those who would take it from us.

We have a lot of catching up to do, too. Most of us have had no financial education at school and may have had bad role models at home. We have been thrown out, clueless, into a world where businesses of all kinds use ever more sophisticated tactics to take our money from us. Supermarkets and department stores use psychologists to work out which smells, colours, lights, sounds and words will make us buy more; banks use our ignorance of financial terms and products to take regular amounts of money from us each month; international fraudsters use clever tricks on the Internet, over the phone and in the mail to swindle money from the unwary. It's war out there, and we're losing the battle because we don't have the weapons to defend ourselves.

With this book and with your continuing interest in financial matters (you don't have to spend years on it, just an hour or two once in a while) you will gradually increase your armoury. You will become your own financial adviser, banker, stockbroker and pension-planner. Most of all, you will have more control over your life, you will have more freedom to do the things you want to do, you will be able to fund your future and that of your family and you will have money to give where it's needed. After all, once you have enough to cover your needs, money is like manure: if you just store it up it becomes a useless, stinking pile but if you spread it around it can turn into something beautiful!

1

What Are You Living For?

'Money is better than poverty, if only for financial reasons.'

– Woody Allen

Money is a part of life and there's no point looking at it in isolation from the rest of your experience. So, before launching into the nitty-gritty of how to spend and how to save it, it's a good idea to step back and consider what's important in your life and how money can help support, rather than hinder, your happiness. Think about what you want in life, what your goals are (if you have any – actually, if you don't have any now would be a good time to set some!), how much money you really need to achieve these things and how you really want to live.

Get the balance

Money is not to be revered or feared. It's not the most important thing in life, but equally it isn't something you should ignore. If you ignore money, it will go away – or be taken away by one of the many institutions that love to take our money from us. Money is an essential for most of the things we need to do and for many of the things we *want* to do. In fact, in terms of importance in our lives, I think our finances rank pretty high – just after health and relationships.

Money is something we need to get right (which, of course, you know or you wouldn't be reading this book), but it's only a *part* of life. It's a good idea to try to accumulate enough over a working life to be independent and secure later on, particularly as we are, in large measure, coming out of several decades of state support and going into a much less secure time of only partial state funding. If you're under forty you won't have had much help with the costs of being a student and you can't look forward to anything like as much financial support for your old age that your parents expected.

However, it's important to see money in the context of your *whole* life. Generally, to amass a large amount of money – unless you inherit it or marry it – you will have to work for it, usually doing something boring but lucrative or doing very long hours to make the extra cash. So ask yourself: are you really aiming at being a millionaire (or rather a multimillionaire, since various surveys recently have found that a million isn't enough to support the millionaire lifestyle any more)? Is it the material luxury life that makes you happy and satisfied? It may be, but it may also be that you would be happier doing much less work and spending more time with the family or with your favourite hobby or charity.

The way to get a balance in your life, financially and emotionally, is to stop and think about your whole life for a while. Think about what you really love in life. Even write a list. You'll find that many of the things – or people – on that list have nothing to do with money. As they say, the best things in life are free – and it's true. However, many things *do* cost, so work out which of the things you love do cost money and resolve to spend your money on those things, and *save* money on the things that don't matter so much to you.

If you love travelling, for example, but you don't care about clothes and cars and gizmos, then save your money for travel and buy your clothes in charity shops or sales, take the bus or walk and pick up things you need at the local car boot sale or on eBay. Whatever you love or don't love in life, though, make sure you never spend more than you need to on the basics of life (household bills, food, cleaning products and so forth). The more you have your day-to-day spending under control, the more money will be freed up for you to invest in your fabulous future and spend now on things that make life worth living.

Take control

Learning about how to run your finances is like learning about nutrition. You don't have to be a fully qualified nutritionist to know how to eat healthily, but you do need to have some of the basic facts about what's a healthy, balanced diet. It's also a good idea to keep up with new, healthy recipes and health discoveries about food. It's the same with money. You don't need to be a financial adviser or City investor with qualifications and years of experience behind you to run your finances properly. However, you do need some knowledge of the basic principles of saving and spending, how to invest and what your rights are. You should also keep an eye on your spending and investing every now and then, checking that you're not paying too much for things and that your investments are on track.

Once you have the principles and your whole mindset has shifted from fear of money or a need to spend, whatever the cost, to a balanced, controlled attitude towards your finances, you'll find yourself becoming much more stable financially. After a while, you'll also be surprised at just how much money you've been able to accumulate without noticing. Once you're armed with the knowledge of where to look for facts, tips and money updates (mostly on websites, as you will see in the rest of the book), you will hardly ever need to consult a financial adviser, investment adviser or a personal banker ever again!

The fact is that no one – not your Mum, not your Dad, not even your best friend and certainly not your financial adviser – has your financial future as much at heart as you do. And no one else knows better than you what is most important to you in life and what you really want to do with your money. So no one is better than you at investing your money. Seriously, once you get the basic facts about spending, saving and controlling your money, you will do better than the City boys at making money for yourself.

What does money mean to you?

As well as thinking about what you really want to *do* with your money, stand back and think about your own *attitude* to money, saving and spending. Most of the things we do in life we do on automatic pilot. Even if we think we make our own decisions, much of the time we don't – we just copy others or pick up on the thoughts and attitudes around us, adopting them as our own. So stop for a moment. Actually question what your attitudes are. Ask yourself why you spend a lot or why you are basically a bit tight (admit it to yourself). Is it because of the way your parents thought about money – perhaps you're copying them or reacting against their behaviour – or are you basically following the general trend in our current culture of spending for the sake of spending?

Our behaviour with money is often impelled by our fears and desires in life. The psychological impulses behind the way we spend or save can be quite deep-rooted but, unlike some other financial writers, I don't believe they're difficult to change. We're not imprisoned by our past or by the thoughts of our parents any more than we want to be. It may take work, but, if you really want to change the way you deal with money (whether you're a tightwad or whether you spend for Britain), you certainly can, and following the instructions in this book will really help you along the way.

Money and happiness

Don't make the mistake that so many of us make of thinking that having a lot of money would solve all your problems and give you a happier life. Having a lot of money can make life easier, but too much can blight a life just as much as too little. Look at the experiences of Michael Jackson, Howard Hughes, Gloria Vanderbilt and Christina Onassis, to mention just a few 'poor little rich people', if you don't believe that too much money can hurt.

The desire to be rich is as old as time and quite reasonable, particularly as it's connected with basic human needs of security, survival and comfort. Certainly, being poor is not something we should aspire to. Being in debt is even worse and health professionals now point to debt as a major cause of stress, which, in turn, can lead to health problems.

However, riches are strongly linked in our minds with happiness, and always have been. That's where philosophers, divines and now even economists tell us we're making a big mistake. For example, the first important study of general happiness in America, by the economist Richard Easterlin, found that, once a country achieves a certain level of wealth, getting richer makes no difference to the general feeling of well-being of the population. And a well-known 1978 study of lottery winners in the US found that, a year after hitting the jackpot, they were barely happier than the rest of us.

Perhaps a person's intense desire to be rich is connected to their lack of a religious life or genuine spirituality. If an individual, or a nation, believes there's nothing outside of matter or material living the obvious conclusion is that the only measure of wealth is the amount of matter that you have. Then, as happiness and a sense of self is so closely linked to material goods and sensations in this way of thinking, the only way we believe we can be happy is to have more material goods, more material experiences and therefore more money to buy them.

In fact, the opposite tends to be true. Once you have enough of an income to cover your basic needs, giving it away tends to make people happier than accumulating more. Happiness studies say time and again that the things that really make us glad include volunteering, going to church, being with close friends and family and taking part in group activities. It's people, basically, and human interaction that lift the heart and make the world brighter, and the more we give (in terms of ourselves, our time and our money) quite often the happier we get.

It's no surprise, then, that the small and intensely Buddhist kingdom of Bhutan is currently, and in all seriousness, trying to work out its Gross National Happiness (GNH). So rather than look at its success as a country from a narrowly economic calculation of Gross National or Gross Domestic Product, it's trying to gauge its richness by the happiness of its people. It's an interesting approach, although, in the interest of balance, I would say that any individual or nation should take note of both once in a while. We need to be happy, but it's hard to be really happy if you can't afford to eat.

The Fisherman

One day a fisherman was lying on a beautiful beach, with his fishing pole propped up in the sand and his solitary line cast out into the sparkling blue surf. He was enjoying the warmth of the afternoon sun and the prospect of catching a fish.

About that time, a businessman came walking down the beach, trying to relieve some of the stress of his work day. He noticed the fisherman sitting on the beach and decided to find out why this fisherman was fishing instead of working harder to make a living for himself and his family.

continues ➤

'You aren't going to catch many fish that way,' said the businessman to the fisherman. 'You should be working rather than lying on the beach!'

The fisherman looked up at the businessman, smiled and replied, 'And what will my reward be?'

'Well, you can get bigger nets and catch more fish!' was the businessman's answer.

'And then what will my reward be?' asked the fisherman, still smiling.

The businessman replied, 'You will make money and you'll be able to buy a boat, which will then result in larger catches of fish!'

'And then what will my reward be?' asked the fisherman again.

The businessman was beginning to get a little irritated with the fisherman's questions. 'You can buy a bigger boat, and hire some people to work for you!' he said.

'And then what will my reward be?' repeated the fisherman.

The businessman was getting angry. 'Don't you understand? You can build up a fleet of fishing boats, sail all over the world, and let all your employees catch fish for you!'

Once again the fisherman asked, 'And then what will my reward be?'

The businessman was red with rage and shouted at the fisherman, 'Don't you understand that you can become so rich that you will never have to work for your living again! You can spend all the rest of your days sitting on this beach, looking at the sunset. You won't have a care in the world!'

The fisherman, still smiling, looked up and said, 'And what do you think I'm doing right now?'

'It's good to have money and the things that money can buy, but it's good, too, to check up once in a while and make sure that you haven't lost the things that money can't buy.'

– **George Horace Lorimer**

2

Control Your Finances, Control Your Life

'I have always lived beyond my means. I am still trying to live beyond my means, but it's getting harder all the time. I am very rich.'

– Allan Sherman

Actually, you've already taken the first step towards controlling your finances, because you're reading this book. The greatest tool you can have for controlling your money – and, incidentally, the most lucrative wealth-creating scheme – is knowledge. Knowledge of the basic rules of money and the ways in which others – individuals and financial institutions – can either make money for us or, more often, take it away from us is your number-one weapon in the war against poverty and dependence.

The basics

Opening your bank statements

Go on! You know you want to. They're in that drawer, still in their envelopes, taunting you with the likelihood of their contents. But be strong, open the drawer, open the envelopes and *study* those statements. You *need* to do this because:

- you won't be able to start controlling your money until you do;

- you will get a pretty good idea of where your money is going just by reading these;

- it's *highly* likely that you can *make* money doing this – banks are notorious for making mistakes with our accounts and you won't know they're losing money for you unless you look; financial fraud is on the rise and someone could be taking money out of your account right now, which you won't know about unless you look; and who knows what direct debits or standing orders you might have going out for goods and services you don't use any more?

So do it, open those statements, get them into date order, put them into a file (you may need a few files to sort out your various financial papers), and *use* them as reference material and as a basis for your budgeting and financial planning.

Still worried about taking the first step? Well . . .

- Remind yourself that going through your bank and credit-card statements *could make you money.*

- Realise that, the moment you get the statements out, ordered and filed in date order (with the gaps filled once you ring up the bank and ask for duplicates), you will instantly feel a little more in control of your money and, therefore, your life.

- Tell yourself you'll write and tell me once you've done it (c/o Piatkus Books, 5 Windmill Street, London W1T 2JA, info@piatkus.co.uk) if that helps.

What to keep

Keep, and file, all your bank and credit-card statements, loan statements, utility and phone bills and council tax bills. Certainly keep receipts for any major purchases, together with any guarantees that come with them. Ideally, you should keep these for about five years (or until you throw away the items you've bought). At the end of each year, or financial year if you're self-employed, put all your bills and statements in a storage box and store them away with the other things you don't look at often. Receipts for major items should be put somewhere you can lay your hands on them quickly. Even if your iron goes wrong after two years, you can often get a replacement or money back under the Sale of Goods Act 1979, which covers you for up to *six* years after you've bought the item. In fact, that's a very useful Act to know about, so do look it up on the Department of Trade and Industry's website at **www.dti.gov.uk**.

How to file

Everyone has a different method that works for them, so the best way to do it is to find a way that you like and then stick to it. One idea is to get a large lever-arch file with dividers and simply put each major bill behind the relevant divider each month. You could have a separate file or envelope specifically for purchase receipts, which you keep somewhere you remember. Some people enjoy tracking their income and expenditure on a computer spreadsheet and then cross-referencing with bills and receipts. Others simply shove *everything* into one big shoebox all year, then put the shoebox in the loft at the end. It's up to you, but do have some sort of filing system that you understand *and will use*, so that you can be in control of your paperwork and able to access relevant information when you need it.

How to budget

All right, I'll admit, the word 'budget' has an abandon-hope-all-ye-who-enter kind of a sound to it. It smacks of reducing your lifestyle, dealing with painful and complicated figures and somehow being transported back into the 1950s with coupons and mangles. But, in fact, budgeting is simply another term for controlling your finances. It helps you get a structure and foundation to your quest to become rich and fabulous. Without a budget – even a rough one put together on the back of an envelope – you don't have a starting point.

It's not hard to do one, particularly now that we have the Internet. The Motley Fool (**www.fool.co.uk**) has a lot of information on budgeting, and on **www.moneysavingexpert.com** there's an extremely useful online budget calculator. This one is particularly helpful because it accepts that some regular payments are made annually or weekly, not just monthly, so you can input your weekly, monthly and annual spends into the list and it then calculates it all as a monthly average. Very sophisticated.

This is how you do it:

- Work out how much you *have* to spend each week/month on things such as mortgage/rent, utilities, phone, food, travel and insurance. In fact, while you're working this out, you could find that at least some of these costs can be brought down by shopping around (see Chapter 4 for advice on this).

- If you're in debt, put in the amounts you pay each month for this.

- Now put in how much you feel you can spend on things such as socialising, clothes, holidays. If you're in debt, though, keep these low (and stick to it). You can bleat about having to have your little luxuries if you like but remember: the longer you take to pay off the debt, the more expensive and miserable it is. (See Chapter 4 for *loads* of help on this – there's really no excuse.)

- You *should* have money left over each month (don't worry, most people don't – you're not alone). If you do, and you have debts, put that extra into paying off your debts sharpish. If not, set up a standing order to transfer that into your savings account and/or an investment product (see Chapter 7 for ideas).

- If, at the end of next month, you find you've got less than you thought, rewrite the budget or, better, cut down on some of your spending. If you've got more than you expected (oh, happy day!), put that into your investments too – the more you put in, the more you'll end up with later on and the smugger you'll feel right now.

Keep a spending diary

Actually, this is something everyone should do for a month once every couple of years, even if they're not in debt. Not only is it a fantastic way of working out how all that money just slips through your fingers, but it can help you manage your money, give you a basis for budgeting and, later, show you how much you could be investing each month if you cut back a bit.

Simply keep a notebook with you wherever you go for a month and write down *everything* you spend each day. If it's a newspaper, or a bus fare, or a coffee or a round of drinks, write it all down. At the end of the month, write down your spending in columns ('newspapers', 'travel', 'eating out', 'coffee and sandwiches') or put it into a computer spreadsheet (clever you!) and you'll see where your money is being frittered away on a weekly basis and where you need to cut back.

Divide up your riches

Everyone is different and it doesn't really matter how you divide up your savings, just so long as you do, and that the way you do it makes sense to you. To give you an idea, though, here are a few different pots you should consider. Have at least three of these and you'll be on your way to an easier life.

Pot 1: A 'rainy day' pot

This is an emergency fund that should not be touched unless you suddenly lose your income through job loss or sickness or similar. Ideally, you should have three to six months' worth of money in it. (*Now* are you pleased you set a budget? You now know how much you need to keep going for a whole month.) In fact, all the big and successful multimillionaire investors say that you should have this fund stashed away before you start investing seriously. This money should be put in a high-interest account – probably in a postal one so that you're less tempted to dip into it every now and then.

Pot 2: Repairs' pot

You know how assistants in electrical shops try to sell you warranties whenever you buy an appliance? These are grossly overpriced and regularly unused, since most appliances don't go wrong for years now, and, even if they do, they usually cost much less to mend than the price of the warranty. Do yourself a favour: set up a small savings account purely to pay repair bills. You could just put £10–20 a month into it. The joy of this system is that you have the peace of mind of knowing that if something does go wrong you'll be able to get it fixed, and if nothing goes wrong you will be making money on your savings rather than losing it on the insurance product.

Pots 3/4/5/6: Holiday pot/car pot/Christmas pot/big-purchase pot

. . . or put all into one general savings pot. Yes, I know it's easy just to stick all these things on your credit cards but that's where debt tends to start – and grow. We've got to get back to the tried and tested method of actually saving for something we want rather than buying it now and paying through the nose for it later in interest payments and fees.

Pot 4 (or 7, depending on how you count it): Future pot

This is where 'savings' crosses over into 'investment' (see Chapter 9). These 'savings' are also your 'retirement fund' – the money you put aside every month into one or more products that will make you money each year and grow into a sizeable nest egg for your golden years. It's up to you how much you put in each month but, as a rule of thumb, you should use the figure that is half your age and use that as the percentage of your net income that you stash away. So if you're 30, for example, you should be investing at least 15 per cent of your before-tax income each year for your future. However, much more on that in Chapter 10, 'Your Future'.

But what if my income isn't regular?

Good question. My income has always been irregular, so I know what it's like. Essentially, you need to do everything suggested above, but more so. When your income is irregular, you need to create even *more* financial stability for yourself than those who are employed.

For a start, you badly need to create a cash cushion for yourself, and it's more urgent that you invest for your future because no one else is going to do it for you. Keep these points in mind:

- Always aim to keep your overheads as low as possible. Get out of debt as soon as you can; cut your outgoings back to a minimum until you have enough money saved to keep you going for a few lean months.

- Set up a separate savings account into which you put 10 per cent of your income each month. This is to cover your tax, which you'll have to pay twice a year.

- In *another* savings account, save up enough money to cover you for three to six months. This is *essential* for the self-employed or those on an irregular income.

- Make sure that you invest enough each month into your retirement savings. Use your age as a guide: halve your age and use that as a percentage of your gross income. Put that amount of money – over the period of a year – into whatever vehicle(s) you are using to create a wealthy retirement.

- Consider how you would keep going if you were unable to work for a year or more. Do you have a fall-back option? If not, look into taking out critical-illness insurance or income-protection insurance.

- Join the union and/or trade association connected to your profession. You can often get free or cheap legal advice and insurance with these as well as the support and connection with others doing the same thing as you.

Create wealth in half a day per year

Keeping your costs down, keeping on top of your finances and, therefore, saving yourself a packet each year really doesn't need to be the time-consuming nightmare it seems. Just spend a few hours here and there checking prices on a few online comparison sites and you'll soon get yourself into the best-value deals all round. This is what you do:

Once a year

Check your major outgoings for cheaper versions on one or more of these websites:

Cheaper everything: **www.fool.co.uk, www.moneysavingexpert.com, www.onecompare.com, www.moneyextra.co.uk, www.switchwithwhich.co.uk, www.moneysupermarket.com**

Cheaper mortgages: **www.moneysupermarket.com, www.charcolonline.co.uk, www.moneyfacts.co.uk, www.easyquote.co.uk, www.moneynet.co.uk**

Cheaper insurance: **www.insuresupermarket.com, www.moneyfacts.co.uk, www.find.co.uk, www.the-aa.com, www.kwik-fit.co.uk**

Cheaper utilities: **www.moneysavingexpert.com, www.uswitch.com, www.buy.com**

Cheaper phone and Internet: **www.moneysavingexpert.com, www.switchwithwhich.co.uk, www.adslguide.org.uk, www.broadbandchecker.co.uk**

Also, see Chapter 5, 'Financial One-upmanship Day to Day', for many other ways of cutting costs all round.

Once a month

File your pay-slips, bills statements and any information sent to you about tax or investments.

Once a week, or more often if you like

- Check your bank accounts and credit cards online, particularly if you make a lot of transactions. Checking your statements regularly will help protect you from fraud because you'll see early on if someone is using your identity or your card. It can also mean that you can stop yourself going overdrawn and being charged through the nose for it!

- Make a mental tally of how much you've spent this week (or have a look at your spending diary). Cut out some luxuries next week if you've overspent. Give yourself a treat if you've underspent your budget.

Useful contacts

The Motley Fool – **www.fool.co.uk**
MoneySavingExpert – **www.moneysavingexpert.com**
BBC website – **www.bbc.co.uk/money**
Financial Services Authority budget planner – look it up at **www.fsa.gov.uk**
Inland Revenue – **www.hmrc.gov.uk**
DWP – **www.dwp.gov.uk**
Directgov – **www.direct.gov.uk**

3

Dump Your Debt, Live Cheaper, Make Money

'I am having an out-of-money experience.'

– Anon

This is the start of your journey towards riches. Really! If you're needing to read this chapter it means that, like millions of others, you're in some level of debt and you want to do something about it. Good. Just by facing the fact that you owe money and need to get free of the debt trap, you're taking a big step towards controlling your finances and, therefore, controlling your life.

Of course, the financial companies don't want you to get out of debt. Billions of pounds are poured into their coffers every month through our interest payments. Never before in history have we had access to such large amounts of cash that's not ours – but, then, never before have we had to shell out so much in interest payments. That said, though, don't start putting the blame entirely on them (blood-sucking parasites though they may be). Face it – no one put a gun to your head and forced you to borrow that money to pay for the new car, the holiday or just nice dinners with friends. We have to take ultimate responsibility for our indebtedness, even though it's always so much more satisfying to blame others for our problems.

Debt is the Devil

Right, get a nice fat wad of £20 notes, tear them up into small-ish pieces and flush them down the toilet. Go on. You know you want to. You must enjoy it because, if you're in debt and paying any sort of interest on it, that's what you're doing with your money on a daily basis.

Really, paying interest on debts is like setting fire to fivers. It's that useless. Not only that but it's probably one of the biggest hurdles to becoming rich in the future. Debt costs – big time – and the longer you have it, the more you'll pay and the less chance you have of making money for yourself. Not only that but, thanks to compound interest (see Chapter 9 for an explanation of how that works), debts can mushroom out of control *very* quickly, trapping you in a net of misery faster than you can say, 'Oh, just stick it on my account.'

Not all debt is terrible, though. Mortgage debt – if it's within reason – is a useful tool for most of us and relatively cheap (although see Chapter 8 for lots of information on mortgages). Raising finance to invest in a business – which may bring in more money – is also an acceptable form of debt. The 'bad' debt is money we've spent on things we didn't actually *need* or things that wouldn't make us money later on. In other words, things we should have saved up for first. That's where our change of thinking really needs to start.

Get out of debt

There's no big and clever secret to getting out of debt. Anyone who knows about it will tell you the same basic things. It all boils down to spending less, earning more and putting any money you have left over into paying off your debts. In fact it's rather like dieting:

- With dieting you need to eat less and exercise more, and to keep the weight off you need to change the amount you eat and exercise *for good*.

- In order to get out of debt you need to spend less and, ideally, earn more. To *keep* out of debt and keep making money instead of constantly losing it you need to change the way you deal with money *for good*.

As with dieting, there are various companies out there that will try to make money out of your problem but will offer no lasting solution. Here are a few in order of unpleasantness.

Consolidation loans

This is the worst solution (apart from local loan sharks – see Chapter 11 for information on how to avoid them or deal with them if they trap you). It's the financial equivalent of having your stomach stapled. With this you take out one big loan to pay off all your other debts, leaving you with just one lender to deal with instead of lots of annoying ones. This *can* work but only if:

- you have closed down all your other credit cards, loans and overdraft facilities so that you won't use them;

- you have started to live – and spend – more sensibly;

- you have a loan that is flexible – that is, you can pay it off early if possible;

- the loan is not 'secured' on your home.

The problem with most consolidation loans is that none of these boxes is ticked when people take them out. They take on the new loan, pay off all the other debts, then start using their old credit cards again, ending up with a worse debt than before. Also, if they've attached the loan to their home (as those horrible ads on daytime TV try to encourage us to do), once they get into problems they find the lender can take away the roof over their heads. On paper it looks like a good idea, but the reality is usually terrible.

Remortgaging

Another form of stomach-stapling, remortgaging should be entered into only if you have done the first two points above. Otherwise, although on paper it may seem like a sensible option, given that mortgage rates are generally so much lower than personal loans, it can put you into a far worse state financially. Remember, the last thing you want to do is jeopardise the roof over your head, and by adding to your mortgage you are doing exactly that. If you add your unsecured debt to your home loan, not only will you increase your mortgage expenses each month but, if you suddenly can't pay for a few months, you could lose your house. At least while it's in the form of credit-card bills and bank loans, they can't take your home away from you.

Debt management

This is like joining Weight Watchers – it can work but it'll cost you. Debt-management companies have become the new big thing in recent years. They're all over the country, doing good business out of debtors' misery. Of course, many (though by no means all) are perfectly legitimate and do a good job, but they charge you for something that you could, and should, get free.

Since debt is such a widespread problem now, there are several government and charitable agencies that exist simply to help you out of debt for nothing. National Debtline, the Consumers' Advice Bureau and the Consumer Credit Counselling Service (contact details below) are all there to help you deal with creditors, learn to budget and, if necessary, file for bankruptcy (see page 40 for more information on that).

What *I* would advise

For most people the answer to getting out of debt is pretty straightforward: spend less, save more and throw everything you save into your debts until you've paid them off.

'But,' you wail, 'where do I start?' Good question. Certainly the free-advice agencies mentioned above are a very good place to start and get some sound advice, but they are often too busy to give *all* the help and support the average debtor needs to keep them going, so, while you're contacting them, get yourself on some support networks online. This is where the Internet comes into its own. Just log on to some of these sites and you'll be amazed at the wealth of knowledge and help that is there.

Free support

- National Debtline, your local Citizens' Advice Bureau and the Consumer Credit Counselling Service (CCCS) – all contact details at the end of the chapter – offer free advice to everyone on how to get out of debt. However, they are all massively oversubscribed and you might have to wait a long time to get help. They all have very useful websites, though (details below), which give you a lot of information while you wait.

- The Motley Fool – **www.fool.co.uk**. Apart from being a generally fantastic site for all things financial and consumer, it has various very interesting discussion boards, including the very busy 'Dealing with Debt'. Have a look at this one and you'll find hundreds of people in the same situation as you – or worse. Also, in the site's 'Get Out of Debt' section there are some useful templates for letters to creditors and an online 'statement of affairs' (see page 29 for more information) that you can fill in.

- MoneySavingExpert – **www.moneysavingexpert.com**. Another favourite of mine, this also has a lot of clear information on how to get out of debt together with literally hundreds of tips on where to get things cheaper. There are also some busy discussion boards on money-saving ideas.

- Good old Auntie Beeb – **www.bbc.co.uk**. There is a very helpful money section on the BBC website with general advice on finance and how to get out of debt.

- The *Guardian*/the *Observer* – **www.guardian.co.uk**. The *Guardian*'s 'Money' section and the *Observer*'s 'Cash' section are, to my mind, among the best newspaper money supplements. They belong to the same company and share a website, which has whole sections on debt, consumer issues, mortgages, saving and so on. Worth a look.

- Friends – and I don't mean the sitcom. If you want to get out of debt it can be very helpful to have a 'debt-busting buddy', in much the same way as it helps to exercise with a friend, so that you egg each other on. Try to get a friend who's in debt, or needing to save, to work with you, share your pain, share your beans on toast and generally make the whole process pleasanter and, probably, quicker.

Then take the first steps – these ones:

Do a 'statement of affairs'

This is essentially a list of your incomings and outgoings so that you can see what your situation really is. You can do it with pen and paper or, as mentioned above, you can do it online on the Motley Fool site (find it in the Get out of Debt centre) or at **www.moneysavingexpert.com**.

If you're doing it yourself, do just two columns. Write down your monthly incomings – salary, income from investments, alimony and so forth – in one and in the other write down your monthly outgoings. In the outgoings it's a good idea to start with the debts – the total amount owed to each creditor, the interest rate you're paying and how much you are actually paying each month. Then put in your essential outgoings such as rent or mortgage, utility bills, phone costs and so on.

Even if your outgoings list adds up to more than your incomings, don't panic. This is just a starting point and you will find a way to deal with it.

Get a plan

All the debt agencies always say that the most important bills to pay when you're in debt are the ones that keep the roof over your head. So pay your rent or mortgage first, your utility bills, your council tax, child support and any hire-purchase debt. Creditors such as banks, loan companies and credit-card companies will send you nasty letters and may be very unpleasant on the phone but their powers are actually quite limited. They certainly cannot take your home away, even if you owe tens of thousands. If you stop paying council tax or keep defaulting on your mortgage, though, you could eventually be kicked out of your house.

Cut all your costs

There are two main ways to reduce your outgoings:

1. buy essential things more cheaply;

2. don't buy other things at all.

The least painful way is to continue having certain essentials but at a lower rate, and you'll be surprised at how much you can save by switching to cheaper versions of the same thing. Start with the essentials:

- Switch your mortgage to a cheaper deal and you can save thousands each year. Speak to an independent broker or check websites such as **www.moneyextra.co.uk**, **www.moneysupermarket.com** and **www.charcolonline.co.uk.**

- Switch your gas, electricity, phone, mobile phone, Internet package, insurances and bank accounts. Look at websites such as **www.uswitch.com**, **www.buy.com**, **www.switchwithwhich.com**, **www.fool.co.uk**, **www.adslguide.org.uk**, **www.insuresupermarket.com**, **www.find.com**, **www.moneyextra.co.uk**, **www.moneysupermarket.com** for any of these alternatives. (See Chapter 4 for more information on shopping around to save money.)

- Buy cheaper versions of the same things. Look at the bottom and top shelves in the supermarket for the cheaper products they don't want you to buy. Buy own-brand goods instead of the expensive special brands. Look at every area of your life and see where you could buy the things you *need* (important point – *need*) for less.

The more painful way – and don't whinge, because if you're in debt you don't deserve these anyway – is to cut out some expenses altogether, until you can afford them again. Things that you *may not* buy until you are solvent again include:

- meals or even just drinks out in restaurants, cafés, hotels or coffee shops – unless someone else is paying or you've got a freebie;

- any clothes you don't absolutely need;

- holidays, unnecessary travel or any entertainment you have to pay for;

- gadgets, CDs, DVDs, ornaments or furniture you don't absolutely *need*;

- any services that you couldn't do for yourself (such as cleaning, ironing, gardening, car-washing).

You don't have to do without totally. You may be able to find a cheap or free alternative. For example:

- join some mystery-shopping (see page 80) companies so that you can get free trips to restaurants, hotels and bars;

- go through your wardrobe and see what you can alter, dye, cut down or mend;

- use air miles that you may have forgotten about or get free flights by being a courier (**www.courier.org**); consider house swaps for a cheap or free holiday (**www.holswop.com, www.homeexchange.com, www.digsville.com, www.echangeimmo.com**);

- use eBay, Amazon and local second-hand shops to sell old books, CDs, DVDs and so forth. Use the money to buy others that you really want;

- barter with friends to get services done that you don't like doing yourself: for example, offer one evening's babysitting for two-hours' of ironing by a friend who enjoys doing it; have a girls' night in where you give each other facials and manicures; swap power tools with neighbours instead of buying your own;

- have a swap shop with friends where you swap such things as clothes and books that you don't want and probably couldn't sell for much;

- call in favours and loans from family members and friends; let them know why you're doing it (most people understand what it's like to be up against it financially).

Whatever you do, cut down your spending as drastically as you are able to. It's up to you, but remember: the less you spend, the more you'll save, the more you'll have to put into your debts, the quicker and cheaper it will be to pay them off, and the sooner you'll be free and able to start building your wealth. Certainly give yourself little treats every now and then to keep yourself going – as you might if you were dieting – but make sure they're little and that it happens rarely.

Snowball your debts

The quickest and cheapest way to get those debts paid is to 'snowball' them. Here's how.

1. First, move as many as possible of your expensive credit- and store-card debts to zero per cent deals (see below for how to do that).

2. Once you know you can't get any of your debts any cheaper (without taking out a nasty consolidation loan), list your debts from the most expensive (the one with the highest interest rate) downwards. It doesn't matter what the size of the debt is, just the interest rate.

3. Use any money you have each month to pay off as much of the most expensive debt as possible. Just pay the minimum on all the others.

4. Once you have paid off the most expensive debt, do the same to the next most expensive, still paying just the minimum on the others.

5. Continue like this with the rest of the debts until they're all paid off. You will find that it gets quicker as you go down the list because you will have more money to throw at them as the first debts are paid off. This is why it's called 'snowballing'.

Zero per cent credit cards

Credit cards that charge zero per cent for a fixed period are a wonderful help to debtors. So long as your credit rating is good enough, you should be able to switch at least some of your debts from expensive credit cards or (worse) store cards on to credit cards that, for a few months at least, charge no interest at all.

Some companies now charge a small transfer fee, but, even if you have to pay that, it's usually worth moving your debt there for a few months. Just before the zero per cent period ends (usually about six months), open another zero per cent credit-card account with a different company and switch the debt over there. You have to keep paying the minimum each month during the zero per cent period but the savings over time can be huge. For example, look at what you would save over two years with these debts if you were just paying the minimum on them each month:

Debt	Saving with 0% card
£1,000 on a store card @ 29%	£580.00
£5,000 on credit card @ 18%	£1,800.00
£8,000 on credit card @ 15%	£2,400.00

Cut up your credit cards

Having encouraged you to take out new credit cards, I'm now going to tell you to cut up all your existing ones – particularly any wicked, evil, they-don't-deserve-to-live store cards that you possess – to stop you using them again. Once you manage to pay any cards off – or you transfer the debt to a zero per cent card – make sure they're closed down too.

However, in case of emergencies, you may keep one (the one with the lowest interest rate), just in case. To save you from temptation, though, you should put this one in a bowl of water and stick it in the freezer. The freezing water won't harm the card although a microwave oven would, so if you need to use it you can just take it out and wait for it to thaw. This means that you will have a couple of hours in which to consider whether you really, *really* need that fabulous, jewel-encrusted wok-polishing kit that you've just seen on QVC. Cool, huh?

Keep a spending diary

You will have seen in Chapter 2 how to do this. If you're in debt it's *very* important that you find out where the money is going and stem the flow. Once you start cutting out non-essentials and changing your spending habits, you'll find you have much more money each month to throw at your debts.

Deal with creditors

One of the most miserable aspects of being *seriously* in debt is the nasty calls, letters and even visits that you get from increasingly irate creditors and bailiffs. That's a big reason why a lot of people pay money to debt-management companies, just so that they'll make the 'nasty men go away'.

But why pay money so you don't have to do something that you *could* do (yes, really, you could) for nothing? It's just a question of knowing how to deal with these people. So, here we go:

- First, realise that credit-card companies, banks and loan companies can actually do very little to harm you. What they *are* good at is making your life miserable by threatening you. As most people think they do have power, this often works for them. Frankly, given that there are many people in the world who don't pay because they don't want to, not because they can't, this is not always a bad thing. It's just miserable if you mean to pay but you're genuinely having problems.

- The worst thing you can do with creditors is to ignore

them. Horrible (even terrifying) though it is, the best, least painful and cheapest way to deal with them is to keep communicating, be polite and respectful and keep them abreast of your situation and everything you are doing to pay the money back.

- Learn how to speak their language. As in so many areas of business, if you know how the other side are thinking, and the words that press their buttons, you will get on much better. The Motley Fool website (**www.fool.co.uk**) has sample letters to creditors written by an actual debt collector, which are really worth using if you need to.

- Contact your creditors before they contact you. If you send a letter explaining your situation and showing how much you are doing to pay off your various debts, many (though not all) will accept your terms and be reasonable.

- Remember: there are some debts that take precedence over others – such as mortgage, rent, council tax, utilities – although even with these you can often arrange to pay smaller amounts for a longer time if necessary.

- As long as you show that you're honestly trying to sort things out the best you can, many creditors will accept an offer of much smaller payments and may even suspend the interest charges.

- Some companies are more aggressive and unreasonable than others, so remember that you do have a right (established by the Office of Fair Trading) to be treated fairly. In other words, they are not supposed to intimidate you with demands for payments that you can't afford or threats to send the bailiffs round. They can't do anything without a court order, and that includes coming into your home to take away your possessions. They know this but they're counting on your not knowing it to intimidate you. If they get really nasty, you could mention that they're not treating you fairly according to the OFT's rules. That'll shut them up for a bit.

Earn more

'Yeah, right, duh!' you say. 'Earn more, huh? If I could do that I wouldn't be in this state, would I?'

Not necessarily true. In fact, be honest: if you earned more you'd probably be in more debt because you'd get more credit and you'd spend more, wouldn't you? However, now that you're in debt it's time to think of ways of boosting your income so that you can throw that money at your debts. If spending less is the equivalent of eating less when you want to lose weight, earning more is like increasing your exercise – it speeds up the process.

So, how do you do it? First, if you're employed, can you get a rise? Think about it seriously because it could be that you're owed one and haven't had it because you haven't asked. Don't ask for a rise just 'because I really need the money at the moment', though. That's not your employer's problem: it's yours. Ask for one only if you think you deserve it and could realistically get it. Could you do overtime? If so, do it – you need the money and, even if it means you have less free time, it's worth it in the long run.

Otherwise it's a question of making money out of what you have. Look at Chapter 6 for lots of ideas on how to make some extra cash, but, briefly, consider these:

- Have a spring clean of *all* your stuff and see what you can sell on eBay, Amazon, **www.gumtree.com** or at a car boot sale.

- Take on evening or weekend work such as babysitting, dog walking, bar work and shop work.

- Make things and sell them – cakes, jewellery, candles, sweets. Sell to friends, on eBay, on a market stall or out of your front garden if you are allowed to!

- Rent out a room or your whole property if you can. If you live near a station you could rent out your driveway for parking.

- Work as a film extra or a life model if you have time off in the week.

- Read my book *A Bit on the Side: 500 Ways to Boost Your Income* (Piatkus, £7.99) for loads more ideas.

- And don't whinge that you don't have the time/energy/need to do extra to earn more. While you're in debt you don't have an automatic right to luxuries – including the luxury of time off and relaxation. Anything other than the necessities is borrowed and is increasing the time and expense of paying off the loan in the long term. Bite the bullet, focus your energies and go for it!

Change your thinking

In spite of all of the above (and it's all true, don't just discard it), none of it will work long term unless you change your whole attitude to spending – and possibly to life generally. So, not much to ask, eh?

Using the overeating analogy again, there's often more going on underneath the problem than we're aware of. Overspending, like overeating (and the same with drink, drugs, casual sex), tends to happen because we feel an emptiness inside that needs to be filled. Psychologists at Sussex University have carried out quite a bit of research into the phenomenon of retail therapy and have concluded that, generally speaking, we shop in order to plug the gap between our actual and ideal selves. The more materialistic we are, the more likely it is that we're going to be big spenders, since it can make us feel more like the person we'd like to be.

It might sound fanciful but, really, it's worth doing some work on your own thinking, your own sense of life and of yourself, to fill that apparent gap with something substantial at the same time as taking the practical steps towards getting out of debt. That way, you really will be a winner in the long run!

If all else fails ...

Bankruptcy stared me in the face, but one thought kept me calm; soon I'd be too poor to need an anti-theft alarm.

— **Gina Rothfels**

IVAs

The number of bankrupts is on the rise in the UK, and certainly the stigma attached to it is lessening, but that doesn't alter the fact that it is, and should be, only a last resort if you are seriously in debt. Some people see it as an easy way of abdicating their financial responsibilities, but there are a number of downsides. Also, the increasing number of bankruptcies is bad for borrowing generally as banks will try to recoup losses by charging everyone else more for loans and will refuse credit to more and more people.

So first, before opting for full bankruptcy, consider an individual voluntary arrangement (IVA). These are effectively glorified debt-management plans designed to give creditors a better return than they would get if you went bankrupt. Essentially, you come to an agreement with your creditors about how to pay off your various debts. It's done under the supervision of a licensed insolvency practitioner (usually an accountant or lawyer), who sorts it all out for you.

The good thing about an IVA is that it stops your creditors from knocking at your door and it helps have more control over how your assets are dealt with than you would with bankruptcy. The very bad thing is that it all costs money – it's likely to cost a few thousand – and that's money that could be spent paying off your debts. Also, they don't always work. Many times IVAs break down a year or so into the scheme and the debtor has to find another way of dealing with things. And, if you default on making payments as per the agreement, your insolvency practitioner has to petition for your bankruptcy. So, consider it very carefully if you want to go down this route.

Bankruptcy

Bankruptcy (known in Scotland as 'sequestration') can turn your life upside down, although, thanks to recent laws, the disruption doesn't last as long as it used to. In fact, most bankrupts are now automatically discharged after just one year. Although you're still liable for your debts for three years after being made bankrupt, after that the debts that remain are written off and you're cleared to borrow money and set up business again.

Once you're declared bankrupt, the majority of your assets are handed over to a trustee, who controls them after that. To start off with, you will deal with the official receiver, who needs to find out as much as possible about what you own and what you owe. You are then protected from your creditors, who can no longer pursue you for money. You might have to pay part of your debts each month, but that will be based on what you can afford.

If your debts exceed your assets the only things you'll be allowed to keep are some basic household items and any tools you need in order to work. If you own your home, the official receiver can sell it off to go towards paying your debts. If you have a mortgage and can't meet the payments, the lender may repossess your home. If you have any income over and above what's necessary to live on, you'll have to hand that over too for the next three years. If you want to have a bank account, you have to tell the bank you're a bankrupt – which means you might not get one at all.

Bankruptcy restriction orders can be imposed on anyone considered to have been dishonest, reckless or blameworthy. In these cases, the orders can last for up to 15 years. Generally, though, you will be debt-free and the slate wiped clean once you are discharged. However, discharge doesn't necessarily happen automatically. The courts can decide to postpone it if you don't co-operate with the official receiver or your trustee. Worse than that, after discharge a record of your bankruptcy will be kept on your credit file for the next six years, which will make getting loans, bank accounts or mortgages difficult and expensive.

And finally ...

Remind yourself:

- Face the demon now: the more quickly you tackle the debt, the quicker, and cheaper, it will be to pay it off.

- Get out of the credit trap. Any time you see the word 'credit' in shops or banks, mentally replace it with the word 'debt', because that's what it is. Suddenly, then, even 'interest-free debt' doesn't sound quite so appealing.

- Do check your bank statements. You'll be surprised how much money you could make just by correcting mistakes the bank has made and closing down old direct debits.

- Don't be afraid to tell your friends that you can't afford things because you're paying off your debt. You need their support and, anyway, they may be grateful that they don't have to spend out either.

- If you don't want to keep yo-yoing between debt and solvency all the time, change your whole approach to money for good, not just until the debt goes.

Useful contacts

Debt advice

National Debtline – **www.nationaldebtline.co.uk**, 0808 808 4000

Citizens' Advice Bureau (CAB) – **www.citizensadvice.org.uk**, or check Yellow Pages for your nearest centre

Consumer Credit Counselling Service (CCCS) – **www.cccs.co.uk**, 0800 138 1111

The Motley Fool – **www.fool.co.uk** (check out the Get out of Debt centre and 'Dealing with Debt' discussion board)

Moneysavingexpert.com – **www.moneysavingexpert.com**

BBC website – **www.bbc.co.uk** (check out the 'Your Money' section for sensible advice on debt)

The *Guardian* – **www.guardian.co.uk** (one of their 'Cash Clinics' is on 'Managing Debt')

Directgov – **www.direct.gov.uk** (look under the 'Managing Debt' section)

Credit Action – **www.creditaction.org.uk**, 01522 699777 (money advice charity)

Bankruptcy and insolvency

www.insolvency.gov.uk – the DTI's insolvency website

www.r3.org.uk – insolvency practitioners

Other information

Experian – **www.experian.co.uk**

Equifax – **www.equifax.co.uk**

In January of this year, I decided to try extreme budgeting. By bringing packed lunches to work, cutting back on unnecessary luxuries (such as take-away meals), I attempted to slash my everyday expenses to zero. With the help of 'Spend Nothing Days' and 'No Cash Withdrawal Days', I managed to spend less than £40 in 31 days. Normally, I would get through about £400 a month on top of my regular bills, so this was some achievement!

My financial detox also had another benefit because, by avoiding alcohol, tobacco, fast food and snacks, I was inadvertently undergoing a physical detox, too. By the end of the month, I'd lost half a stone, boosted my energy levels, and felt terrific. What a bonus!

– **Cliff D'Arcy, personal finance writer, fool.co.uk**

4

Saving and Borrowing

'Rich or poor, it's good to have money.'
– Sid Lance

Whoever said 'neither a borrower nor a lender be' must have had a trust fund from Mummy and Daddy and no idea of the realities of adult life. Unless you have a private income, it's likely that you'll spend a large part of your life as a borrower, even if it's just a mortgage, although I hope you'll be a saver for a much longer time.

Saving is a very important part of being financially (and mentally) secure. It's not the same as investing (see Chapter 9 for that) because you save for the short term, for specific things and as a back-up to life, rather than aiming to make money for the long term. That said, money in your savings account(s) should be growing, thanks to compound interest, even in the short term.

Borrowing is one of the necessities of life and certainly of business. Actually, the word 'borrow' is a little misleading because really we 'buy' money when we borrow it. A lender gives us a sum of money and we pay for it over time by adding on a certain percentage to the amount we pay back each month – in other words, we pay *interest* on that money. The total amount we pay depends on how much we've borrowed, the interest rate we're being charged and, particularly, how long we're borrowing it for.

With saving *and* borrowing, the most important thing to look at first is the interest rate. Generally, with saving, you need to go for the highest rate you can find. With borrowing, you need to go for the lowest, although there are other factors to consider. With both saving and borrowing, though, the key to getting the best deal is to shop around (see below for a list of very useful comparison websites).

Saving

> 'With money in your pocket, you are wise and you are handsome and you sing well, too.'
> – **Yiddish proverb**

Saving seems to have gone out of fashion in recent decades, but for those in the know it's still an important part of being wealthy – or at least being financially secure. The best way to save (once you've got out of debt, please – no point saving if you're *in* debt) is to have a few 'pots' into which you regularly put money for different things in your life. 'Regularly' is a very important word with saving. Even if you put just a small amount away each month, the action of putting it in regularly is a great discipline and will help your money grow almost without your noticing it. Here are some of the pots you should consider setting up.

Safety-net savings

All the big and clever investors say the same thing: you should always have a cushion of money put by to cover your living expenses for three to six months before you start investing. If you currently have debts, get rid of those first. Once they're out of the way, work out how much you need to keep going each month, set up a high-interest savings account (probably with an online bank or building society) and keep putting money into it until you have enough as a safety net for three to six months.

This is your rainy-day savings pot and it shouldn't be touched unless you lose your job or fall ill and need to pay your way. In fact, to avoid temptation, it may be best to put this money into a postal account or a 90-day-notice account so that you really can't get your hands on it without a lot of thought.

Big-purchase savings

Set up another savings account for Christmas or your holiday or a new kitchen or whatever else is looming on the horizon. Some bank accounts now offer you a multiple 'savings pot' facility, which can be useful for this type of saving, but there's nothing to stop you starting accounts with a few different financial companies and setting up a different monthly standing order into each one. The amount you put in depends entirely on you – how much you can afford and how much you need to make.

Insurance savings

You can get insurance for almost anything these days, but most of it isn't worth the money. The worst type of insurance is the retail warranty: those bits of paper that shop assistants are desperate to sell you when you buy a new TV or oven or other electrical item. Always say no because (a) you already have a manufacturer's warranty for the item in the packaging, which can be extended; (b) most electrical goods now don't go wrong in the first two years; (c) you are already covered by the Sale of Goods Act 1979, which says that an item should be fit for use 'for a reasonable amount of time' (this is not defined and will depend on circumstances); and (d) the amount they charge for these warranties is usually much more than the cost of getting the item mended (according to the Consumers' Association). After all, the assistants make commission out of them and the insurance companies make billions each year out of them, so the money has to be coming from somewhere!

A far better and cheaper way to deal with possible repair bills is to set up a savings account specifically for this. Put a small amount of money into this each month and if you need to get something mended you can just dip into it. If you don't, you'll have a nice pot of money left over with which you can buy yourself something sensible such as 100 pounds of chocolate!

A few points:

- Always shop around for the best (that is, the highest) interest rates. Look on the Internet or in the 'Best Buy' tables in the Sunday newspapers.

- Keep an eye on your savings accounts. Financial companies often drop their rates without warning, so, if this happens to you, vote with your money and move to a better account.

- Remember to take tax into account when calculating how much you will make on your savings.

- If you want to avoid paying tax on the interest you make, keep your money in a cash ISA (individual savings account). Check out **www.mrc.gov.uk** for the current annual limit on how much you can save in one of these.

- If you want to save but like to have a flutter too, consider Premium Bonds from National Savings and Investments (**www.nsandi.com**). The average return is actually around the same as you'd get from a normal building society (after tax) but returns are tax free, you don't lose your money as you do with normal gambling, and there's always the possibility that you could win the big one! The one big drawback, though, is that the longer you keep your money there, the more it's eroded by inflation, but if you make some good winnings along the way that'll balance it out.

Borrowing

'If you'd know the power of money, go and borrow some.'

– Ben Franklin

There are many ways by which you can borrow money – if your credit is good. In fact, there are probably too many ways in which we can borrow nowadays, which is why we have such a serious debt problem in this country. Before you borrow ask yourself:

- Do I *really* need the thing I want to borrow money for?

- Is there a cheaper, or free, way I can get it?

- Could I wait another 6–12 months or so to give myself the chance to save for it?

- What would be the total amount I would spend if I borrowed the money for it – would it be worth that amount?

That last point is very important. Unless you're borrowing money for nothing (using zero per cent credit cards or from Mum and Dad), the item you're buying will actually cost you more in the end – maybe much more – than the ticket price. Let's look at an example. Say you buy a car for £6,000. You put down £1,000 deposit and get a loan of £5,000 over three years at 13.9 per cent APR. The total amount repayable will be £6,072.48 as your interest bill is £1,072.48, and so the car will cost you £7,072.48. Great!

However, if you still want to borrow, keep these points in mind:

- Shop around.

- Go for the cheapest rate you can find.

- Go for the most flexible loan you can find (one that you can pay off in full early if you're able to).

- Don't borrow money against your home if you can possibly avoid it.

- Don't borrow any more money than you absolutely *have* to. The more you borrow, the more interest you'll pay.

- Good borrowing is money that will be used to invest in something that will make you money or improve your life or your children's lives later on. Bad borrowing is money that will be used on short-term pleasures such as holidays, clothes, toys and even a car if it's not completely necessary.

If your credit rating is good (see page 53 to find out about that) there are various ways to borrow.

Credit cards

Incredibly, one of the cheapest ways to borrow now is on credit cards. Not the usual ones, but the new zero per cent credit cards, some of which charge no interest for an initial few months on purchases. These deals come and go and they're certainly not available to everyone, but you can find them on any of the money comparison sites in the list on page 363. If you can, take one out, buy the item you want, and, when your zero per cent deal is coming to an end, transfer your remaining balance to a 'zero per cent on balance transfers' card, and keep doing that until you've paid it off.

Otherwise, though, credit cards are one of the more

expensive ways of borrowing money (if you don't pay the amount owed in full each month – bad idea). Not only will you have to pay interest but they're *very* quick to slap on the charges if you're just a day late. If you *do* pay off your debt each month, cards can be a very useful way of paying for things: you tend to get free insurance on the stuff you buy; you usually have at least a month's grace before you have to pay it off; and some cards even give you cash back when you use them.

Personal loans

There's huge competition in the personal-loan market now. People used to just go to their bank and get grilled over what they were spending it on. Now, you can go online and get a loan as cheap as a mortgage (often with catches, of course, so you have to watch what you're doing) and you don't have to justify it to anyone. However, there are a few important points to remember:

- Don't bother trying to get a loan from your high street bank. They have the worst rates. Go online instead and get the cheapest that way.

- APRs (annual percentage rates) are a useful way of finding the cheapest loan, but a more accurate way is to compare the TAR (total amount repayable) for the various loans. If this isn't written down in the loan offer, ask them for the figure – they have to give it to you.

- Don't go for a loan that is set against your home, because it could jeopardise the roof over your head.

- Don't get conned into buying one of their add-ons such as PPI (payment-protection insurance). These are where the banks make their profits (up to 90 per cent of the deal is profit to them in some cases) and they're useless for most borrowers.

- Beware of 'typical' APRs. Although legally two-thirds of borrowers must be given the advertised typical rate, you might not qualify for this if you don't fit their ideal customer profile.

Overdrafts

This is a useful form of short-term, easy borrowing but it's a lot more expensive than most people think. The banks make billions of pounds every year by charging us interest on authorised overdrafts and exorbitant one-off fines and extra interest for going over the limit – even by one penny for one day!

A bit of forward planning could help you avoid punitive overdraft charges either by arranging a bigger overdraft when you know your spending is going to be higher than usual, or by calling your bank as soon as you've gone into the red and asking for a temporary overdraft increase. If all else fails, according to Cliff D'Arcy, of the Motley Fool website – who used to work in financial services – complain about the charges because, he says, 'the banks secretly admit that they are out-rageous. On the occasions that I've threatened to challenge these charges in my local court, banks have backed down swiftly every time.' Check out bankchargeshell.com for more help.

On the other hand, if you find yourself being charged a fortune in overdraft interest and charges, it's probably worth your while switching to another account. It's not as complicated as it seems and many newer banks make it very easy indeed to switch to their service.

Store cards

Store cards are evil and must die. There, I've said it and it's true. The only point in having them is to get the 10 per cent discount on your first purchase and, perhaps, the odd sale preview here and there. They're appalling for borrowing, though, and, in the main, are the most expensive mainstream way to borrow money, charging six or seven times the Bank of England's base rate. If you're ever tempted to buy things with them, always make sure you pay your bill right on time.

Remortgaging

'Surely you don't think remortgaging is worse than store cards!' you exclaim incredulously. Actually, in many ways, yes, I do. Although a remortgage, on paper, certainly looks like one of the cheapest ways to raise some cash, there are a few big disadvantages to it:

- It puts your home at risk in a way that all 'unsecured' loans can't do.

- It usually doesn't address the main issue – overspending – so you carry on spending on credit cards while your monthly mortgage payments have gone up.

- Ideally, mortgages should be paid off as quickly as possible, not given even more time to accumulate interest.

Of course, the time when remortgaging is a very good idea is when you're out of the fixed period with your current mortgage and you want to get a better deal. That's fine and very sensible, particularly if you're not increasing the original amount you borrowed at all. But, if you're remortgaging in order to free up some cash to pay for anything other than improving your home to make it worth more (in other words, for investment purposes), then it's a very, *very* bad idea. Don't do it – do without for a while and save up for that holiday, that car, or that new sofa.

> ## Remember
>
> - The only reason you should remortgage is to switch to a cheaper deal.
>
> - You should pay off a mortgage as fast as you comfortably can. It shouldn't be used as a cash machine any time you want to make a large purchase.
>
> - Don't just take out a loan for another 25 years. Make sure it's the same length as the time left over for your original loan or, ideally, even less.
>
> - Arrangement fees are going up all the time. If you're going to remortgage, make sure it's worth the costs.

The dreaded credit file!

Any time you apply for some sort of loan – including a mortgage – the bank or lender will check your credit history to see if you're a good bet. There are two main credit reference agencies they turn to: Experian and Equifax (contact details below). Between them the two agencies hold details on some 44 million people in the UK – and I mean *details*! Your file includes information about your other credit cards, your mortgage and your bank accounts, as well as facts and figures on any unpaid bills, failure to pay hire-purchase debts and County Court Judgments (CCJs).

Importantly, your credit file also records whether you have applied recently for several new loans or credit cards, and this can make a difference to your application. Financial companies are like sheep and, if they find that you've been turned down by a few other lenders, they're likely to turn you down too. They also get worried if you made several applications for credit and loans at the same time, because it makes you look as if you're in a desperate financial situation. If the first couple of lenders turn you down, then the third might wonder what's going on and turn you down as well.

Lenders will look poorly on you if they see you have CCJs against you or that you have regularly defaulted on mortgage or loan payments in the recent past. Other than that, though, there are few hard and fast rules as to what's good and what's bad on a credit record. Some lenders like students with lots of debt, for example. Others won't touch them and go only for people in established jobs and, ideally, their own homes. Amazingly, if you've never borrowed in your life, never owed money and don't own any credit cards, many lenders will view you with immense suspicion. Sometimes it seems that you just can't win!

Essentially, companies give you a credit 'score': they award you points or take them away. The more points you get, the more likely it is that the provider will lend you money. You get points for paying loans off on time, for having a good job and for living in a 'posh' postcode area. But you get points taken off for defaulting, for being young (sometimes) and even for not having a phone. However, all providers have different criteria. While one may give you 40 points for being married (some lenders think that makes you a stable and reliable person!), another may not give you any points at all. Other criteria include how long you've lived at a particular address (the longer the better) and whether or not you're on the electoral roll.

Your credit file can contain mistakes and, as you're allowed to correct any factual errors, it makes sense to get a copy of your file to check it. You're also allowed to add a brief statement to your file to explain a problem that might count against you, for example, why you briefly fell behind with your mortgage payments six months previously. Since fraud and identity theft is on the rise, it's possible that someone else created a credit problem for you somewhere along the line, so you should have that explained on your file too. It costs just £2 to get a copy of your credit record (although both companies will try to sell you one of their more expensive, deluxe versions if you don't watch it) so it's not going to break the bank to get a copy every now and then.

Cleaning up a bad credit history

If you've ended up with a bad credit history, for whatever reason, it's possible to improve it, although it can take time. There's a growing market for 'sub-prime' lending – that's companies who will lend, at a very high interest rate, to people with poor credit histories. If you take out a credit card, for example, with a high rate but make sure you pay off the full amount on time every month, you can gradually improve your rating (and it won't cost you anything if you pay it all off each month). You could get a mortgage or loan with one of these sub-prime companies but the rates tend to be high – to reflect the level of risk they're taking on – so you would lose money by borrowing from them. However, if this is what you have to do, bite the bullet and just make sure that you pay on time every month and don't default at all. After at least six months of 'keeping your nose clean' your credit rating will improve.

Alternative methods for borrowing and saving

Bank of Mum and Dad

If you've got generous parents (lucky you!) who can afford to stump up some cash for your latest 'must buy' (even luckier you!), then this is often the cheapest and least-hassle way of borrowing money. Increasingly now, young people are borrowing large amounts from beleaguered parents to get on the housing ladder. The pros of this kind of borrowing are that it's cheap, flexible and often immediate. The cons are that it makes you even more beholden to your parents, possibly stops you learning the value of money and could make them poor in their old age if you don't pay it back. It's up to you.

Credit unions (CUs)

Credit unions have never quite taken off in this country, thanks to some of our finance laws, although they're big in America, Ireland and a number of developing countries. They're somewhere between a bank and a co-operative. They're owned and controlled by their members and run for the benefit of their members, all of whom have a common bond such as living or working in the same area or in the same business. Basically, everyone pools their savings and these savings provide the funds for loans.

They're usually thought of as organisations for people on low incomes but a recent *Which?* magazine report showed that the rates of return for savers are often higher than those offered by the main banks. It's also pleasant to know that profits on your transactions aren't being pocketed by City fat cats.

Interest on loans is also charged at competitive rates and there are no early-redemption penalties; nor do you have to watch out for hidden extras such as overpriced payment-protection insurance. Usually, you have to build up a history of saving with a CU before you can borrow, but this can be as little as three months.

Zopa

Crazy name, crazy concept – it seems. In fact, Zopa is the first online financial 'exchange' in this country, attempting to shake up the banks' hold on lending. It works by putting individuals like you and me together to lend to each other directly. By joining Zopa, you can either become a lender or borrow money from other members. Their charges are low, which means that, on the whole, lenders get a high rate on their savings and borrowers get a competitive rate, too.

You set your own rates for borrowing and lending and you can choose the kinds of people you lend to. Both lenders and borrowers are credit-checked, as with any other financial organisation, but the whole process is a little more humane than the usual way financial institutions operate.

Where *not* to borrow from

See Chapter 11 for a list of lenders you shouldn't touch with a bargepole, including pawnbrokers, loan sharks and anyone who advertises on daytime TV.

Useful contacts

There are several useful websites that compare rates for savings accounts, credit cards, loans and overdrafts. Look at:

www.moneysavingexpert.com
www.moneysupermarket.com
www.moneyextra.co.uk
www.moneyfacts.co.uk
www.find.co.uk

You can also work out the best bank account for overdrafts and savings at **www.switchwithwhich.co.uk**.

For more help and advice on borrowing and saving like a professional, go to **www.fool.co.uk**.

To get a copy of your credit file or find out more about credit ratings go to either of the following:

Experian – 0870 241 6212, **www.uk.experian.com**

Equifax – 0870 010 2091, **www.equifax.co.uk**

To get redress for bad charges go to **www.bankchargeshell. com**

Alternative methods of saving and borrowing

The Association of British Credit Unions Limited – **www.abcul.org**
Credit Unions Online – **www.creditunionsonline.com**
Zopa – **www.zopa.com**

5

Financial One-upmanship Day to Day

'Money can't buy happiness, but it can buy you the kind of misery you prefer.'

– Anon

As I mentioned, on average, we're each ripped off to the tune of about £500,000 through our lifetime. That includes paying too much for food, travel, insurance, banking, clothes, mortgages, household goods and so on, as well as being sold underperforming pensions and investments that make money for the sellers but not for us. For the most part, retailers, banks, service organisations and even governments are able to fleece us because we let them. Individually we don't shop around enough, we don't go for the best deal, we don't defend ourselves against sharp selling practices and we're too confused or lazy to ask the right questions.

A very important part of controlling your money is to learn new habits of spending (or not spending) on a daily basis. That way, instead of automatically overpaying for goods or buying things we don't need, we are more alert, question more and naturally protect ourselves from being 'mugged'. Here are some ways in which you can help yourself.

Daily spending rules:

- When you go to buy something, ask yourself, 'Do I really need this or do I just want it?'

- Could you get this cheaper or, even better, free somewhere else?

- Any time you run across something you absolutely *must have*, just wait a little while. If you take 24 hours, or even a couple of days, to think about it, the desire to have it often subsides.

- If you have real problems stopping yourself spending, cut up your credit cards, set yourself a weekly budget and take that money out in cash from the ATM at the beginning of the week.

- Even if you're not much of an impulse spender, remember that cash is king. You can often get things cheaper if you pay with cash.

- Even in large stores you can often haggle. We're not used to it in this country but many people are open to offers. Don't always take the marked price as the final word on the matter.

- Whether it's insurance or insecticide, cars or candles, shop around for the best price.

- Use price-comparison websites (shopbots) to get the cheapest deal.

- Being 'anti-seasonal' can work well: that is, buying goods at the 'wrong' time of year, such as Christmas presents in the summer.

- Play sellers off against each other – this works particularly well in cut-throat areas such as car sales. You can phone one salesperson and say the car is being sold for so much less in the showroom in the next town. Then phone the next showroom with the price quoted by the last until you get to the genuinely bottom price.

- Ignore zero per cent finance deals – they always make their money back somewhere, usually by marking up the price. Better to offer cash and insist on a discount.

- Try to get free add-ons, particularly if the shop hasn't given you a discount. Can they deliver it free instead or give you some free extras?

- Sometimes it's worth buying online from a high street store, but only if they offer discounts and you can get free delivery or pick it up from the shop yourself.

Smart spending

Once you get the principles of shopping around, not buying what you don't need or love and not being pressured into buying, you'll find that you can apply these to pretty much all areas of life. Also have a look at Chapter 16 ('Ethical Money') for more tips on living more cheaply by living better – the two really are connected!

To give you an idea of how to get good deals on most things, here's a list of a few of the things we could get more cheaply, and how to do it.

Insurance

Most people in this country are either over- or underinsured. It's not surprising really given the bewildering array of things you could possibly insure. For example, you can get insurance against having twins or triplets, insurance against rain (pluvius insurance) and one enterprising Scottish insurance company now offers insurance against being bitten on the bum by the Loch Ness monster!

When deciding what insurance you need ask yourself a few questions:

- Am I legally required to have this? Answer 'yes' for motor insurance, for example.

- Would I have the funds to cover repairs or replacements if the worst happened? Answer probably 'no' for buildings insurance but 'yes' for TV repairs, for example.

- Would I sleep better if I knew this was insured?

Most insurance policies are renewable each year and it's certainly worth having a look online or checking over the phone with a broker to see if you can find a better deal than you currently have. With insurance, cost is not always the main consideration. You also want good service.

There's massive competition in all areas of insurance so shopping around will always get you a better deal, even if it just makes your usual insurer offer a discount.

- *Car insurance*: Try insurance broking sites such as **www.the-aa.com**, **www.kwik-fit.com**, **www.confused.com** and **www.insuresupermarket.com**.

- *Buildings and contents insurance*: Have a look at **www.find.co.uk** for all kinds of insurance companies, also brokers such as **www.kwik-fit.com**, **www.insuresupermarket.com**.

- *Life assurance, critical-illness insurance and so on*: Think about which of these you really need. For example, if you have children you should have life assurance, unless your employers have a good package. Look at **www.lifesearch.com** for life assurance. For critical-illness insurance, it's probably best to go to an independent financial adviser (IFA) or independent insurance broker (not one owned by a bank), because there are so many different versions it's hard to compare like with like. Again, some employers offer insurance if you are incapacitated or seriously injured, so check this out.

- *Travel insurance*: Never bother with the insurance offered by the tour operator you use. It's always overpriced. Shop around on sites such as **www.insuresupermarket.com**, **www.moneysavingexpert.com** and **www.moneyextra.co.uk.** If you travel more than twice a year you would definitely be better off going for an annual multi-trip policy. Remember, too, that your credit card covers you for purchases – including holidays – costing over a certain amount (usually about £150), so that can cover you if the tour operator goes bust while you're away.

Motoring

You never stop spending when you have a car, but you can cut costs by shopping around and watching how you drive.

- Don't go for a new car if you want to save money. You lose around 20 per cent of the value as you drive it off the forecourt.

- To get better deals on new and used cars, check out some of the many car websites around right now, such as **www.jamjar.com**, **www.autotrader.co.uk**, **www.dixonmotors.co.uk** and **www.drivethedeal.com**.

- Never bother with any financing deals they offer you. Like banks, car salespeople make more money from the add-ons such as financing than they do selling the actual product. Look in Chapter 4 ('Saving and Borrowing') for cheaper ways to borrow money if you need to.

- Avoid paying extra for car warranties – they're far too expensive and you should get them to include them for free in the total price.

- See Chapter 16 ('Ethical Money') for many more ways to cut motoring costs and help the environment.

Holidays

For cheaper flights, hire cars, holidays and hotels, check out **www.cheapflights.co.uk**, **www.ebookers.com**, **www.expedia.com**, **www.lastminute.com**, **www.opodo.com**, **www.teletextholidays.com**, and **www.travelocity.com**.

House swapping is increasingly popular and is a very cheap way of taking a holiday with the whole family. Try **www.homeforexchange.com**, **www.holswop.com**, and **www.homeexchange.com**.

For really cheap flights try being a courier. To find out about how to be one and how much you could save on normal air ticket prices go to **www.aircourier.co.uk** or **www.azfreight.com**.

Household goods

Try **www.kelkoo.co.uk**, **http://uk.shopping.com** (part of eBay), **www.pricerunner.co.uk**, **www.froogle.co.uk** (part of Google), **www.123pricecheck.co.uk** and **www.check-aprice.com**.

Books, audio and video

There are specialist sites for certain goods, and new ones turn up all the time. For example, for books you can go to **www.amazon.co.uk**, **www.bookbrain.co.uk**, **www.abebooks.co.uk** and **www.bookbutler.co.uk**; for CDs and DVDs look at **www.dvdbrain.co.uk**, **www.dvdpricecheck.co.uk**, **www.find-dvd.co.uk**, **www.cdwow.com** and **www.play.com**.

Clothes

Clothes are getting cheaper all the time because of foreign competition. Apart from sticking to the less expensive stores you can also get bargains at factory outlets (go to **www.shoppingvillages.com** for a list of them), at charity shops in posh areas and also on eBay. If you have a sewing machine, then making clothes can be cheap and more personalised and for free gear have a swap shop with friends where you swap the outfits you just don't want any more.

Also, if you know what you want to buy, try websites such as **www.bbclothing.co.uk**, **www.swerve.co.uk**, **www.designerdiscount.co.uk** and **www.designersalesdirect.com**.

Christmas

A time of stress and misery for many but a time of big business for retailers, Christmas has become so far removed from a simple religious festival and so much, now, a festival of Mammon, that it needs a lot of thought to stop us spending crazy amounts of money for nothing.

- If you love to splurge during this season, spread the cost over the year, either by buying presents, decorations and so on from January onwards or by setting up a savings account specifically for it.

- If friends and family agree, set a spending limit on presents for each other – perhaps no more than £5 or £10 each – particularly if there are a lot of you.

- Agree with friends and family that you will all give to charity this year instead of giving to each other (see Chapter 16, 'Ethical Money', for ideas on charitable giving).

- If you're caught short in December and need to spend on a credit card, make sure it's one that gives zero per cent on purchases for a fixed period. At least that way you won't pay extra in interest.

- Take your annual holiday over the Christmas period – escape the need to give and receive presents or spend on entertaining.

How to get the most out of 'all you can eat' salad bars:

- Never feel guilty about going back for more (if a server stops you explain you have multiple personalities that need feeding).
- Create a false wall with carrot batons and cucumber slices to increase the dish's volume; push the potatoes down with a spoon; squash the lettuce up.
- Don't forget night-time munchies – stuff a few sausages in your pocket on your last trip to the table.
- If you're really hungry, pull your chair up and eat straight from the buffet trolley – saves time and effort.

Money back

There are various shopping sites that pay cashback or give you points when you use them to visit and buy from other websites. This can be helpful, although, of course, they will try to entice you to buy things or services you don't really need by offering more points, so make sure you guard against that. The main cashback sites are **www.bighair.co.uk**, **www.greasypalm. co.uk**, **www.mutualpoints.com** and **www.rpoints.com**.

Loyalty cards in shops can be useful, although most are not that helpful. The Boots loyalty card is the best value, but with the others, if you're going to buy things in their shops anyway, why not use the loyalty card and get a fiver back every now and then?

Some credit cards also offer cashback, although, again, these tend to be relatively small amounts. However, if you're buying large items it helps to know you'll get at least a few quid back later on. Also, thanks to Section 75 of the Consumer Credit Act, you get extra legal protection when buying goods costing between £100 and £30,000 or a credit card.

Resisting temptation

It's a tragic truth that currently shopping is Britain's number-one leisure activity. I say tragic because this is part of the reason why we have such a debt problem. We need to understand that *shops are not our friends*. In fact, for a while, large retail chains have been working on more and more subtle ways of persuading us to part with our money without our realising that we've been effectively hypnotised.

In his excellent book *Influence – Science and Practice*, the psychologist Robert Cialdini itemises some of the sneaky ways in which our buttons are pressed by individuals, businesses, governments and other organisations to make us respond automatically and unthinkingly. In the case of shops and salespeople, there are all kinds of psychological techniques that they can and do use. In shops, special lighting, flattering mirrors, positioning of items, ambient music, smells and enticing posters are just part of their money-grabbing armoury. Supermarkets are particularly adept at turning us into mesmerised morons as we wander through the aisles putting expensive, branded products we don't need into our baskets.

As a general rule, remember that shopping is war. You need certain products at the best price, they want you to have more at the top price. They will win unless we defend ourselves against their tactics. Keep some of these points in mind when you next go shopping:

• Always shop with a list, particularly in supermarkets. If you think about it beforehand and stick to your list, you'll be less tempted by 'special offers' and other money losers.

- In the supermarket, look at the bottom and top shelves more than the ones at your eyeline. They put the better-value goods on the less accessible shelves.

- Do your supermarket shopping online. You have to pay a few pounds to have it delivered but that can be outweighed by the petrol and time you would waste going to the shop. You're also less likely to be tempted to buy outside of your list.

- Don't shop with a spendthrift friend who will encourage you to buy things you don't need.

- Don't shop if you're tired, hungry or depressed.

- Try to do your food shopping at markets rather than supermarkets. On average their prices are 30 per cent lower than the high street stores.

- Once a year, decide to use up all the things in your kitchen cupboards, buying fresh foods only to go with those items.

- If you find yourself buying more than you should in certain shops, just don't go through their doors! If you're not in the shop you're not going to be persuaded by their goods, mirrors, lighting and ambient music into buying what you don't need and can't afford.

- Sometimes buying in bulk can be cheaper but not always. Consider the space you have available and just how much you would save per unit if you buy a lot. Also beware of BOGOF (Buy One Get One Free) offers. Do you really use this brand or would a single unit of another brand be cheaper and better?

- When dealing with any salespeople (including your

'personal banker'), insist on having time to think about any product they're trying to sell you. Take paperwork away with you, ask friends or, better, experts and think about it outside of their office/shop before actually buying.

Useful contacts

www.tesco.com
www.sainsbury.co.uk
www.ocado.com
www.fool.co.uk (for more tips on canny shopping)

Getting your money back

Whether you've been sold a duff kettle or a substandard endowment policy, you can not only get satisfaction but, in some cases, you could be better off than before – if you know how to complain about it constructively. The trick is to know how to do it, and where to go if you need more help. Here are the main rules for successful complaining.

- Taking a faulty item back to the shop should be a relatively straightforward matter, although in some cases, such as when the item is out of the guarantee period, you may have problems getting satisfaction. Remember, though, that the trader will still be liable for any breaches of contract such as the goods being basically faulty. In some cases the shop could be liable to compensate you for up to six years!

- Try to point out, and get redress for, the bad product or service as early as possible. It puts you in a stronger position than if you hung around for a few months.

- Before you go to the shop or pick up the phone, get a clear idea of what you want to achieve. Should you have your money back, a replacement or compensation? Write down a list if necessary.

- Try to stay pleasant and don't lose your temper at any time. Don't be a pushover, of course, but most assistants will be happier to help someone who is nice to them than someone who is not. Particularly, try to keep your cool if you are transferred from department to department and cut off along the way.

- Get the name of everyone you speak to – although be aware that some will deliberately give you a wrong name to avoid comebacks – and keep a record of the name and number everyone gives you.

- If you don't get satisfaction by going through the usual channels – customer service, customer service manager and so forth – then write to the chief executive and copy the letter to the PR department and head of customer service if you feel like it. Again, keep the letter balanced, back it up with your written records of phone calls and copies of any correspondence you have had.

- If you have any professional contacts who could have more leverage, then use them. For financial products, perhaps your financial adviser should get involved on your behalf. Otherwise, try getting one of the 'complaining' websites to take up the challenge on your behalf (see below for contact details).

- You might think that poor financial products would be a more complicated matter to complain about but in fact that is not necessarily so. Financial institutions have some quite clear and sophisticated guidelines for handling complaints and all you have to do is write a letter. Once you do that, it's then in the system and it's up to the company to go through the complaints procedure. Don't just phone them, though, because records of that contact are likely to get lost in the system.

- The website **www.financevictims.co.uk** has a lot of

information on how to get redress for financial misselling, including lists of ombudsmen and a discussion board where you can find out about other consumers' experiences. The Financial Services Authority's very comprehensive website, **www.fsa.gov.uk**, also has answers to most questions you would have on how to complain about bad financial products.

- Don't necessarily take yes for an answer, particularly in the case of financial products. The first offer of compensation may not be the highest one, even if it is described as 'final'.

- Whatever happens, don't take no for an answer and if necessary use all the professional help available if you need it. There is a lot to be had.

Contacts

www.howtocomplain.com
www.complaindomain.com
www.getmethemanager.co.uk
www.financevictims.co.uk
www.tradingstandards.gov.uk
www.fsa.gov.uk
www.bankchargeshell.com

Dealing with sales calls

Sick of rushing to the phone while in the middle of making dinner only to hear an indeterminate accent on the end of the phone wanting you to switch your electricity provider/buy a new kitchen/buy double-glazing from 'our salesperson who is in your area right now'?

You can stop the nuisance before it starts by registering with the Telephone Preference Service (TPS) at **www.tpsonline. org.uk** or phone them on 0845 070 0707. Under the Privacy and Electronic Communications (EC Directive) Regulations

2003, it's unlawful to make unsolicited marketing calls to any-one registered with TPS. They have to pay a large fine for even one call, so you only have to tell them that you've registered to get them scurrying off the phone. Stop unwanted faxes at **www.fpsonline.co.uk** too.

Stop mounds of junk mail by registering with the Mailing Preference Service (MPS) at **www.mpsonline.org.uk** or calling 0845 703 4599. You can even attempt to cut down email spam by registering your email address at **www.dmaconsumers.org**.

Come-backs for cold callers

Want to get your own back on nuisance callers and have some fun at the same time? Use one, or all, of these satisfying retorts to get them slamming the phone down:

- Pause for a moment then say, 'What are you wearing? I'm not wearing anything right now.'
- After you've answered the phone don't say any more words, just bark and meow and give the occasional purr. Every now and then hack up a furball.
- Occasionally interrupt to ask, 'Did you hear that?' in a rather distressed voice. When the caller says 'no' say 'oh' in a mournful tone. Later start saying, 'Why are you doing this to me? Why do you lie? Am I just your plaything?'
- For no reason at all start describing your latest operation or particularly gruesome health problem. If you haven't had one, talk about someone else's – a difficult birth is always a good one.
- Say, 'Yes, I'd love to talk to you for as long as you like. Have you been saved?'

6

Making That Bit Extra

'If you can build a business up big enough, it's
respectable.'

– **Will Rogers**

Everyone needs to make a bit on the side once in a while!
Whether you're dealing with debt, saving up, investing in
your future or just sick of running out of money before the end
of every month, on the quiet we all yearn for a bit more cash.

Money from nothing

Go through every room in your house and pull out anything
you don't want any more. Sell it on eBay or Amazon or go and
do a car boot sale for a day. Do that at least once or twice a year
and you will have a clearer home and some useful cash every
now and then, just using stuff you have already.

The other great resources *you already have* are your own abilities and talents (yes, you do have some), and that's a great way
to start on your money-making quest. Use your hobbies and
the qualifications, training or experience you already have to
make money. Think laterally, too. If you have carpentry skills

you could turn them into toy making, or if you are a great cook, and you have given birth at least once you could become a doula (birth partner or post-birth partner – see page 299). Just a long-time interest in something can be a money maker if you work at it. A gardening fanatic who is totally self-taught can still make money propagating seedlings or doing some gardening or hedge cutting for people in the neighbourhood.

So if there's something you've always wanted to do – teach English as a second language, for example, be a stand-up comedian or run some fun parties – don't let your lack of qualifications or experience stop you. If you can afford it, this is the time to get that training or experience and go for it. Even if you don't make masses of money and you spend more time on it than you meant, at least you will have had a go and you won't get old and grey wishing you'd tried.

When you're looking for a way to earn some extra cash, don't just look at the bottom line. Look at the expenses in terms of the money you will have to invest, the effort and time you will have to take

It's quite likely that you will end up doing a few different things, not just one, to make a bit on the side. Some of my friends seem to make *all* their money just doing 'bits on the side', particularly writers and performers who make very little at their 'main' job but keep themselves going as film extras, market researchers, mystery shoppers, buskers, waiters, virtual and real secretaries and babysitters. It's an honest living and at least they get variety!

Down the back of the sofa

You could have hundreds or even thousands of pounds that you've forgotten about. According to the Unclaimed Assets Register (UAR), an organisation run by the credit agency Experian, there are at least £15 billion in unclaimed financial assets lying around, of which £5 billion sit in dormant bank and building society accounts and another £3 billion in unclaimed shares and dividends. There may be as much as £1.2 billion in windfall shares from demutualising building societies and insurers. So why not spend a bit of time looking through old papers and bank books. It could make you money.

- There's thought to be about £1 billion in loose change in Britain's homes. Grab your share! Trawl through the nooks and crannies of your home and you might find you're in the 88 per cent of people who reckon they've got at least a tenner in small change in jars, biscuit tins and down the back of the sofa.

- Look through your boxes of papers to see if you've got old building society and bank pass books. If you find them, cash the money in or switch to a better rate elsewhere.

- If you vaguely remember that decades ago you deposited a small sum in a long-closed branch of a bank, you can ask the bank to search for the money by using the special form available from any branch. For more details check out the British Bankers Association website at **www.bankfacts.org.uk**. The Building Societies Association – **www.bsa.org.uk** – also has information on how to trace lost or forgotten savings accounts.

- If you suspect there are all sorts of accounts, old policies and even shares you've forgotten about, contact the UAR. They charge a nominal amount for a search of their records for old accounts, life policies, share dividends, unit trusts and so on. This includes one search when you apply and a second one 12 months later. You can find more information on their website at **www.uar.co.uk**.

- The UAR also estimate that we've let slip £3 billion of pensions, so, for a fee of £35, they'll check their database and inform you if you have any unclaimed occupational pensions or personal pension products. Or you can investigate it yourself if you want to by contacting the Pension Schemes Registry at **www.opra.gov.uk** to use its free service.

- For information on lost National Savings certificates, National Savings accounts and unclaimed Premium Bonds prizes you should apply to National Savings. To obtain details of certificates, write to National Savings, Durham DH99 1NS. For all other accounts, write to National Savings, Glasgow G58 1SB. To discover whether a Premium Bonds prize is waiting for you, write to Premium Bonds, National Savings, Blackpool FY3 9YP. Alternatively, if you know your holder number, search the National Savings website at **www.nationalsavings.co.uk**.

- If you like to buy Lottery tickets (shame on you!) and you think you might have won something while you were away, you can check your numbers on their website at **www.national-lottery.co.uk/player/p/results/winCheck/ winCheckerStart.do**. However, remember, that tickets expire 180 days after the relevant draw and odds of winning are tiny.

- If you think that you might own some shares or be entitled to dividends, the first thing to do is to contact the registrars for the company. The three main registrars are Lloyds TSB (**www.shareview.co.uk**), Computershare (**www-uk.computershare.com**) and Capita IRG (**www.capitaregistrars.com**). If you have an old share certificate, the registrars can update it, usually free of charge. If you've lost the certificate, but find that you own or are entitled to some shares, the registrar can issue a new share certificate.

- If you find some old share certificates you didn't know you had for years and you're feeling generous, send them to the charity Sharegift (**www.sharegift.org.uk**, 020 7337

0501). They'll take your unwanted shares – however small in number or value – and will add them to others of their type, sell them and distribute the money to various charities with which they are connected. After all, if you haven't missed them for all those years, you won't miss them from now on.

Make money with zero per cent credit cards

Credit-card companies make billions out of us every year, but there's a way you can get your own back and make some money at the same time – so long as your credit rating is good enough.

First, open up a zero per cent credit card (that's where you need the good credit rating). Find out what credit limit they'll give you and then get them to transfer the full amount they'll allow into another credit card that you already have (which actually has no debt on it), i.e. your original card. Once the money is transferred over to your original card get *that* company to put that extra money into your own bank account. Then for the next six or nine months, or however long the zero per cent period lasts on your new card, you leave that money – which you've been given, for nothing – in a high-interest account somewhere. Make sure you pay off the minimum each month and just before the end of the zero per cent time, you pay all the rest back. You can make hundreds of pounds this way – I know people who do – but you do have to be disciplined.

Confused? Try this example. You've got a credit card with Big Bank plc., which you haven't used for a while, so it's currently standing at £0. You find an offer from Whopping Bank plc. for a credit card that offers zero per cent for balance transfers for nine months. You take out that Whopping Bank credit card and they offer you a credit limit of £10,000. You ask them to transfer that £10,000 to your Big Bank credit card, which they do electronically (they don't check to see if you really have any debt on your original credit card because they don't care – they just want your debt). Leave it for three or four days, then ring Big Bank and ask them to transfer the £10,000 that you suddenly have in your account to your bank account (it's legally your money now, so they can't argue). Once it's in your bank account, transfer it again into a high-interest account, unless your own bank account has a decent rate. Pay back the minimum amount you're asked for each month to Whopping Bank, and then, about two weeks before the end of the zero per cent period (about eight and a half months later), transfer what's left of the £10,000 back into the Whopping Bank credit card and close it down.

This way, you've made some interest on the money and haven't had to pay anything, other than a possible transfer fee that some credit-card companies are now charging. This process is called 'stoozing' and it's very popular with people with good credit who are disciplined. Mind you, even if you're not that disciplined, at **www.moneysavingexpert.com** you can set up a 'tart alert', which means they'll send you an email reminder before the end of your zero per cent period so that you can send the money back in time.

Big ideas and little contacts

Seriously, the ways in which we can make some money on the side are endless. There are many obvious ones (some of which I have itemised below) but everyone is different and everyone – yes, even you – has their own individual talents and abilities through which they can make some cash. Even if you think you can do nothing other than listen to others, you can still make money out of that – in fact listening is a very valuable skill, don't forget it!

The ways of making money fall into two basic categories: selling things and selling services. Even selling your time is selling a service – for example, you can hire yourself out as a house sitter or someone who will wait in for parcels or tradesmen. Use your skills, use your hobbies, use your spare time and use the space or things in your home to make money when you need it. Here are a few ideas that pretty much anyone could do at any time, but you can find many more in my book *A Bit on the Side: 500 Ways to Boost Your Income* (£7.99, Piatkus).

Sell your hair

Extensions, wigs and hairpieces are increasingly popular and many are made out of real hair. European hair is particularly sought after as it is rarer in type than, for example, Asian hair. If you have long flowing locks, and you wanted to get them cut anyway, why not make money out of them! According to Banbury Postiche, also known as Wigsuk.com, the fees are £3 per ounce if your hair is 6–12 inches long and £5 per ounce if it is more than 12 inches long. Wigsuk.com – **www.wigsuk.com**, 01295 750606.

Medical experiments

Drugs, creams, cold remedies – they all need testing on humans and the money is quite good. If you don't mind swallowing pills for money this can bring in hundreds of pounds at a time. Check out Biotrax – **www.biotrax.co.uk**, 0161 736 7312 – a very comprehensive website with information and support and a directory for those wanting to get involved in clinical trials. **www.hotrecruit.com** is a website with many and varied clinical trials that you can get paid for.

Police line-ups

It used to be that you could make about £15 quite often by taking part in police line-ups. Now, though, thanks to technology, you just get a one-off fee of £10 for taking part in a video 'line-up' but it's better than nothing. Just go down to your local nick and ask how to do it.

Film/TV extra

Anyone can be a film extra or walk-on part. You don't need any acting ability or particular looks. Simply contact some extras agencies and get yourself on their books. You can find a comprehensive list of agencies in *Contacts* (£10.99, Spotlight Publications), although you should be careful whom you sign up with. The basic is £64.50 per day but you can get up to £200 with 'add-ons'. Try the Casting Collective – **www.castingcollective.co.uk**, 020 8962 0099.

Market research

You may be irritated by smiling people with clipboards stopping you in the shopping centre and asking you your opinions on mayonnaise, but if you were paid to talk about it, in a pleasant room with food and drink laid on, that would be a different matter, wouldn't it? You can make around £50 cash for a couple of hours' chat about a product or service. Contact Saros Research – **www.sarosresearch.com**.

Mystery shopping

You may see exciting adverts on the Net about making money and getting freebies just for shopping. This is true, and there are lots of opportunities to make some money in your own time through mystery shopping, but it's not necessarily the big shop-fest they like to make out! You can make anything from £10 to £500 a week plus a few freebies doing this. Try any of these agencies: Retaileyes – **www.retaileyes.co.uk**; TNS – **www.tns-global.co.uk**; IMS – **www.ukims.co.uk**; Cinecheck – **www.cinecheck.com**, 0800 5870520; Field Facts Worldwide – **www.fieldfacts.com**, 020 7908 6600.

Dog walking and pet minding

If you hate the gym but want to get out and about, then this is an excellent idea. Full-time jobs and busy lives mean that many people don't have all the time they need to look after their pets. Charges depend on the area you are in and what you think people can reasonably afford. Dog walkers in London can charge up to £15 per dog, per session.

Poll clerk

This is an important job that many people don't think about. Election day polling stations have to be staffed in order for a government to be elected! Admittedly, these days don't come up very often, but when they do you can earn £230 just for the day! Get in touch with your local council now for a form to fill in and, come the next election, you could find yourself earning a good amount for a day's work!

Write articles

You don't have to be a card-carrying journalist to write for newspapers and magazines. Anyone can do it. You just need to be able to write (not necessarily as easy as it looks) and be able to withstand the many brush-offs your ideas might get from editors. Fees vary from a paltry £25 for 1,000 words for small-circulation, specialist magazines and websites (if they pay at all) to £1,000 for 1,000 words for some national Sunday newspapers.

Create a TV game-show format

TV companies are always looking for game-show formats. Really successful ones such as *Who Wants to Be a Millionaire?* can make millions for the TV company and they'll pay top dollar for an idea they think will run and run. Think up an idea and sell it! There, how easy is that? No really, a good TV game show format is a remarkably difficult concept to come up with. Some people try for years before breaking through. Essentially, the idea should be simple but fun. You should be able to fit the description of it onto one A4 sheet, so it is up to you to come up with an idea that is not already being aired, hone it down to some simple rules and a few fun gimmicks and send it to TV production companies or direct to TV channels. If you managed to come up with a winning format that was sold around the world you could pretty much retire on the proceeds!

Competitions

Anyone can do them. You see them on the backs of soup packets, on chocolate bars, on tissue boxes and attached to cars. Coming up with a witty and appropriate line to finish off a sentence can be a great way of winning money, a car or household goods.

Check out **www.competitions.com**, which is a very useful site for anyone interested in comping. Lots of tips, rhymes and contacts.

Being a business

If you have the time, the energy and the money-making ideas, you may find yourself running a whole little business 'on the side'. A lot of people do this, either because they need to or they want to or a bit of both. If you do get into the area of running a proper business – however small – it'll really help keep your stress levels down and help you make more money if you get clued up on a few basics before starting (or while doing it, if you've already started!).

Is it for you?

Do you really have the time and energy to devote to a small business? Do your partner and family feel happy about it and would they help in any way? Can you organise yourself and your time? Are you tough enough to cope with difficult customers and tricky suppliers? Are you willing to do what it takes to make it work and make some money?

If the answer to all or most of these questions is yes, then you have a chance of making the business work. If there are a few nos, then you should look to cut your expenses more or find a higher-paying full-time job than the one you have now. Either that or confine yourself to doing bits and pieces to make money. Don't knock it, by the way, as some people make a good living and keep their families going simply doing lots of different bits and pieces throughout the week.

Make a plan

It helps to do a few costings and make estimates on how much time you would need to devote to a business, how much you could make and so on before you start. On the whole, it's best to try to make money out of something you enjoy, something you do already (gardening, toy making or yoga, say) and something you don't need to spend too much time and money on before you actually set the business up.

However, if you've always wanted to try your hand at singing in clubs or being a dog trainer and money isn't your prime object, then go for it. If you make money at it, too, that'll be a bonus!

Try to be strict with yourself and pick worst possible scenarios when you're working out costs, effort and possible profits. Best to go into a venture with your eyes open! If you have a partner, make sure they're happy with what you're doing and, ideally, could help. There's no point bothering if you won't have support at home.

Decide whether you're going to be a sole trader – this gives you lots of freedom and flexibility, but you'll be completely responsible for any liabilities you incur in the business, which means your personal as well as business assets may be at risk – or a partnership. In a partnership you can share a lot of costs and responsibilities but you will have to do everything by consensus and you need to know that you can trust the other person absolutely. If you do go down the partnership route, make sure you draw up a partnership agreement with the help of a solicitor – however much you trust each other at the start!

If you are going to do things on a largish scale, make a business plan. This should be brief and easy to read and include all the relevant information that you and any possible financer will need. It should be a useful guide for you as you run your business and can be as invaluable to a small sole trader as it is to a multinational company. There are many books and websites that give help on writing a business plan. Go to your local library and pick out one of the books they have on it, or look at Lloyds TSB's free website **www.success4business.com** or **www.businessbricks.co.uk** or **www.entrepreneur.com/business-plan**.

Try to test out the market you're going for before launching into the business proper. If you're already doing this activity in a small way, you will be doing that anyway. Also, check out the viability of your idea with your local Business Link. They have a lot of free or cheap one- or two-day courses for business start-ups and it's often worth attending one of them.

Keeping your books

Many, many good businesses fail simply because they haven't kept a wary and regular (sometimes you need to do it daily) eye on their accounts. Whatever the size of your business, you need to know your costs and your income exactly to ensure that you're making a profit and not in danger of running into financial problems.

There are several good accountancy packages on the market that you could use, although many small businesses find that a simple spreadsheet set up on Microsoft Excel is quite good enough. Do have a look at Quickbooks (**www.quickbooks. com**), Microsoft Money or, if you have a big and prosperous business, Sage (**www.sage.co.uk**). You can find reviews of other accountancy packages at **www.accounting-software.qck.com** as well.

Unless you have a background in finance or accountancy, you would do well to employ an accountant, too. Accountants come in all shapes and sizes – good, bad and totally useless – so go by recommendation if you possibly can. Even those with qualifications up to their armpits can be expensive and hopeless, so be careful.

If you decide to go for it completely and you give up your day job and set up as a self-employed leg waxer or whatever, you should speak to your local tax and benefits offices about changing your coding to Schedule D and setting up National Insurance payments for yourself. Go to **www.hmrc.gov.uk** and **www.dwp.gov.uk** to find your local branches.

Bank accounts

If you're working for yourself it's helpful to have a separate bank account for incomings and outgoings to do with your business. It doesn't have to be an actual business account – most banks charge extra for those – but just a separate account, perhaps called your 'Number 2' account. Some of the smaller banks now offer really good deals for small businesses, though, so ask around or look on the Internet at websites such as **www.reviewcentre.com** and **www.startups.co.uk**.

So, with your personal account you pay your personal and household bills, but with your 'business' account you pay business expenses and pay in money from clients, and you can also pay yourself a kind of wage (known to accountants as 'drawings'). Also, if you pay for things out of your personal account you can add that up and pay yourself back from your business account.

There's no law to say that you *have* to work this way, but it makes it easier in the long run for tax purposes if you keep it all separate.

Advertising

You can lose a lot of money buying expensive ads or ads in the wrong places. You can also lose by having ineffective or misleading ads, so be careful. Many small businesses may need only a listing in Yellow Pages, a small website (one you could create yourself) and some word-of-mouth 'viral marketing'.

Look at where competitors are advertising and how they are doing it. That should give you an idea of the useful places to be. Try an ad in a paper or website if you're not sure. You will notice from the amount of enquiries you get whether it is worth it or not. On the whole, when you start off it is not worth spending large amounts of money on advertising. Keep your costs low until you know you could sustain more expensive publicity.

If at all possible, use PR, which is free, rather than advertising (see below). You will probably need to do both if you have a proper business on the go but, wherever possible, pay as little as you can!

Marketing

Marketing covers all kinds of things – printing, exhibitions, logos, websites, telemarketing, direct mail, among others.

If you're a great designer yourself, feel free to design your own logo, website, headed notepaper and so forth, but if not it's really worthwhile finding someone or a small design company that will do it all for you. Brand is important these days, particularly where there is a lot of competition, and the more you push your brand – on your website, your logo, your headed notepaper, your gifts – the more it will advertise for you.

The best marketing strategy is to allow some amount of time each week to talk to existing and past customers, talk to possible customers, check out what the competition is doing, talk to staff and suppliers and look for opportunities to promote your service or product.

PR

If you can do it, PR is – as we saw above – the best and cheapest form of advertising. Gaining column inches or airtime for your product or service for nothing is incredibly valuable. If you have lots of money you could hire a PR agency to run a campaign for you but (a) they tend to be expensive – even if they are one-person operations – and (b) there is no guarantee that they will get you into the media.

If you have a journalistic or any sort of writing background it can help. Essentially, you need to come up with interesting and even exciting press releases that will hook local and/or national media. Try to think from their point of view rather than your own. Your product or service may be the most interesting thing in the world to you but to others there is very little newsworthy in it.

Think around the topic. If your business is picture framing, for example, you could find out which are the most popular prints that people have on their walls, send them out to the media as a 'Top Ten' (journalists love those, particularly 'Top Ten Tips') and mention, in passing, that you can frame any of these prints – or anything else for that matter – for a fraction of the price of high street shops. 'Oh, and here are my website and contact details.'

Which annual events are important to your business? Think of a fun story featuring your business for Christmas or Valentine's Day or Easter or the summer holidays. If you offer tours around your town, offer a special deal with champagne and small boxes of chocolates (possibly brought in free through a deal with a local chocolate shop) for couples coming on the tour in Valentine's week. You could also research 'lurve' facts about your town and send them to local media as a fact sheet (journalists love those, too) with bullet-point bites of information about romantic happenings around your town in history.

Just be creative, think laterally and find out names, numbers and email addresses of journalists in local or national media that you particularly want to be featured in. Personal contact goes a long way, just so long as you don't irritate them with constant pestering.

There are several books on the subject of PR and it's worth reading one to get some ideas.

Insurance

So much of insurance seems like a waste of money that it wouldn't be surprising if you've forgotten all about this. However, with some businesses, if you don't have certain types of insurance you can actually be breaking the law.

You may need public liability insurance, motor insurance, employer's liability insurance, cover for fire, flood and other perils, cover for goods in transit, professional indemnity, cover for computers and other business equipment and so on.

If you belong to an association or federation for the sector you are in, you could get cheaper insurance through them. Otherwise, check websites such as **www.insuresupermarket.com**, **www.the-aa.com**, **www.moneyfacts.co.uk** and **www.find.co.uk** to compare prices and get the best deal.

Getting paid

For most sales, you will need to invoice your clients for payment. It is up to you to set a date for the payment – some businesses insist on payment within 14 days, which is perfectly acceptable so long as your potential client knows it beforehand

and agrees to it. The legal limit is 30 days from the date of the invoice and now, thanks to the Late Payment Act of 1998, you are within your right to charge interest for invoices paid after that date. See how much at www.late-payment-law.co.uk.

If you're being paid by the hour, keep track of the hours you work each day and include the total in the invoice. This helps your client see what has been done for the money. Many accounting packages offer templates for sales invoices that you could use, or make up your own.

Your invoice should include the date, an invoice number, your name or business name, your address and, if you like, your National Insurance number. It should have the terms of payment (for example, 'payment within 30 days') and the name and address of the person who should pay it. It should also include brief details of the work done or products sold and the total price (including a breakdown of charges if necessary). You may also like to include details of your bank account for BACS payments, since more and more people now prefer to pay that way.

If you are having difficulty getting paid, simple persistence usually works. Close to the final payment date, start ringing your client every other day reminding them, in a friendly way, that they haven't paid yet. Quite often just one phone call will do the trick, but for stubborn non-payers you may need to keep sending new invoices with interest slapped on before they pay.

If you have problems getting paid after that, look into factoring. This is where you sell your debts to raise cash and get a certain percentage – up to 80 per cent – of the value of the invoices. The balance, minus a factoring fee, is paid when the debts are collected. However, you will probably need a turnover of around £100,000 a year to make this a viable option.

Useful contacts

Business Link – **www.businesslink.gov.uk**
Small Business Service – **www.sbs.gov.uk**

Federation of Small Businesses – **www.fsb.org.uk**
Small business advice – **www.smallbusinessadvice.org.uk**

Books

Working for Yourself – Godfrey Golzen and Jonathan Reuvid (Kogan Page, £12.99) – a bestselling guide for people going it alone.
The Which? Guide to Starting Your Own Business (Which Guides, £10.99)

7

Student Finances

'I'm so poor I can't even pay attention.'

– Ron Kittle

'Be a student and** control your finances? Surely not a possibility!' you cry. Admittedly, it's a tough one, but, with some knowledge and a determination not to let the system get you down, you can do it.

The bad news 1

Being a student is not good for your bank balance – at least in the short term. Let's be honest, going to university entails signing yourself up for three or more years without pulling in a living wage. Not only that but you'll have to pay a hefty whack in the form of tuition fees for the privilege.

So why do it? Good question – and please do think hard about it before you go through the application process. University really isn't right for everyone and it's costing more each year, so don't rush into being a student if your heart's really not in it.

However, if you *are* keen you can console yourself with the fact that there's more to being a student than just cold, hard cash. It's a whole way of life. As well as picking up a degree, you'll get to immerse yourself in a subject that you (hopefully) enjoy, widen your career prospects, meet a bunch of like-minded people and have a lot of fun while you do it. And, if that's not enough to tempt you, you'll boost your potential earning power no end. The average graduate earns bags more cash over their lifetime than a non-graduate. Estimates of exactly how much more vary, but figures of up to 50 per cent have been bandied around. There's a lot of variation within this: studying highly sought-after subjects such as medicine, dentistry and architecture statistically set you up for a more secure future than an arts or humanities degree (check out **www.grb.uk.com** or **www.prospects.ac.uk** if you're interested in finding out which degrees lead to the most lucrative salaries).

That's all very nice to know, but what about the here and now? Students have long had a reputation for being hard-up scroungers who scrimp by on a diet of watery beer and own-brand baked beans – and that was back in the day when forking out for your own tuition and living costs was but a glimmer in a junior government minister's eye. Going to university has become increasingly expensive in recent years. However, the range of funding sources available and ways to ease the financial burden have also increased, if not enough to cover the costs of studying, then at least enough to make it doable. Whichever way you look at it, it's never been more important to find out exactly what university is going to cost you, and what help is available.

The bad news 2

There are two main things to find money for: tuition fees and living costs.

Tuition fees

Things are changing all the time in the wonderful world of tuition fees. It used to be that all students were charged a flat fee wherever they studied, taking various factors into account such as how much their parents had. Now, for anyone starting their degree in or after 2006, universities in England and Northern Ireland are allowed to set their own fees, within reason. These universities don't – yet – make home students pay all of their tuition costs. Putting on a university course is reckoned to cost an annual five-figure sum, as seen by the higher fees charged to international students (and those at private institutions such as the University of Buckingham or a handful of specialist colleges, which are few and far between).

However, English and Northern Irish universities can now ask for a greater proportion of the fee, rising each year at no more than the rate of inflation (until 2010, when things are set for a review). Unlike under the previous system, everyone will have to pay something, regardless of how poor or rich their parents are. But, also unlike under the previous system, no one will actually have to hand over the cash until after they've graduated. If you want to pay the fees straight away, year by year, then no one's going to stop you. But, for those without the ready cash to hand, there is a deferred-loan system, whereby the government 'pays' the fees for the student upfront. The graduate then has to pay back this money to the government once their salary goes over a certain amount. But more of that later.

With this in mind, it's worth looking at the cost of different courses and different universities. As in any marketplace, things are changing all the time. Although most universities need to haul in as much dosh as possible and charge the maximum possible fee, some institutions may undercut their rivals or offer unpopular courses more cheaply. That said, however, getting too caught up in tuition-fee savings is probably a false economy, especially while fees are capped at a relatively low amount. Short of a Lottery win or a generous parental trust fund, going to university is going to mean getting into a lot of debt. Far better to take on a marginally bigger debt in order to study what and where you want, rather than go into the red for what is, to you at least, a second-rate option.

Things are different for students in Wales and Scotland. Universities in Wales kept out of the 2006 increase in tuition fees, at least when it comes to students from Wales. Instead, they are introducing fees of up to £3,000 in 2007, but at the same time making Welsh students who study in Wales eligible for a tuition fee grant to cover the increase. In real terms, that means their fee payments would be unchanged.

Scottish students studying in Scotland don't pay tuition fees. They do, however, pay a fixed fee, known as a graduate endowment, at the end of their course, although certain groups (mature students, lone parents, disabled students and students on some courses) are exempt.

Living costs

The other area of expenditure – and the one where you have far more leeway – is living costs. Basically, this means rent, food, study materials (books, computer, pens, pencils, fluffy pink notepads), travel, clothes, toiletries, entertainment and hobbies, going out, and anything else you feel you can't live without. Unlike tuition fees, these costs have to be paid for while you're at university.

Many of these costs vary for students in different places. Your university or students' union should able to supply estimates. Loads of websites offer online budget calculators to help you work out how far your loan and – if you're lucky – grant will stretch. Try **www.ucas.ac.uk** or **www.studentmoney.org** for starters. Also, see Chapters 3, 4 and 9 for advice on budgeting, saving money and spending smartly. If you've read them already, read them again!

There are also a few extra things that students need to be aware of:

- Accommodation is usually your single biggest expense. To a large extent, how much you have to spend will depend on where in the country you study. As a big generalisation, the north is cheaper than the south, and the south-east and London are the most expensive of all. Check with your university when applying.

- Student housing takes many forms, from traditional university-owned halls of residence through private purpose-built student flats to privately rented houses and bedsits. University-run accommodation is usually a good bet, since it may be subsidised, or at least run on a not-for-profit basis. Catered student halls may charge a bigger weekly or termly rent than a room in a private house, but often work out cheaper once additional costs such as food, bills and insurance are factored in.

- If you live away from home, you're not covered by your parents' TV licence. Even if you live in a hall of residence with a communal TV area, you're not licensed to hide away and watch your own TV in your room. You need to stump up in order to avoid a hefty fine – see **www.tvlicensing.co.uk** for details and how to pay. You may be able to claim back some of your licence fee if you're away for three consecutive months, such as over the summer.

- Student houses, unoccupied during vacations and often packed to the gills with computers, TVs and other thief-friendly pickings, can be prime targets for burglaries. Students' unions are a good source of advice on simple steps to improve your house security. Insurance is a must. Endsleigh (**www.endsleigh.co.uk**), which was started by the National Union of Students (NUS), has special policies for students, as do most banks that cater to students.

- If you rent through a letting agent, minimise the likelihood of losing your deposit by using those that are members of the Tenancy Deposit Scheme for Regulated Agents (TDSRA) – see **www.tds.gb.com** for more information.

- An NUS or students' union card is your new best friend. Have no shame: flash it to bag as many discounts as you can – in high street stores, travel agencies, pubs and restaurants, on everything from cinema tickets to driving lessons to haircuts. Every little helps.

The good news: where to get the money from

The main chunk of your money will come from the government in the form of a loan and, perhaps, grants. Let's look briefly at some of the help available.

Loans

Everyone on their first degree can apply for a basic maintenance loan (that's the one that you get in cash to cover your expenses, not the one that the government 'gives' you to pay your fees). Students from poorer families are also entitled to an extra, means-tested portion.

However, how much of this you get also depends on whether you've been awarded a maintenance grant – those who are given a grant might not be allowed to borrow quite as much money, so they don't end up with that much overall. Final amounts, and just how these pieces of the financial jigsaw will fit together, are still being decided. Basically, depending on family income, you're likely to be able to get just the non-means-tested portion of the loan (richest families), the full loan (less rich families) or a full grant and some of the loan (poorest families). Or, because these things are done on a sliding scale, somewhere else between the two extremes.

There are a couple of extra things to be aware of. Because of the high cost of living in the capital, students in London are entitled to a bigger loan. Students living with their parents won't get as much money, because their living costs are seen to be cheaper (free or cheap rent, Mum's cooking and so forth). Check the official websites for up-to-date information.

Grants

The higher-education grant – that's free money from the government, with no repayment plan and no strings attached – is available to students from poorer families. Money is given on a sliding scale according to household income. The full grant is similar to the maximum amount of tuition fees being charged in England and Northern Ireland.

Applying for grants and loans

Don't delay! Look into it when you apply to university – there's no need to wait until you have a confirmed place. Application deadlines change each year, and getting your forms in late may mean you're still waiting for money at the start of your first academic year. See **www.dfes.gov.uk/studentsupport** for the latest deadlines, as well as downloadable forms and application packs. The information can also be found at **www.studentsupportdirect.co.uk**, and there's also an online application facility here if you prefer. Get in touch with your local education authority (LEA) – details from **www.dfes.gov.uk** – for more specific queries.

Wales and Scotland

As with tuition fees, student support arrangements are different for students in Scotland and Wales. Eligible Welsh students studying in Wales get an Assembly Learning Grant to help with their living costs. Loans are available, and vary depending on the place of study. A national bursary scheme for students going to university in Wales is being introduced in 2007.

Scottish students studying in Scotland get a means-tested loan towards living costs, and young students from poorer families get part of their living costs in the form of a non-repayable young students' bursary (YSB). Other grants are available for mature students, student parents and disabled students.

Official funding information/applications

For students in England

www.dfes.gov.uk
Student loans company: **www.slc.co.uk**
www.studentfinancedirect.co.uk
www.aimhigher.gov.uk
www.studentfinance.direct.gov.uk

For students in Wales

www.elwa.org.uk
www.studentfinancewales.co.uk

For students in Scotland

www.student-support-saas.gov.uk

For students in Northern Ireland

www.delni.gov.uk
NUS in Ireland: **www.nistudents.org**

Other students

Student funding is far from simple at the best of times. But, for students from a whole range of groups with slightly special circumstances, it gets even more complicated, with slightly different rules being applied or extra funding being available. If any of the following apply, or might apply, to you, then check **www.dfes.gov.uk/studentsupport** (or your local equivalent if you're from Scotland, Northern Ireland or Wales) for the latest information (other possible sources of advice are also listed below):

- part-time students;

- students spending part of their course abroad;

- mature students;

- married students;

- students with children or adult dependants;

- students with disabilities;

- certain courses – currently social work, some medical and teaching courses – have special bursary arrangements (check with your university).

National Bureau for Students with disabilities: **www.skill.org.uk**
Mature Students Union: **www.msu.org.uk**
Study placements abroad: **www.erasmus.ac.uk**
Teacher training: **www.tda.gov.uk**

Cross-border issues

Different rules, particularly in terms of tuition fees and eligibility for bursaries, apply for students from part of the UK going to study in another. If, for example, you come from Northern Ireland but want to study in Wales, or from England but want to study in Scotland, the rules are currently a veritable minefield. Check with your local authority for the latest arrangements.

Postgrads

Postgraduate study is a whole different ball game. Tuition fees have to be paid, and you won't (unless you're doing a Postgraduate Certificate of Education) get a loan. However, there are more generous bursaries available than to undergraduates, but to qualify you need a great academic track record and/or be studying something that's valuable to a business or the country.

There are two main types of postgraduate degree: taught and research. Application cycles are more flexible than at undergraduate level, but the earlier you get in, the more likely you are to get funding.

Some postgrads study part-time; the course takes longer, but you can work at the same time. Here are some other possible sources and ideas.

- First, look for funding at the university department in which you wish to study.

- Then try the relevant government-funded research council (**www.rcuk.ac.uk**).

- Trawl the sources of education grants listed below under 'Bursaries, scholarships and sponsorship'.

- Look at **www.prospects.ac.uk** and **The Grants Register** (Palgrave Macmillan) updated annually **www.palgrave.com**.

- Some employers may sponsor staff through courses such as MBAs.

- Many banks offer postgraduate loans at good rates of interest (that's good compared with another type of commercial loan, not the virtually interest-free student loans given by the government to undergrads). Those doing vocational courses may also be eligible for a career development loan (see **www.lifelonglearning.co.uk**).

Repayment

It may mean starting your working life in a stack of debt, but, as far as borrowing goes, a student loan is one of the best offers you're likely to get in your life. First, the interest on the loan is pegged to the rate of inflation. Although there is interest to pay, this is supposed just to reflect the changing value of money you borrowed rather than actually getting more out of you. If, for example, you borrow £1,000, the amount you eventually pay back is supposed to be the equivalent of £1,000 in today's money.

Secondly, you don't have to pay back the money until your salary reaches a certain level. Loan repayments will then be deducted from your pay packet on the amount you've earned above the repayment threshold. If a couple of years later your salary drops down below the threshold – because, say, you're made redundant or take time out to travel, your repayments are automatically suspended until you get back to earning megabucks. And, if the worse comes to the worst, your nearest and dearest won't be expected to pick up the tab: if you die with outstanding loan repayments, or if you're still owing money 25 years after the April after graduation (except for arrears), the debt will be cancelled for good.

Basically, this is a loan that needs to be paid back but as it's a relatively cheap loan you don't need to bust a gut to do it terribly quickly. Better to concentrate on making it in your chosen career and paying off any expensive loans you've acquired such as credit-card debts or overdrafts before concentrating on this one.

Other money

Whatever way you do the sums, your full loan (and maybe grant) entitlement isn't going to be enough to live the high life. Or even much of the low life, for that matter. It's likely to make up much of your cash, but there are other sources of money available to supplement your income.

Bursaries, scholarships and sponsorship

A bursary is, basically, a gift of money to help you study. Britain doesn't have such a well-established tradition of bursary funding as the USA, but there's still a fair pool of money sloshing around for those who take the time to look. And, even better, the pool has got much bigger in recent years and is likely to carry on growing. Just as going to university has become more expensive, more bursaries have, handily, been introduced.

Some bursaries are open to anybody who feels like filling in the application form, and others have specific criteria: coming from a low-income background or a family with no tradition of higher education is a common factor, though others can be as specific (and bizarre) as playing a brass instrument and living in a town no less than three miles from a river. Other bursaries are available for those with particular academic or extracurricular skills such as musical or sporting ability – these are often (though not always) also known as scholarships.

The law that brought in higher tuition fees from 2006 also meant that universities that charge the maximum fees allowed are obliged to provide some kind of bursaries for poorer students. In practice, many choose to make these bursaries bigger than they have to.

If you have a good idea of the career you're heading for, it could be worth looking for sponsorship in that field – some employers will help pay for your studies if you agree to work for them during and/or after university. There's not a great deal out there, but, if you don't ask, you'll never know. How likely you are to get the cash depends on the industry – specialised technical or scientific subjects, big businesses and the military are the best bets.

How to get your hands on them

- Start with the university/universities to which you are applying. Check their website (links to UK institutions at **www.hesa.ac.uk**). Look for general university funding, anything specific to your department or course, any links with employers or local industry (particularly if you're doing a course that involves a work placement).

- Search the databases (and get some general money advice) at **www.studentmoney.org** or **www.scholarship-search.org.uk**. Also try the Educational Grants Advisory Service (**www.egas-online.org**).

- Get to the library and leaf through **The Educational Grants Directory** or **The Directory of Grant Making Trusts**, which are published by the Directory of Social Change (**www.dsc.org.uk**).

More possibilities

Access to Learning Fund: This is an extra pot of money designed to help those who find themselves in dire financial straits while studying. It's more an emergency fund than something to rely on when drawing up your budget, and priority is given to people seen to be in most need, such as mature students, students with children, students from low-income backgrounds and final-year students. Apply for the handout through your university – it's up to them how much to give you and whether to shell out a lump sum or pay the money in instalments. They do not usually have to be repaid.

Parents: You get the maximum amount of financial support only if your parents' income is below a certain threshold. That's because it's conveniently assumed that your parents would like to give their student offspring extra money if they're able to. In practice, many do, perhaps paying their rent, giving a monthly allowance or simply throwing extra pounds their way when things get tough. But there are no guarantees. Not all parents want – or can afford – to bail out their kids, no matter how the government has done its sums.

If they're willing and able to help out, then it'll be easier for you to work out a budget if you know how much you'll be getting from them – and when. A useful starting point is to look at your financial assessment from the local authority – if your parents' income is high enough to stop you from getting the full, non-means-tested amount of money, it would be helpful for them to give you at least enough to make up the difference.

Work: Earning some money while studying is becoming increasingly common: about 40 per cent of students do some kind of part-time paid work during term time. Most of these find work in catering, retail and hospitality. A small proportion find work that uses the skills they have learned on their course, such as teaching or nursing.

Many universities understand that some students need to work, and even offer help in the job hunt. The level of help can vary from a dedicated job shop that acts as a casual employment agency to a tiny noticeboard in the corner of the careers service. Students' unions often hire students to work in their bars and other facilities, which can be handy, because they tend to be more sympathetic to things like the need to cut down hours as exams loom.

Universities and/or individual university departments often put a limit on the maximum number of hours of paid employment their students should take on. Even if rarely enforced, these recommendations are worth heeding. Take on more than 12 to 14 hours of additional work a week, and it's likely your studies will feel the impact. Ultimately, this will be self-defeating. Also bear in mind that academic workloads tend to increase each year, and some courses involve more contact time than others and so will be harder to squeeze part-time work around.

There's also plenty of time to top up the coffers during

vacations. The long summer holiday is the safest bet – the length of Christmas and Easter breaks varies from university to university, and can fall when you're up to your ears in course-work assignments or exam preparation. Part-time jobs, particularly for big employers, may let you go full time over the holidays – although, if you live away from home, remember to factor in the extra costs of rent and food. Internships or work placements can be a useful way of getting some CV experience while earning money – depending on your area of study, they might be lucrative, or might not pay you at all.

Also check out Chapter 6 ,'Making That Bit Extra', for more ideas for boosting your student income.

Useful contacts

Sources of work

www.activate.co.uk
www.e4s.co.uk
www.justjobs4students.co.uk
www.summerjobs.co.uk
Work placements:
www.step.org.uk
www.work-experience.org

Advice on work and rights at work

www.morethanwork.net
www.worksmart.org.uk
National Association of Student Employment Services – www.nases.org.uk

Look out – the bankers are coming!

Banks love students. Not because you're going to deposit vast sums of cash in their coffers in the foreseeable future, but because they want to snap you up and hang on to your business in anticipation of the day you'll be a high-earning graduate in need of lots of financial services. Consequently, there are a load of student bank accounts on offer promising everything from sizeable interest-free overdrafts to free gifts when you sign up. It's these gifts you need to be wary of. Some are far more valuable than others – and it's not necessarily the ones that look nice and shiny. A discount rail or coach card will probably pay off better long-term dividends than the latest technological toy. But, really, any free gift should be at the bottom of your list of priorities when choosing an account. Here are some more important things to look for.

- *The interest rate when you're in credit.* It makes sense to make what little money you do have go as far as possible, so look for the account that will pay you the most when your loan's just been paid in. Or consider a separate, high-interest savings account.

- *The interest-free overdraft.* How much extra cash will your bank let you use for free? How much will it increase every year? Is this guaranteed, or a discretionary amount subject to review? Might they extend your limit if things get tight? How long will they let you keep the overdraft after graduation? What happens if you go over the limit – how much interest will they charge you?

- *Credit cards.* Does the account include one? Do you trust yourself to use one? What's the limit, and what's the interest rate?

- *Any extra charges.* How much would it cost if your cheques bounce?

- *Proximity.* It's also handy if there's a branch near where you're living or studying, especially if you're on a campus or out-of-the way university.

In general, the Internet banks and former building societies offer the best rates for overdrafts and savings, so make sure you look at what they have first. The exact packages for all the banks change year by year, though, so shop around on the money websites for the latest offers in current accounts. Try **www.switchwithwhich.co.uk**, **www.moneysupermarket. com**, **www.moneyextra.co.uk** or **www.find.co.uk**.

Taxes and other joys

Council tax

Full-time students are exempt from paying council tax. Part-time students are not, though you can claim relief if your income is low enough. The situation can also get trickier if you live with a non-student. Check with **www.nusonline.co.uk** and get in touch with your local council for advice and any exemption forms you might need to fill out.

Income tax

Student loans, grants and scholarships are not taxable, which is handy, since there's not much money in them to go around in the first place. Earnings from paid employment are subject to tax. However, unless you've got a plum job or are really putting in the hours, you're unlikely to earn more than your personal tax-free allowance. If you work only in the holidays, you may qualify for a student exemption form to stop tax being taken out of your pay. Otherwise, you will be taxed under PAYE, but may be eligible for a refund if you've overpaid during the tax year because, say, your hours vary over the year. Check with the Revenue **www.hmrc.gov.uk** for the necessary forms and information. See also Chapter 14, 'Taxation'.

Benefits

Students aren't generally entitled to social security benefits, either in term time or holidays. There are a few exceptions. Those with children under 16, students with certain disabilities and pensioners should be able to claim housing benefit and income support. Students who have to suspend their studies because of illness or caring duties may be able to get housing benefit and jobseekers' allowance. Conditions apply: check with your university, students' union, or look online at **www.dwp.gov.uk**, **www.dfes.gov.uk/studentsupport** or **www.direct.gov.uk**.

Debts and bankruptcy

Although debt is an almost inevitable fact of student life, all debts are far from equal. Taking out a student loan and paying your tuition fees after graduation are designed to be as painless as possible. But students are also susceptible to credit-card debt, loan sharks and most of the horrors that 'grown-ups' face. However, see Chapter 3, 'Dump Your Debt, Live Cheaper, Make Money', for all the advice you need to deal with it.

As a student you can also get specialist advice from the NUS (**www.nusonline.co.uk**) or your university student advice centre. The Consumer Credit Counselling Service (**www.cccs.co.uk**) run a student debtline – get free advice by calling 0800 328 1813.

Bankruptcy is generally a bad thing for students or graduates to go into (see the advice in Chapter 3), even though many are now touting it as an easy way to spend what you like now and not have to pay for it when you graduate. In fact, it's also not the solution to wiping out student debts. It was, for a time, possible to cancel some student loans by declaring yourself bankrupt, but this loophole has now been closed throughout the UK. Because student debt is public money, you'll still have to repay it if you declare yourself bankrupt.

In theory, bankruptcy is taken from your record after a year, but in fact it can stop you getting loans, mortgages and even bank accounts for a number of years after that. Worse, it can stop you getting jobs in certain sectors, including banking, the police force and local council and government offices. Also, more and more potential employers are now doing credit checks on applicants as well as all the usual background checks.

Other useful contacts

Universities UK (represents universities, surprisingly enough): **www.universitiesuk.ac.uk**
Universities and Colleges Admissions Service: **www.ucas.com**
Office for Fair Access: **www.offa.org.uk**
Higher Education Funding Agency for England:
www.hefce.ac.uk
National Union of Students: **www.nusonline.co.uk**
Funding advice: **www.support4learning.org.uk**
Course information: **www.hotcourses.com**
The Times Higher Education Supplement: **www.thes.co.uk**
Education Guardian: **www.educationguardian.co.uk**
Money advice: **www.studentmoneynet.co.uk**
Information on being a student, including finances:
www.studentuk.com, **www.student123.com**,
www.push.co.uk

8

A House or a Home?

Buying a property used to mean simply buying somewhere to live. Now, though, we think of it as an investment as much as a dwelling. Not surprising, given the astounding rises in prices over the last 30 years – although, as with the stock market, you can't guarantee the same or even similar rises over the *next* 30 years. In fact, if you look at it over the last *50* years, you'll see that property has returned an average of 9 per cent per year while the stock market has returned an average of 11 per cent over the last 100 years.

If you're thinking of buying property, make sure you're quite clear about why you're doing it. If you're going to live in it, forget the investment aspect. The important thing is that you like it and it suits your needs. If you make money on it later, that's just a bonus. If you're buying a property purely as an investment, on the other hand, the opposite applies: your tastes are of no interest here, you simply need to buy what you know will rent and what you think is likely to grow in value.

Should you be your own landlord?

We're so obsessed with owning our own property in this country that it's easy to think that it's the only way to go. In fact, it's not right for everyone and there are many downsides to owning property. So, before you even start down the road of property purchase, first ask yourself some questions:

- Do I really want to tie myself into a mortgage and a single geographic location for the foreseeable future, or do my lifestyle and career choice demand more flexibility?

- Can I afford – and do I want to pay for – all the extra costs such as legal fees, building and decorating, repairs, furnishing and the like?

- Can I afford a place that I would really like to live in now, or should I work hard and save hard for the next year or two to put together a deposit for somewhere that I would genuinely be happy to live in?

If you answer 'no' to any of the points above then you're better off renting – at least for the time being. After all, it's the way in most of the rest of Europe and why buy here just because everyone else seems to do so? There are things in life other than property ownership. However, if you've done your sums, decided you really want to be a homeowner and know you could afford something, then go for it.

First rung of the property ladder?

Whatever you do, don't overstretch yourself when buying your first property. As house price inflation has slowed, people's mortgages have started to hurt for much longer than they used to. Think about it: in olden times (the eighties and nineties) you'd buy a place with a 90 per cent mortgage and after a year of house price growth your 90 per cent mortgage would have shrunk to just 80 per cent of the value of your home. You can't expect that now. So really consider waiting for a while before you buy to save enough of a deposit to bring the mortgage payments down.

Some questions

Sit down with a pen and paper and ask yourself what your incomings and outgoings are. Where can you make savings? How can you earn more? Take a good hard look at what your goals are and how you can reach them. What kind of property would you like to buy and, realistically, *could* buy? How much of a mortgage could you get and, therefore, how much do you need for a deposit (keeping in mind that 100 per cent mortgages are also much more expensive than 90 per cent or even 95 per cent mortgages)? Set yourself a realistic time frame for saving up the necessary deposit (it could be a year or two, so be patient). Consider the fact that, even if house prices do go up a lot in your area, it's still more helpful to have a wad of cash to put down as a small deposit than to have no deposit at all. Apart from anything else, you'll have to pay for solicitors' fees, surveyors' fees, mortgage arrangement fees and, possibly, stamp duty, so you'll need some cash to cover all of that.

If you knew the total cost of servicing a mortgage – in other words, the total amount of interest you would pay on the capital over a 25-year repayment period – you would be horrified. Interest rates fluctuate wildly from year to year, but say we pick a rate of 8.65 per cent (the average, apparently, for the period between 1945 and 1996). If that was your average interest rate on a £100,000 mortgage, which you took 25 years to pay off, you would pay a total of £238,038 – that's the basic £100,000 loan you borrowed in the first place plus a staggering £138,038 in interest (a.k.a. 'money thrown out of your purse into the lender's "holiday in Barbados" account'). This is the joy and thrill of compound interest working against you – and we don't want that, do we?

The deposit

Aim for a deposit worth at least 5 per cent of the value of the home you could go for, plus an extra £4,000, *at least*, for stamp duty, solicitors' fees, surveyors' fees and other joys.

Mortgages and how to get one

The important thing to know about mortgages is that they are simply big loans – whopping great debts – so all the rules that apply to your approach to a loan or debt repayment also apply to your mortgage. In other words:

- go for low interest rates (but don't be taken in by short-term, low 'headline' rates that suddenly jump up after a few months);

- don't borrow more than you can comfortably afford to pay off (taking into account possible rises in interest rates later on);

- remember that the sooner you pay off the mortgage/debt the cheaper it will be.

Whichever type of mortgage you plump for, though, make sure that you take into account the possibility that the interest rate could rise either in the short term, if you have a variable rate, or later on when your fixed interest period finishes. If you've borrowed the absolute, outside, not-a-penny-to-spare maximum amount you could get for your mortgage, you could find that interest rates double or even triple in the next few years and you have terrible difficulty meeting your monthly payments. So don't borrow a frighteningly high amount of money, and do try to test out the numbers to see if you could afford the payments if the rate goes up by 3 per cent or 4 per cent. You could be horrified at how much the repayments jump up.

The last thing you should do when looking for a mortgage is to go to your bank, ask them what they have got and just choose from their limited offerings. Tragically, this is what a lot of people do, and they are losing so much money this way I'd like to grab them all gently by the neck and *shake them*! There are about 8,000 different mortgage packages on the market and several of them could be right for you. Certainly, many of them are bound to be better than anything your own bank could offer.

The best way to make the most informed decision is to do a load of background research yourself. It's easy to find out what's around on websites and in mortgage magazines. At the back of the mortgage magazines there are lists of mortgage lenders with the packages they have on offer, together with the rates and other useful bits of information, such as whether there is a fixed period and if so how long, whether there are penalties attached and how the interest is calculated (whether it is calculated daily – good – or annually – bad). The Sunday broadsheets are also useful for up-to-date 'best of' mortgage lists.

If all this talk of doing it yourself sounds too worrying to you, then by all means get the advice of an independent financial adviser (IFA) or mortgage broker – sometimes they have access to mortgages that aren't on the general market anyway. But make sure you've done your homework first and know what sort of a mortgage you want and what you definitely don't want. Also, make sure you have some fairly good ideas about mortgages you are interested in so that if the IFA doesn't mention them you can bring them up in the conversation and show that you're not a pushover.

It's important to find a reputable, independent broker who charges upfront fees. Beware of other kinds, because a broker claiming to be independent who doesn't charge upfront fees will make their money from commission and may offer the products of only a handful of lenders who pay good money. Ask the broker at the start if they have access to any mortgage on the market. They're legally required to let you know if they are paid a commission by the company they recommend, but it's still a good idea to ask that question yourself.

Information point

Find loads of mortgage and house-buying information at:

www.fool.co.uk
www.bbc.co.uk
www.charcolonline.co.uk
www.firstrungnow.com
www.direct.gov.uk

Magazines: *What House, What Mortgage, Mortgage Advisor, Your Mortgage, BBC Good Homes*

Different types of mortgage

There are so many different types of mortgage on the market, and so many lenders, that it's hard to know where to start. Once you get down to it, though, you realise that there are three basic decisions you need to make.

Decision 1

Will you go for a 'repayment' or 'interest-only' mortgage?

- Repayment mortgages are the most popular. Part of your monthly payment covers the interest on the loan and the rest eats away at the capital. It means that at the end of 25 years (or whatever the term of the loan) you will actually own your home outright.

- Interest-only mortgages are slightly cheaper than repayment ones, since your monthly payments pay only the interest on the loan. This means that at the end of the term you will still owe the amount you originally borrowed. For this reason most people set up a separate payment each month into an investment vehicle (see Decision 3') that will grow as the mortgage term continues.

Decision 2

Which payment rate will you go for?

- *Fixed rate*: This is useful for first-time buyers, because you're guaranteed that, no matter what happens to the Bank of England base rate, your mortgage will stay the same for a fixed period of time. This is great if the base rate goes up but disappointing if it goes down. These deals tend to be inflexible and will impose high charges if you leave before the agreed end time. Also make sure you *never* go for a deal that ties you to the company after the fixed-rate period finishes. This means they can charge you a ridiculously high rate (and they do) and you won't be able to get out of it without paying a high penalty.

- *Capped*: These mortgages have a variable interest rate but there's a fixed upper limit, which can give you the best of both worlds. The cap lasts for a fixed period within which, again, you are tied to the lender and charged high fees if you try to leave. It's a useful kind of mortgage if you think mortgage rates might fall but you don't want to be exposed to the risk that they could rise.

- *Variable*: This is the standard mortgage rate that lenders usually offer. It could go up or down, depending on what the base rate does and how much money the mortgage company feels like making. The advantage of this kind of loan is that it tends to be flexible and you can opt out at any time. The disadvantage is that it's generally a lot more expensive than other deals.

- *Discount*: these offer a discount on the lender's usual variable rate for a fixed period. They can be cheaper than the norm, but you still have the disadvantage that they could go up, albeit at a discounted rate, if the lender's variable rate goes up in that period.

- *Tracker*: This mortgage sets an interest rate that is just above base rate and goes up and down exactly as the base rate does. So if it's set at, say, 0.75 per cent above base rate and base is 5 per cent then your mortgage will be 5.75 per cent. Trackers are great if base rate is going down, of course, and your mortgage rate will change as quickly as base rate changes. They're not so good, though, when base rate is going up!

- *Offset and current account*: A recent development introduced from Australia, offset mortgages bundle up your current account, savings account and mortgage in one product. This means that any credit in your current or savings accounts is 'offset' against your mortgage, which means that, although you pay the same amount into your mortgage each month, more of that money goes to paying off the capital of your debt rather than in interest, as the company charges you interest only on the amount of the mortgage that's left after your savings are taken into account.

- *Flexible*: More and more mortgages include some flexibility now, in that you can overpay or underpay – or even have payment holidays. These can be useful if you're self-employed or expecting some life changes in the near future.

Decision 3

Do you need extra products to back up your mortgage or an alternative style of mortgage?

- *Endowment policy*: This is one way of paying off an interest-only mortgage. Very popular (with mortgage brokers) in the 1980s, the idea is that the product generates enough money to pay back the whole loan and gives you life assurance to cover your debt should you die before the end of the term. However, these policies tend to have high charges, often underperform and could leave you with a shortfall once the mortgage needs to be paid off.

- *Pension and ISA*: These are also ways of paying off an interest-only mortgage. Either you can take out an ISA (individual savings account), which will grow (one hopes) enough to pay off the final mortgage debt, or you can link part of your pension (up to 25 per cent of the lump sum) into your mortgage so that it can be used to pay off the outstanding debt. You cannot access the money till you reach 50, but it's a tax-efficient form of investment.

- *Sub-prime*: If you've got a dodgy credit history or you're self-employed and normal lenders won't give you any money, you can still go to one of the growing band of mortgage companies who will lend – at a price – to people whom no one else will touch. The big disadvantage of these is that they tend to be much more expensive than normal mortgages but at least you can get the money and, possibly, switch to a cheaper deal a year or so down the line.

- *Guaranteed*: Could Mum and Dad guarantee a larger-sized mortgage than you could afford on your own? Or could you do it for them? This mortgage is for people who can't afford a large enough mortgage (on paper) but a relative could guarantee the rest for you.

- *Self-cert*: If you're self-employed and your accountant saves you tax by making your income look small, this can stop you getting a decent-sized mortgage. With self-certification mortgages (self-cert) you say what your real income is and the mortgage company lends on the basis of your say-so. Again, the rates for these loans tend to be higher than the norm because they're riskier.

- *100 per cent (or more)*: Does what it says on the tin – you can borrow 100 per cent of the value of your property and some lenders offer up to 130 per cent so that you can pay off other debts at the same time. Any mortgage over 95 per cent tends to be a lot more expensive than others, because of the risk involved, and if you take out one of these you're much more likely to suffer negative equity (this means that the value of your house falls below the amount outstanding on your mortgage).

- *Cashback*: So desperate are mortgage companies to get your custom that they're offering all sorts of incentives, including a percentage of your mortgage back as a cash lump sum (usually about 3–5 per cent). This can be worthwhile but there's always a downside, usually that you're tied into the deal for a long time with heavy penalties for pulling out and a higher interest rate.

There are other unusual ones on the market that could suit you too: sharia mortgages for Islamic borrowers; 25-year fixed mortgages, whereby you fix your interest rate for the full 25 years; rent-a-room mortgages, whereby they take into account the income you would get from renting out a spare room; and even divorce mortgages, whereby the interest is frozen for the first six months because people getting divorced have a lot of extra expenses at the start. Lenders are getting so creative that the next new mortgage could be specifically for 30-year-old blonds called Brian living in the north-east.

Mortgage payment protection

Mortgage companies aren't allowed to force you to take out mortgage payment-protection insurance (MPPI) but they might make it difficult for you to get a loan if you don't. This insurance, as ever, is designed to protect the lender more than you and, of course, it's an extra cost on top of your mortgage payments.

Before jumping to buy insurance, find out what your employer offers if you can't work because of accident or illness. Even if there's no great deal to be had there, remember you can, and should, build up an emergency cash fund yourself of at least three months' salary to cover crisis situations anyway.

If you still think you need insurance there are two main options:

- *MPPI*: Most policies don't pay out until a month after you're unable to pay your mortgage and the payouts may last for only a year. If you're self-employed, you can get cover, but, if you claim, you'll need to show that you've ceased trading.

- *Permanent health insurance*: More expensive, but PHI pays out indefinitely in the event of accident or sickness. You can bring down the premiums by choosing a slightly longer deferment period – the length of time following a claim before the policy starts to pay out – but make sure you have enough savings to cover the interim.

Higher lending charge

This is what used to be known as mortgage indemnity guarantee (MIG). If you borrow more than 75 per cent of the value of your property you may have to pay the Higher Lending Charge (HLC), which can add hundreds or even thousands to the total amount of your mortgage. Try to avoid it if you can, because it insures the lender against your being unable to pay – it doesn't help you (again), even though you're the one who will pay the premium each month. Lenders say the fees are there because the loan is 'high risk'. They say HLCs protect them against the dangers associated with lending a high percentage of the property's value. The fact is, though, that there are so many mortgages on the market for you to choose from that really you can tell any lender that insists on HLC to take a running jump!

Special life insurance (descending term insurance)

Another thing you don't need is special life insurance to go with your mortgage. In fact, if you keep your mortgage down to 75 per cent or so there's a good chance the mortgage company won't require you to have any, although they may still try to sell it to you because sales of life insurance carry impressive commission levels. If you don't have dependants, you almost certainly don't need it. If your mortgage outlasts you, then the lender can get its money back when the house is sold. If you do have dependants, then you still might not need *more* life insurance. If you already have life insurance (and you probably do if you have children), then you don't necessarily need to add another policy but if you do go for an assigned one, shop around. Don't let anyone force you into it. By avoiding unnecessary life assurance you can save yourself sizeable sums, which you can add to your savings or pay into your mortgage, which are far better places for your money.

Get someone else to pay your mortgage

If you can bear to share your personal space with another human being, having a lodger renting a room in your home can be a pretty painless way of earning money and paying the mortgage. As a move to lift the burden of demand on affordable housing, the government introduced a tax incentive to prospective landlords a few years ago, allowing them a few thousand pounds in rental income per year tax-free. Check on the Inland Revenue's website, **www.mrc.gov.uk**, to see what is the current amount you're allowed each year. That way you should see how having rent from someone else can substantially increase your monthly income and in some cases cover your monthly mortgage payments for you. Financially, it's well worth considering.

Getting a leg-up!

There are cheaper alternatives to buying property the usual way. If you can't afford the kind of place you want, consider some of these.

Auctions

Properties that need a *lot* of work or places that need to be sold fast go to auction. If you know what you're doing (and particularly if you're good at building), you can pick up a real bargain here. But there are problems:

- You won't be able to get a mortgage for *really* tumbledown properties, so you'd have to be a cash buyer to get anywhere with them.

- For other properties you need to have at least a 10 per cent deposit ready to put down on auction day. The rest has to be paid within 28 days, so it's best to have a mortgage sorted out beforehand.

- Ideally, you should have a property surveyed before even bidding, and that can be a large cost down the drain if you don't win.

- It's easy to get carried away with the excitement of the auction room and bid too much for the wrong property.

- You could end up with a complete lemon.

For more information on how to buy at auction look at
www.bbc.co.uk/homes
www.propertyauctionnews.co.uk
www.propertyauctions.com
www.ukauctionlist.com
www.eigroup.com

Bank of Mum and Dad

Parents with money to spare could be helpful either as guarantors of your larger mortgage or by buying a share in your property as an investment with you, perhaps, paying a small rent for their share. Some parents give the money as a gift outright, essentially paying out part of the child's inheritance early on (after all, if they survive for another seven years there'll be no Inheritance Tax to pay). Others will buy jointly with their offspring and take their cut of the profits when the property is sold.

Buying with a friend/lover

Two incomes are better than one when it comes to getting a decent mortgage, but buying with a friend, and especially with a lover, can be fraught with problems. Obviously, you need to know you can stand living with them day in, day out, but, even if they're wonderful, you should get things on a proper legal footing from the start to protect you both.

In legal terms, you can own a house with someone else either as *joint tenants* or as *tenants-in-common*, and it's a very important distinction.

- With *joint tenants* two people simply own the whole house between them. There's no technical division of the property and, if one dies, ownership of the house passes automatically to the surviving partner regardless of whether there's a will. Essentially, it means you cannot 'gift' your share of the property to anyone else.

- Usually, when married couples buy a home together, they do it as joint tenants regardless of who's actually paying the mortgage. It's so common that solicitors handling the purchase sometimes even forget to suggest the alternative option! And, because lots of people don't bother to make wills, this at least covers the problem of dying intestate, since there'll be no arguments about who subsequently owns the whole house – often the main asset in a relationship.

- With tenants-in-common you both own half each of the house (or a different percentage, depending on what you agree). It's obviously a technical 'half each' but it does mean that each tenant-in-common can leave their share of the house to anyone they like and the other person can't just sell the house and get all the money. It has to be divided up equally. If you're cohabiting, or you're just friends pooling resources, this protects you both.

Housing associations

Shared ownership is one great way of getting on the housing ladder cheaply, and for the most part this can be done only with a housing association. What happens is that you buy a share of a property and pay a small rent on the rest. You can then go on to buy further shares, and eventually own your home outright. There are usually long waiting lists for these schemes, particularly in London, so get on a list – or several – as soon as you can. They usually operate on a kind of points system and the longer you've been on the list the more points you have. You also get extra points in some areas if you're a 'key worker' (such as a teacher, nurse, social worker or the like) or if you have dependants or currently live in a home that is demon-strably bad for your health.

To find out about buying a home in stages from a housing association, and from some trusts and co-operatives, contact the Housing Corporation office covering your area. They'll send you a list of registered social landlords (RSLs) operating these schemes in your neighbourhood. Phone them on 020 7292 4400 or look them up at **www.housingcorp.gov.uk**.

Ex-council properties

If you're lucky enough to get a council property you may be eligible to buy it, although be careful. Some council properties – particularly those in large, poorly maintained blocks, may be very difficult to resell and won't hold their value. Long-standing tenants (at least 15 years' tenancy) may be eligible for substantial discounts of up to 70 per cent of the value, so it can make it very worthwhile. But you may have difficulty getting a mortgage on certain properties – mainly on those hard-to-resell properties – and you may have to pay a share of huge repair bills.

The starter-home initiative

If you're a key worker, such as a nurse, police officer or teacher, you could benefit from the £250 million starter-home initiative brought in by the government in October 2001. The initiative was designed to help people doing 'key' jobs buy homes in expensive areas and has been very useful for those who qualified for help. The scheme was brought in because in general teachers, nurses, social workers, police officers and other essential staff earn too much to qualify for social housing. But most earn too little to afford to buy a home by themselves in an increasing number of property hotspots around the country – London in particular.

There are various ways in which key workers can be helped with accommodation under this scheme. Have a look at the government website **www.housing.dtlr.gov.uk**, where you can find a fact sheet on the scheme and contact details for your area. There's also lots of useful information on the *Guardian* newspaper's website at **http://society.guardian.co.uk/key-workers**.

Self-build

More than 25,000 people build their own homes each year. It may seem a bit extreme but you don't have to be a builder yourself, just be willing to look for land, bring in an architect and have the patience to project-manage the works while the house is being built (probably 12 to 18 months). There are more and more mortgages on the market for self-build schemes and many will lend up to 95 per cent. A well-run self-build project should see the final value of the home increase by 20–30 per cent on the actual building and land costs once it is finished. So, if you're prepared to wait and do the work necessary, you can make some sensible money on it. For more information on how to go about building your own, home check out the online magazine *Build It* at **www.selfbuild.co.uk**, and also look at **www.ebuild.co.uk** and **www.homebuilding.co.uk**.

Alternatively, make it easier for yourself and get a flat-pack home. These are increasingly popular and there are now lots of designs to choose from. There's still a lot of building involved but a lot of the work is done for you. The kit home – where a major part of the house itself is manufactured in a factory somewhere – is just another example of the prefab building, but rather nicer and more solid! There are all sorts of companies around the world making kits in all kinds of materials (timber, obviously, but also metal structures and some using former freight containers!), and it's worth spending some time researching what's out there. Find out more about kit houses from **www.channel4.com/homes**.

For any type of self-build, though, remember that you'll have to buy land as well. Beware of companies trying to sell you land without planning permission in the hope that it'll qualify for some later on. This is extremely risky and some of the companies are frankly dodgy.

Useful contacts

www.bbc.co.uk/homes
www.direct.gov.uk
www.rics.org.uk

The buying process

Looking for a property to buy can be a huge effort and hassle, but at least there are more alternatives now to just signing up with a range of estate agents. Look at ads in newspapers, look in selling magazines and websites such as Loot (**www.loot.com**), your local version of the Gumtree (**www.gumtree.com**), **www.findaproperty.com**, **www.hot-property.co.uk** and **www.propertytoday.co.uk**. Many property websites now are directly linked to estate agents, so they don't give you much of an advantage except that it means you can do some searching from the comfort of your own computer.

Once you've found a property you like it's simply a question of making an offer – probably through the agent – and, if it's accepted, you then need to have a survey done, find a mortgage (they will want to do a valuation survey too), instruct a solicitor or conveyancing practitioner (see below) and wait.

In Scotland property buying is quite different. The seller will invite 'offers over' a certain price and you have to make a sealed bid for it. You have to have a mortgage before you start home hunting because, if your bid is successful, you're legally obliged to buy. You also have to have a survey done before you bid. Some properties come on the market with a fixed price but the majority sell in this bizarre and unhelpful way!

The survey

There are three types of survey:

- the mortgage lender's valuation;
- a homebuyer's report;
- a full structural survey.

Valuation: If you've applied for a mortgage the bank will send round a surveyor to carry out a valuation, and sadly you have to pay for it – usually at least £150. This is very basic and won't tell you about the fabric of the building or anything really useful to you.

Homebuyer's report: This gives you much more information about the property, particularly the structural health of the building. It typically costs upwards of £250 and covers the general condition of the house, major defects and any maintenance needed.

Full structural survey: This involves extensive investigation of the property and costs between £400 and £1,000. You really should get a full structural survey on any building over 100 years old, more than three storeys high, or of unusual construction, such as thatched or timber.

Lawyer or conveyancing specialist?

The legal side of buying a home, including the transfer of ownership, is known as 'conveyancing'. Some people do their own conveyancing but it can be hideously complicated, so most are happier paying someone else to do it – either a solicitor or licensed conveyancer. In both cases, their job is to check the legal documents and carry out a search for any local authority plans that could affect the home: a proposed new bypass, for example. They'll also agree what is included in the house sale, arrange the completion and exchange of contracts, and oversee stamp-duty payments.

Solicitor

Ideally, you should choose your lawyer as soon as you start looking for a place to buy, so they can be ready to start work on your case the moment your offer is accepted. Ask family and friends for recommendations or use the Law Society's online search facility (**www.lawsociety.org.uk**) to find solicitors' firms in your area who do conveyancing work. If you're lucky, you might find a 'no sale, no fee' deal, where no charge is made if the transaction falls through. Not many solicitors offer this – hey, they're lawyers, what do you expect?

When looking for a solicitor, get several quotes but don't make your decision based on price alone. You'll want to get on with the person you're dealing with, who should be able to explain the process clearly and whom you trust to do a good job – actually, just doing the job at all seems like an impossibility for some solicitors.

Licensed conveyancing practitioner

Specialist firms of conveyancing practitioners are quite new to the marketplace, but they are growing as building societies also set up conveyancing sections within their companies. These practitioners can be less expensive than traditional solicitors, but bear in mind that they won't be able to help with anything in the purchase that falls outside the remit of property law. To find one, run a regional search on the Council for Licensed Conveyancers' website (**www.theclc.gov.uk**).

Stamp duty and other joys

You pay stamp duty land tax when you buy residential property such as a house or flat. Not everyone has to pay it: cheaper homes are exempt but after the basic rate the tax goes up from 1 per cent to 4 per cent depending on the price of the property (check **www.hmrc.gov.uk** to find out what the thresholds are at the moment).

Useful contacts

www.firstrungnow.com – all kinds of ideas on less conventional ways of becoming a homeowner; also news articles and links to mortgages and legal advice
www.fool.co.uk
www.bbc.co.uk
www.moneysupermarket.com
www.charcolonline.co.uk
www.direct.gov.uk
www.hmrc.gov.uk
www.theclc.gov.uk
www.lawsociety.org.uk

For a free guide, 'How to Buy a Home' or 'How to Buy a Home in Scotland', phone the Council of Mortgage Lenders on 020 7437 0075 or 020 7434 3791 or go to **www.cml.org.uk**.

Selling property

Selling a property is much less stressful than buying one, although to do it well you should follow a few basic points:

- If you sell through an estate agent go through personal recommendation if you can. If not, have a look at signs outside houses with 'sold' on them rather than 'for sale'. Go for the one with the most 'sold' signs.

- Read the agent's contract's small print carefully, as you may find yourself signed up and legally bound to stay with them for a long period of time. Insist on a time period of your choice. Month to month or even week to week if you can get away with it!

- If you decide to use more than one agent also check the small print on their contracts. They may insist on 'sole selling agreement', which means that even if you sell your home privately or through another agent, you'll still be charged a commission fee. Not good.

- Most properties are sold through estate agents but there's nothing to stop you selling privately. Take out ads in local papers or even national ones if it's an expensive property, or try the cheap websites such as **www.loot.com** and **www.gumtree.com**, or the specialist property sites such as **www.fivepoundahouse.com**, **www.thelittlehousecompany.co.uk**, **www.mypropertyforsale.co.uk** or **www.houseweb.co.uk**.

- Don't just go for the highest valuation an estate agent gives you. They might just be telling you what you want to hear. If you're unsure, have a look at how much similar properties in your area have gone for at **www.landreg.gov.uk** and **www.upmystreet.co.uk** or ask your neighbours!

- Negotiating a low fee with an agent could be a false economy, because it won't necessarily generate the high levels of enthusiasm needed to get the best result. A full asking price deserves a full fee, but you might want to agree a downward sliding scale if offers fall below it.

Seller's pack

A newish joy for anyone selling property is the legal require-ment to fill in a 'home information pack' (HIP), which everyone calls a 'seller's pack'. This has been brought in to speed up the buying process – so many sales used to fall through, or be held up, because buyers would find horrors in the survey that they didn't know about before and have to withdraw or re-negotiate. With a seller's pack, a buyer, instead of undertaking their own search and surveys after an offer's been accepted, will have the information they need when they visit the property. The pack must include a surveyor's report on the condition of the property and results of any local authority searches. Importantly, the seller will have to pay for these (a few hundred pounds) which should stop quite a few putting their properties on the market just to test the water.

Capital gains tax

One good piece of news is that you don't have to pay capital gains tax on any profit you've made through the sale of your own home. If it's a second home or an investment property then you'll have to pay a significant chunk of tax on that profit.

Useful contacts

Royal Institution of Chartered Surveyors – **www.rics.org.uk**
www.gumtree.com
www.loot.com
www.findaproperty.com
www.landreg.gov.uk
www.upmystreet.co.uk

Property as an investment

Contrary to popular belief – encouraged by TV programmes and people at dinner parties – property will not automatically make money for you. However, it can be a very good investment if you do it right. Chapter 8 has more information on property as an investment, but, to focus your mind, here are some of the pros and cons of investing in property, particularly buying to let.

Pros

- You should get the double whammy of money coming in each month from the rent *and* capital growth in the property itself over the years.

- Britain is already an overcrowded island and there is likely to be even more pressure on the property market in years to come as people move towards more single-person occupation, and immigration increases. This should drive prices up in the long term.

- Property has generally leaped in value over the last 30 years across the country, although it has been patchy. The growth is likely to be less steep in the next 30 years, but there is likely to *be* growth.

- Everyone needs somewhere to live. Even if you have to drop the rent, you can still get some money for it.

- This is one of the few investment products for which it is acceptable – and even advisable – to borrow money. This means you can make money by using other people's (the bank's) money.

Cons

- The property market has been grossly inflated over the last few decades and the growth is likely to flatten off considerably over the next few years.

- There is no guarantee that property won't actually fall in value at any stage, just like any other investment.

- There are many costs and risks connected with property. However sturdy it is, all property needs some maintenance, painting and mending each year. You may even have to replace boilers, heating systems, drains or roofs. Some tenants can cost you money by wrecking the place or refusing to move out and creating massive legal costs. You may find the place lies unrented for months and you should insure the property and, possibly, your rental yields.

- Many people have piled into buy-to-let in recent decades, which has caused a glut in rental property in some areas, bringing rents down.

- Property is a very illiquid asset. In other words, it can take a long time to sell it and convert it into cash. This means that you can invest in it only money that you don't need to put your hands on for a few years.

- Given the price of property now, you can properly invest in it only if you have a large lump of cash to put in, since deposits are much larger than they used to be. With shares, bonds or building society accounts, you can invest a relatively small amount to start off with.

Yes, I really want to invest in property

Right, in that case, the first thing to do is to have a good, hard look at your own financial situation. Since there are many potential downsides to renting out a property – such as bad tenants, void periods and expensive maintenance emergencies – you need to think whether you could cover these expenses for a few months if everything went pear-shaped. If you're already in debt, just ignore the idea of investing in property at the moment. Concentrate on paying off your debts, then think about it. Getting property if you're already in debt will only add to your burdens.

If you can manage the investment, though, you first need to think about where you want to buy. The first three rules of buying residential property are: location, location, location. Investing in buy-to-let property is first and last a business decision. As with any major investment, the first thing you should do before launching into any rental market is to speak to the professionals. In this case it's the local letting agents (not estate agents – beware of them!) who will know which are the best kinds of property and which are the best locations. To start with, they will be able to tell you whether there is a demand for rental property in their area and, if there is, what kind is the most popular.

Think of this as a business transaction, because that's what it is. Look at the property you want to buy in terms of its proximity to transport links and also whether it is in the kind of place that tenants in that area want. After that, it's the size and type of property that is most important and can vary enormously depending on the tenants you want to attract.

Financing a buy-to-let

The first thing you need to consider is finding a deposit. This can be tricky, because mortgage lenders tend to want you to put down at least 20 per cent of the value of the property, sometimes even 30 per cent, although there are more and more who will take just 15 per cent.

If you're in the lucky position of having enough cash knocking about, then great – put that down as a deposit. If you have, say, £100,000, and a 20 per cent deposit for easily lettable properties in your area would be £50,000, you have the choice of using it as the deposit on something worth £500,000 or, cleverly, using it as the deposit for two properties worth £250,000 each. This way, not only will you be spreading your risk – in terms of rent and so on – but also you will make more money in the long run than you would if you put it into one property. Also, you'll save on tax, because you'll have more mortgage interest to set against the rental income.

Borrowing a large amount to invest in something is called 'gearing'. It means you put the smallest amount of your own money in and borrow the maximum you're able to, then use the rent to pay off your loan. Remember, though, high gearing is no use if the rental income doesn't cover the mortgage. You need to work out very carefully first just how much *realistically* you're going to get from the rent and whether that will *easily* cover the mortgage payments. There needs to be some slack – ideally about 20–30 per cent extra rental above your mortgage payments. Mortgage rates can go up or down and even small movements upwards can greatly increase your monthly outgoings.

If you're looking to invest in a buy-to-let property, it's likely that you already have a property that you live in that probably has some equity in it. With new mortgage deals coming on the market every week it's quite possible that you can remortgage, free up some extra cash and still pay less each month to pay off the loan.

Again, though, make sure your own personal mortgage isn't hiked up to the sky. Rates could go up at any time and it's no good bankrupting yourself just so that you can invest in something else.

The mortgage

Finding the right buy-to-let mortgage is easier than ever now, thanks to the Internet. The popularity of investing in property has meant that more and more mortgage companies are offering buy-to-let deals at ever more competitive rates. A good mortgage broker will be invaluable here. However, you can do a lot of research yourself and you should. Again – check out the Internet:

www.moneysupermarket.com
www.charcolonline.co.uk
www.fool.co.uk

www.moneyfacts.co.uk
www.moneyextra.co.uk

As a prospective landlord you will have to choose between an interest-only and a repayment mortgage.

Interest-only

Interest-only mortgages are cheaper but you will need to invest in another vehicle, such as an ISA, extra pension or endowment policy, to pay it off at the end of the term. Or, like many owners, you might take the view that as house prices go up you will have enough to pay the mortgage off when you sell. It takes a strong nerve to do that, though, since nothing, including a rise in house prices, is ever guaranteed in this life!

Buy-to-let is considered a business venture and so you are allowed to offset the mortgage interest payments against any tax you might be liable for on the rental income. Bear in mind that this tax benefit applies only to the *interest* and not to any repayment of the capital. This is why a lot of property investors use interest-only mortgages most of the time.

Repayment

So the advantage of a repayment mortgage is that the property will be all yours when you come to the end of the mortgage term. The risk is that you will have less money to play with should you need some of the rent for other purposes and it's also not as tax-efficient.

Do get your sums right. Will the rent cover borrowings and costs after allowing for time when tenants don't pay up or when the property is empty? You'll need to keep some cash spare to cover void periods and repairs to the property. And don't forget tenants who fail to pay their rent too – not only does it mean you're subsidising their housing when they don't pay up but it's an expensive business to have them evicted from your property.

Useful contact

The Association of Residential Letting Agents (ARLA) – **www.arla.co.uk**, 0845 3455752

Book

Renting Out Your Property for Dummies – Melanie Bien (Wiley, £14.99)

Buying abroad

If you can't afford to buy in this country, or you want a place in the sun or you think there's more potential for house-price growth abroad, by all means look into buying overseas. If you think buying here is a fraught process, though, you'll be shocked at the extra nuisances surrounding buying abroad.

By far the most common destination for holiday home buyers is Spain, followed by Greece, France, then Italy and Portugal. America is increasingly popular now, too, particularly Florida. But, before you leap on the next flight to Barcelona clutching a fresh mortgage in your hot little hand, remember that there are costs and several pitfalls to buying foreign property, however cheap it may at first appear to be. Here are some examples.

- If you buy in France you have to allow for a whacking 12–15 per cent on top of the actual purchase price in expenses. First, the *notaire*, a lawyer who acts on behalf of both buyer and seller, will charge 6–7 per cent for their work and for the property transaction tax – like our stamp duty. Then the estate agents, who make our besuited bovver boys look like pussycats, slap on another 5–6 per cent of their own. This you can avoid by buying privately, but, if you do, you must make sure you have good legal advice to protect you.

- In Spain, Italy and Portugal you should allow for 10–11 per cent in fees and expenses, including proper legal advice. As you would expect, there are a few nasty surprises in the conveyancing laws abroad and, unless you are a native, it is easy to make a terrible mistake. In France, for example, once you have signed a *compromis de vente* (agreement to sell) you are essentially bound to buy the property unless you are happy to pay a huge fine.

- In Italy, one of the oddest legal processes is agreeing a valuation for your property. Because everyone tries to avoid tax, the official valuation can be as low as half the purchase price. This way the various taxes associated with the sale are cut down for you.

- Under Spanish and Portuguese law, any debts on a property automatically go to you on completion. This can mean that any previous mortgage on the property that has not been cancelled could become your liability. It is therefore essential that you get a good professional to do thorough searches for you before you buy.

Ask yourself why you want to buy a home abroad. As with property here, it's easy to get carried away with the flow and make a move that isn't actually right for you. Ask yourself:

- Do I really want to go to the same place every year?

- Do I mind the hassle of looking after the property when I'm there or paying a local to maintain it?

- What do I really want from it – sun, sea and relaxation or a good investment?

- Can I afford the expenses involved in having a holiday

home? Remember: budget airline flights may not remain at rock bottom for ever.

- Could I cope if the value of my home abroad went down?

It's possible that you'd be better off putting money regularly in the stock market to build yourself a nest egg and just renting holiday villas in various different places during the summer.

However, if you do go ahead and buy a place in the sun, keep these points in mind:

- If you're looking at buying a home as an investment as well as a place to escape to, you need to research the market before jumping in. Prices of property in France, for example, vary wildly but buying in the popular areas such as Paris or the Cote d'Azur is generally a better investment than buying a cheap farmhouse miles from anywhere, which will be hard to resell.

- Buy as the natives do. In Italy, for example, if you buy in the centre of Milan it's going to be expensive but it will hold its value. Look at the popular areas that the Italians buy in, such as the lakes or picturesque villages that are a short drive from an airport.

- Any house purchase abroad should be thought of as a long-term investment. With the costs involved in buying and moving properties you should expect to stay there for at least five if not ten years before you even think of selling.

- Decide whether to have a UK or a local mortgage. UK mortgages can be cheaper and easier to arrange but you could lose out if exchange rates change wildly. Also, in some countries you'll be allowed tax relief against rental income for the interest on a local mortgage but not on a UK mortgage. Look into this.

- Get a preliminary mortgage agreement before you look.

In some countries, if you pull out of a sale because you can't get a mortgage this can put you in breach of contract.

- Even 'preliminary' or 'reservation' contracts should be checked before you sign them. You think lawyers and estate agents are bad over here – just wait till you see what they're like in Eastern Europe, for example!

- If you want to let the property or alter it you will probably need permits, which can be hard to get in some countries.

- Decide who should own the property – you, you and your children, a trust or just you as a couple. There are usually tax implications for all of these, so get it right before you sign the contract.

- What would you like to happen to the property if you die? In some countries you're not allowed to leave your property to whomever you choose. Make a local will at the same time as you buy the house – don't just trust your English will.

- Get a survey done – particularly if the property is old.

- Always get relevant advice from an independent lawyer and listen to the experts on the ground – so long as they are not connected to the sale of the property.

- Does the property have the necessary permissions and licences? More importantly, is the property allowed to be sold? Recent horror stories recently show that it's quite possible to buy a villa in Spain built on land that wasn't owned by the vendor in the first place, and which can then be taken from you.

- Take out the right property insurance. Depending on what you do with the property you'll have to have different kinds of insurance.

- Be prepared for how long it can take to buy a place. Buy property in France and it could take up to 20 weeks to complete the transaction. In Spain, Italy, Greece and Portugal it'll average 12–18 weeks.

- Always give yourself a cooling-off period if you see a must-have property and are tempted to put down a deposit there and then.

- If you're arranging finance on the property, make sure you have an opt-out clause in the contract if the loan isn't agreed (so that any deposit paid is refunded).

- If you rent out your property abroad, income will have to be declared to the British taxman. Check out the tax laws of the country you're buying in. There may be implications if you rent or sell the house. Many countries have reciprocal tax agreements with the UK so that you don't end up paying tax twice.

- Think about combining your cash with friends or family: it could bring a villa with pool rather than just an apartment. It also cuts down the running costs.

- Open a bank account in your chosen country and get a certificate of importation for the money you bring in.

- Set up standing orders in a local bank account to meet bills and taxes. Failure to pay your taxes in some countries, such as France, Portugal and Spain, could lead to court action and possible seizure of your property.

Useful contacts

The Federation of Overseas Developers, Agents and Consultants – **www.fopdac.com**
The Law Society – **www.lawsociety.org.uk**

Books

Buying Property Abroad – Liz Hodgkinson (Kogan Page, £12.99)
Fiona Fullerton's Guide to Buying, Selling and Moving House –
Fiona Fullerton (Piatkus Books, £9.99)
Fiona Fullerton's Guide to Buying to Let – Fiona Fullerton (Piatkus
Books, £9.99)

Make a will

As soon as you have any property, or investment, you need to
make a will. It doesn't matter if you're only 19, if you have
property (lucky you at that age!), then you need to make a will
just to stop the government getting its mitts on your family's
money.

Sadly, people pop their clogs at all sorts of ages for all sorts
of reasons. If you have nothing to leave anyone then you don't
need to think about it, but the moment you have something
valuable to leave to family or friends you should make a will.
If you don't leave a will stipulating what should go to whom,
the government will take its very substantial cut from your
property – 40 per cent in fact – before your loved ones see any
of it.

See the section on 'Making a Will' in Chapter 12 for advice
on how to go about it quickly and painlessly.

9

Make Your Money Make Money

'A billion here, a billion there, and pretty soon you are talking big money.'

– Everett M Dirksen

Whether you are on a top salary or just struggling through on the basic wage, before you even think of investing you should first make sure that you have got rid of all non-mortgage debt and that you have some money saved for a rainy day.

All the top investors say that it's vital to save up enough money to cover you for three to six months in case of emergencies before you start investing. This means that if you lose your job, become ill, or your marriage breaks down, you could keep going for a few months without having to worry. If you don't have this kind of emergency money, you could find yourself having to sell your investments just to get cash quickly. This is not a good idea, because you may find that you need cash just at a time when your investments are not worth as much as they could be at a later date.

So, as mentioned in Chapter 4, 'Saving and Borrowing', sit down and work out how much you would need, realistically, to keep going and start putting money away in a high-interest building society or bank account until you have that amount saved. It used to be that only the postal accounts or long-notice accounts gave high interest, but now quite a few instant-access accounts offer the better returns, so go for one of those. Once you have your financial 'cushion', you can start on the fun stuff!

Information point

Find the best savings rates online at websites such as
www.fool.co.uk
www.moneyextra.co.uk
www.moneyfacts.co.uk
www.moneysupermarket.com.
Or have a look at the savings tables in the money sections of Sunday broadsheet newspapers.

Where and how to invest

Investing, as opposed to saving, means putting money into something that you hope will make more money for you over the long term. And that's the key difference between investing and saving – in fact it's the key difference between investing and gambling, too. Real investment means leaving your money in something for a long time, ideally a minimum of five years and preferably a lot longer. It's done with an eye to providing yourself, or someone else, such as your child, with a large amount of money at a particular time. It can be to give yourself a pot of gold when you retire or create a lump sum to pay for your child's education some way down the line, or even to give yourself the necessary cash to set up your own business when you've spent a few years in your current employment.

However, although investment is an excellent idea that

most of us agree with, it doesn't work as well as it might for everyone. This is generally because of our ignorance of the basic principles of investing, which makes us sitting targets for companies and individuals who want to sell us investment products that make *them* lots of money but keep *us* poor. So read and digest the following to protect yourself and keep you on the straight and narrow investment path.

Basic principles

- It's important to think long term, and it's particularly important to invest in products that will increase in value and keep up with inflation – that's the buying power of your money – over the long term. Not all do. Cash investments, for example, tend to lose value over time (see below).

- It's also very important to spread your investments where you can. This is easier when you have more money to spread, of course. To start with, you may need to just put your money in one kind of investment vehicle. But, as your income and savings increase, try to diversify your investments (some in shares, for instance, some in cash, some in property and so on). This way, if one or two of your investments go belly up, you will still have the others to fall back on.

- Never invest in anything you don't understand. Even if that nice, smart adviser tells you the product is bound to grow and give you security later on, if you don't understand how it works, don't commit money to it.

- Never invest in anything advertised on TV. TV advertising is *very* expensive and companies who can afford it are clearly making too much money out of their clients.

- Be wary of investments advertised in newspapers and

billboards. This is cheaper advertising but it still costs. Most of the best, simplest and cheapest investments are hardly advertised at all because they don't make so much money for the financial companies.

- Never ignore the downsides to any investment. When investing in shares or other 'invisibles' such as bonds and cash, be aware that one of the biggest factors that determine the performance of your investment is the charges. With equity funds (funds invested in shares), for example, the charge is taken out of your money before it is invested, which cuts down on the amount you can make in that year. Try to keep charges below 1 per cent if possible. With property and collections (such as art and antiques) you have many potential costs such as repairs, insurance, lack of tenants for your property and so on. Even if they grow in value, you still have to weigh up how much you lost in costs.

- Try to use cut-price brokers – you can save on some of the initial charges if you use one of these. These brokers bulk-buy and can therefore negotiate decent reductions with most fund managers. Also, because they are simply processing orders rather than giving advice, they will give back some or all of their own upfront commission and make their money on the annual commission alone (bad enough on its own I think but at least you will save on the initial charges). You can find more information on these at **www.iii.co.uk**.

- *Never* invest in something just because everyone else is. In fact, when everyone else (heralded by reports in the media) is investing in something (technology shares, say, or property) that is precisely the time that you need to stay away from it. The Motley Fool website has a lot of information about this 'contrarian' way of thinking (**www.fool.co.uk**) and top investors such as Warren Buffet (see his company at **www.berkshirehathaway.com**) ignore popular opinion and invest only in what they personally believe to be sound ideas.

So where do you put your money?

Well, that depends on you! We're all different and we all have our own attitudes to risk and reward, so, even given the same information, none of us will behave in the same way. That's why it's important that you do your own research first, find out the facts and then make up your own mind as to what you want to invest your money in. No one else really knows (or cares) as much as you do about your money and how you see your future. So consider the following different options – and do more research elsewhere if you like – and then put your money in one or (better) several of them.

Cash

By cash I mean basically bank savings accounts or building society accounts. For most of us it's the closest we've ever got to 'investing'. Perhaps your mum and dad opened a building society account for you when you were a kid and when you've been feeling sensible you've put some money in here and there and got a bit excited once a year when your statement showed the extra few quid you got in interest. It's safe, it's easy to understand and you know you can make some money on it. But, sadly, because it's safe, the interest you're paid is relatively low and, over the long term, the return on your money is not too hot. This means that generally cash is a very poor place to invest if you want to make yourself rich in later years.

Long-term building society returns just about match the long-term rate of inflation after you've taken tax into account but, if you also consider average earnings growth, cash really is a loser. In other words, the amount you end up with after a few decades won't seem anything like as impressive as the same figure would today. Even if you keep reinvesting the interest you get each year, over time the real spending power of your little pot of money will actually decrease. If we're thinking long term (and we always are for investments, aren't we?), keeping your money in banks or building societies is only slightly better than sticking it under the mattress.

What's an APR/AER?

APR stands for *annual percentage rate* and it shows you, essentially, how much your loan will cost you per year including any charges.

AER, which is quoted more often than it used to be, stands for *annual equivalent rate* and it's used in descriptions of savings accounts. Really, it shows what the notional interest rate *would* be if the interest were compounded and paid once a year. Jane Mack from the Motley Fool website explains, 'If the bank pays you interest every month, it's the difference between you taking the interest out of the account each month or leaving it in there to build up over the year, in which case you'd get interest on the interest as well as the capital as each month goes by.'

Bonds

Strange and rather dull-sounding things, bonds tend to be more popular with older people than with the young, because they offer guaranteed returns over a fixed period of time, which is useful if you are living off the money rather than looking for growth. Bonds, like cash, are a nice safe-ish place in which to put your money, and you do get a better return on the whole than with ordinary savings accounts, but it's still not great.

Bonds are essentially loans you make to large institutions that can be bought and sold on a market. The most common are government loans, or gilts (see below). But you can also trade corporate bonds, which are loans to large companies. Essentially, you lend the company a sum of money to use as they will. They agree to pay the money back to you at a specified date in the future, plus an annual amount of interest. Unlike with shares, where you are basically buying a small part of the company itself, with bonds you are just *lending* money to a company, so you don't have a stake in that business.

Bonds have different safety ratings depending on the riskiness of the company you're lending to, but mostly, if you stick to big, solid companies, you'll find they're pretty safe – although, of course, the safer they are, the less they give you in interest. If you wait until the bond's term is up before cashing it in, you should get your money back in full if you bought it at the right price to begin with. However, if you try to sell it before the end of the fixed period, its value will depend on the current yields on bonds and the time remaining to the redemption date.

The capital value of bonds moves up and down in relation to interest rates. It's like the opposite of taking out a fixed mortgage: the point of a bond is that you get a fixed rate of interest over a fixed period of time. So if you are promised a return of, say, 5 per cent over the next three years and the savings accounts are offering 4 per cent today that will look like a good deal. But, if interest rates go up in those three years to 8 per cent, your 5 per cent return will seem pitiably little. So bonds are not a totally safe bet, but they give a half-decent yield with very little risk, which is why retired people, or those approaching retirement, like to transfer some of their money from shares into bonds.

Most of us don't bother trading in individual bonds. We tend to invest in bond funds – the kinds of things that banks and building societies advertise with the words 'high', 'builder', 'extra' and 'yield' in their titles. As with stock market funds, these invest in a basket of bonds of different levels of risk. Ideally, they should be safer because they spread the risk over, sometimes, hundreds of different bonds.

Gilts

These are a kind of bonds subset. They're also known as government bonds – basically, loans to the government. As we're living in a civilised country with a relatively stable, democratic government, not in one of those places where the leader has a special salute and a predilection for tight uniforms (although give it time ...), lending money to the government is generally considered to be a pretty safe bet. Therefore, the return on gilts, though nice and secure, is even smaller than that on company bonds. Still, these are very useful investments if you want to have guaranteed returns right now and in the future. They're just not helpful for long-term investing.

With-profits bonds, endowment policies and anything packaged!

If there's one thing that financial companies *love* doing it's creating clever-sounding and often complicated investments that sound just right for your needs. It keeps their marketing department busy and often brings in nice, healthy profits. The only real losers are the mugs (you and me) who buy them.

Products such as endowments and with-profits have come in for a lot of criticism in recent years. And rightly so. They are highly inflexible beasts that require you to commit to investing a regular amount over a long time. That's no bad thing in itself but if you don't manage to keep up the payments you end up paying heavy penalties. Worse than that, they tend to have high charges, which means they are inefficient and give you a poor return for your money. These charges are often front-loaded (a large amount taken out in the first few years your investment period), too, which means you don't even start making money for at least a couple of years. The way they are designed – particularly the endowment policies – means that it's often hard for the investor to work out what the charges are, and therefore how much they are losing, so they often don't find out until it's too late. What delightful little animals they are!

With-profits bonds attempt to smooth out the return of the stock market by awarding annual bonuses that cannot be taken away. But the largest bonus is kept right until the end and many people don't get that far. The problem also is that over long time periods the stock market tends to rise, so these 'guaranteed' annual bonuses offer little value anyway. Therefore, you pay a lot in charges for something that probably won't be necessary. As if that weren't enough, the guarantees often turn out to be less than rock-solid, as the events surrounding Equitable Life have demonstrated.

Watch out for what are called 'guaranteed-income bonds', too. They might give you a guaranteed income, as they say, but they don't guarantee the *capital* you originally invested. That means that, in order to pay you the guaranteed income, when times are tough they could pay you out of your own money. So at the end of the term, if the investments have generally done badly, you could end up with nothing left, just the income paid from the money you originally invested.

Equities

Equities, or shares, are what they say they are: a share of a company. Whenever you buy a share you buy a piece of a company. The amount it costs depends on how much the company is considered to be worth when you buy it. If the company is worth £100 million, and there are 50 million shares of it around, then each share is worth £2 (usually described as 200p) when you buy it. After that its value can go up or down depending on what happens to the perceived value of the whole company. The more shares you own, the greater your share of that company, of course, and if, as with pension funds, you end up owning a decent percentage of a company, you can have quite a say in what that company does or doesn't do. Even small shareholders get to comment on the company at the annual shareholders' meeting, if they so wish.

For long-term investment, historically nothing has done better than equities. Numerous studies have been done about the rates of return that each of the main types of investment have made down the years. Over and over again they've shown that shares give far and away better returns than cash, bonds or gilts. For example, in the UK a study by CSFB (Credit Suisse First Boston investment bank) came up with the following figures for the period 1918 to 1999. The rates shown are the annual rate of return after taking off inflation, otherwise known as the real return. It's the 'real' return because it represents the real value of your money – spending power now versus spending power in the future.

Cash	1.6 per cent
Bonds	2.3 per cent
Equities	8.2 per cent

Yes, in the short term shares are much riskier than cash or bonds, but in the long term the risks are cancelled out and the market (in the past at least) has simply grown steadily over the years. If you look at the stock market for the last 30, 50 or even 100 years, you'll see that it has gone steadily upwards. Certainly there have been dips, sometimes quite substantial, such as the infamous 1929 crash and the Great Depression that followed it, Black Monday in October 1987 and the Asian Crisis of 1998. There was a dip in 1974 when, overall, shares lost 50 per cent of their value, but then the very next year they rose 149 per cent and in 2000 and 2001 UK shares fell by around 25 per cent. In fact there have only been 10 years since 1918 in which shares have lost 10 per cent or more. The point is that the *general trend* over the years has been upwards and for those who invested for a long time those bumps got smoothed out and made relatively little difference in the long run.

There are two really important things to consider when investing: one is that the longer your money is invested, the more it makes, thanks to compounding (see below for an explanation of compound interest); and the second is that even small differences in the interest you get each year make a big difference in the long term. So even a real rate of 'just' 8 per cent can produce a large sum if you give it enough time. For example, look at what would happen to £10,000 invested over 20 years at the above rates, in real terms.

Cash	£13,770
Bonds	£15,760
Equities	£48,360

Quite a difference, huh? As small differences in the annual return make a big difference in the long term, one thing you have to keep in mind is the charges that are made each year to run any of your investments. All else being equal, the lower the charges you pay, the higher you can expect your eventual return to be. Unfortunately, here in the UK we have a financial services industry that has a talent for both charging high rates and hiding the fact that it is doing so. So read the small print, since all investment products have to lay out their charges in what is known as a *key-features document*. The industry is moving towards a clearer and fairer charging structure, but we've got a long way to go.

Taxation can also take a big lump out of your investments each year, so see Chapter 14 ('Taxation') for ways of minimising the amount the Revenue can take off you.

How do you invest in shares?

There are two main ways to invest in shares – either you can buy shares in individual companies or you can invest in funds that include shares from various different companies. If you invest in individual shares then you will need to use a stockbroker of some sort – either a person in a company that you call on the phone or one of the newer online services that tend to do it more cheaply for you. There are various ones you can try including Barclays Stockbrokers (**www.stockbrokers.barclays.co.uk**), Squaregain (**www.squaregain.co.uk**), iWeb (**www.iwebsharedealing.co.uk**) and Hargreaves Lansdown (**www.hargreaveslansdown.co.uk**).

Investing in individual shares can bring you big money or it can lose you big money. The best way to do it is really to study it properly beforehand, maybe including running a 'virtual portfolio' first whereby you pretend to put money into shares, then watch how they do over a year or even two years. (Yahoo has a virtual portfolio service.)

You should learn how to read company reports, what a P/E ratio is (the price to earnings ratio which is worked out by dividing the share price by the earnings per share), what a dividend yield is (the percentage of a company's share price that it pays out as dividends over the course of a year), how your chosen sector (pharmaceuticals, retail, tech stocks, for example) is doing and how to tell if a company is a good long-term bet. There are loads of books on investing, some better than others, and also the Motley Fool website has a *lot* of very useful information on how to invest and learn about companies (**www.fool.co.uk**).

The other, easier, way is to invest in a fund that has done the choosing for you already. This is a less risky way of doing it, since the more shares you invest in, the more the risk is spread. It tends to be less lucrative than stock picking, though. There are two basic types of fund that you can invest in: managed and index-tracking.

Managed funds

Also known as 'actively managed funds', the managed funds are just that, managed by highly paid individuals who spend their working lives studying the market and deciding which shares to invest in for a particular fund and how much money to put into each. There are hundreds of these around and you've probably seen adverts for them on billboards and in broadsheet newspapers. Some do well but the majority don't make very impressive amounts of money. In fact, three-quarters of them underperform the stock market itself, which is disappointing. One of the reasons for this is that they often levy high charges for the privilege of messing around with your money, and that reduces the amount you end up with. The other reason is simple human fallibility. The stock market is notoriously fickle and it's very hard to work out whether a company will do well and whether its shares are worth the money.

People who invest in managed funds tend to get excited about a particular fund manager and invest in their funds even if they move to another company. The general cleverness of one manager is about the only thing you have to work with when deciding which fund to go for, apart from the particular sector they invest in. If, for example, you think that pharmaceuticals are the way to go you will probably look for funds that invest specifically in this sector.

There are two main types of managed fund that most people invest in. First, there are open-ended funds, known as OEICs (open-ended investment companies), which are as big or as small as the number of people invested in them. There are hundreds of different OEICs (which have replaced the old 'unit trusts') and most are managed but some are tracker funds (see below).

There are also 'investment trusts'. An investment trust is a managed fund, which is an actual company itself. The company doesn't produce anything, though: it just invests in a portfolio of shares of other companies. Shares in investment trusts can be bought and sold like ordinary shares and there are index-tracking investment trusts, although they tend to have more charges than basic trackers. Investment trusts are often riskier than OEICs, but over the long term they can bring in better returns – if you pick the right ones! Find out more from the Association of Investment Trust Companies (**www.aitc.co.uk**).

Index-tracking funds

The index-tracking funds are cheaper than the managed ones and tend to perform much better. They can charge less than the managed funds (you shouldn't pay more than 1 per cent a year for your index tracker) because they're run by computers, which don't demand a new Porsche Boxter and a holiday in the Bahamas each year.

The way they work is that they put a small amount of your money (depending on a complicated mathematical formula) into each company in the index you've chosen, depending on where that company ranks in the index. The fund should then largely follow the movement of the index (i.e. go up as it goes up and down as it goes down). Because the charges are low you are likely to make more money with this kind of fund, although one disadvantage is that the indices tend not to include the dividends from individual companies in their calculations.

There are funds that track the FTSE All Share, the FTSE 100, the FTSE 250 and the FTSE Tech Mark. There's nothing to stop you investing in funds that track indices in other parts of the world too. Foreign funds tend to have higher charges but if you want to spread your investments then go for it. In the US major indices include the Dow Jones Industrial Average (the Dow), the S&P 500 and the Nasdaq (the technology index). Other well-known ones are the Nikkei (Japan), the Hang Seng (Hong Kong) and the Dax (Germany).

ETFs

ETFs are *exchange-traded funds*. Like tracker funds, these also track a particular index, except they're actually shares themselves. It represents a portfolio of investments that are designed to track a specific index (such as the FTSE 100). When you invest in a tracker fund you put money into an OEIC, but ETFs can be bought and sold through stockbrokers (like investment trusts – see above). They're a relatively recent investment product but are fast gaining in popularity with regular investors because they have very low charges, often just 0.5 per cent, and are not liable for stamp duty. See **www.fool.co.uk** for more

Compound interest

This is what makes your money grow when you invest it in building society accounts or shares. It's also what makes your debts grow if you don't pay them off fast! The principle of compounding works like a snowball. Your initial capital (the money you've put in) collects interest (a percentage paid back to you for the loan of the money) over a year. If you keep it there, that means that your original capital has grown a little by the end of the year. That means that in the next year you earn interest on a larger sum, so the interest you receive is slightly greater, and so it goes on each year with the amount on which you are earning interest growing exponentially every 12 months.

With investing, the more you save and the longer you save, the more you'll end up with. You start off just getting interest, but then you earn interest on that interest and then you earn interest on the interest on the interest, and so on. The two things that create

continues ➤

wealth for you are the level of interest you're getting (big numbers are better than small here, so a 10 per cent return is going to make you much richer than a 5 per cent return), and the length of time you keep the money there. Over long timescales, with compound interest working its magic, it all really adds up.

In the case of shares this is why it's important to reinvest dividends you receive from your shares each year. If you buy more shares with your dividends then that's more shares you have the next year to produce more dividends with which you can then buy more shares and so on and so on until you're so rich Bill Gates is asking you for the price of a cup of tea.

ISAs

The ISA (individual savings account) has replaced TESSAs (tax-exempt special savings accounts) and PEPs (personal equity plans) as tax-saving investments. ISAs are not investments in themselves: they're just 'wrappers' that you wrap around a cash- or shares-based (equities-based) investment to protect it from tax. As explained in Chapter 14, 'Taxation', there's an annual limit (within each financial year, 6 April to 5 April) to how much you can invest through an ISA. Currently, you can invest up to £7,000 – either the whole lot in equities (Maxi ISA) or divided up into £3,000 in cash (Mini ISA) and £4,000 in equities (Mini ISA). It's not really complicated, particularly as most financial companies offer investments that are 'pre-wrapped' in an ISA, so if you have money to invest do yourself a favour and put the first £7,000 into something that is ISA-wrapped so that you can make more money by not wasting it in tax payments.

What does the FTSE mean?

It's the Financial Times Stock Exchange (sometimes called the Footsie). The 'Index' part of it is simply a way of showing how well the stock market is performing. There are hundreds of different indices around the world, and quite a few within this country. For a start there is the FTSE All Share, which, obviously, measures how all the quoted companies in this country as a whole are doing, then there's the FTSE 100, which measures the top 100 companies as a lump (names such as Vodaphone, Shell and BT are in there). There are less well-known ones too, such as the FTSE 250, which measures the 250 companies after the first 100.

When they say on the news that 'the FTSE has risen 100 points today', it means that the perceived value of the FTSE 100 has gone up that day. In fact, the top 100 companies in the index account for around 80 per cent of the value of the whole index, so it's a pretty good measure of how big business is doing in the country. Say the index rises by 100 points from 5,000 to 5,100. That means it has gone up by 2 per cent. So that means that overall, after all the buying and selling of shares in big companies that day, the overall value of those companies has gone up by 2 per cent.

How do I buy into these products?

Cash

You can invest in building society or bank accounts at branches, in the post or through the Internet. For maximum returns do shop around (and keep an eye on the account you have to check that they haven't sneakily dropped the rate while you weren't looking) and look on the money comparison sites such as **www.moneysupermarket.com**, **www.moneyextra. co.uk**, **www.moneyfacts.co.uk**. Also, for maximum return, invest through an ISA, unless you're using up your annual quota in equities-based investments.

Bonds/gilts

You can buy actual gilts and bonds through most stockbrokers, just as you can buy shares. Most smaller investors don't buy and sell bonds directly, though. They tend to invest in bond funds, which you can buy through banks, building societies or through money websites. Look for them at **www.moneysuper- market.com**, **www.moneyextra.co.uk**, **www.moneyfacts. co.uk**

Shares

If you're investing in individual shares you'll need to do it through a third party – a bank, a broker, an IFA (independent financial adviser) or an online dealer. With all of these, by the way, if you want your investment wrapped in an ISA, you only have to say.

If you know what you want to buy and you don't need any advice on it, thank you very much, you should ask for what is known as an *execution-only* service. That means they'll do the buying or selling for you but they won't tell you whether they think it's a good idea or not. 'Who wants to know what they think, anyway?' you might say. Quite. You will still have to pay for this service but not too much, particularly if you do it through one of the really cheap online brokers (check out **www.fool.co.uk** for a list of nice, low-cost ones), which are cer- tainly the quickest and best-value way to go.

However, you may lack confidence in your ability to pick stocks (if so, why are you doing it?), which means that if you still want to buy them you should go for an 'advisory service', which costs a lot more than the execution-only one, but then you do get more of an actual service. This tends to be offered by private client stockbrokers who have posh offices and expensive suits. They will recommend which shares you should buy or sell and will probably contact you every now and then with further recommendations. Or you could have a 'discretionary service', whereby you just hand over your money to them and let them buy and sell shares on your behalf without bothering you about it.

Of course, as they do this for a living, you would expect professional stockbrokers to know a thing or two about the market, and some of them do, although remember that generally they're called a 'broker' because, when you use one, you are. If you still want your very own stockbroker to keep and love and cherish, though, ring the public-information department at the London Stock Exchange on 020 7588 2355 for a list of them.

Tracker funds/managed funds/ETFs

Funds are even easier to invest in. The only hard part is choosing one. With tracker funds, there's not a lot to choose between them (although the FTSE 250 seems to have outperformed the other indices since it has been in existence, so check that one out). The main thing to consider, therefore, is the annual charges – just go for the cheapest. Several well-established financial companies offer various types of tracker fund and most come pre-wrapped in an ISA. Just make sure you mention it when you buy into one. You can buy over the phone, by post or through the Internet, although if you do it by phone or Internet you will have to sign paper forms for it later on.

It's the same with managed funds, except that they're much harder to choose. If you're determined to invest in one of these, either you will need to study the form closely – read money pages in the broadsheets, ask around, read their tedious literature – or you should take the advice of a (good) IFA who will do the necessary paperwork for you, for a fee. If you do it yourself it's a question of investing through the phone, Internet or post again.

Here is a selection of fund providers but you can find more at **www.fool.co.uk**, **www.moneyextra.co.uk**, and **www.moneysupermarket.com**.

Tracker funds

Legal and General – **www.landg.com**, 0800 0920092
M&G – **www.mandg.com**, 0800 390390
Scottish Widows – **www.scottishwidows.com**, 08457 678910
Virgin – **www.virginmoney.com**, 08456 101020
Fidelity – **www.fidelity.co.uk**, 0800 414161
Gartmore – **www.gartmore.co.uk**, 0800 289336

Managed funds

There are hundreds to choose from but you can start with:
The Investment Management Association –
www.investmentuk.org
The IFA Association – **www.unbiased.co.uk**
The Association of Investment Trust Companies –
www.aitc.co.uk
www.find.co.uk

When the stakes are high

Apparently, being a 'functional psychopath' can help you be a better stock market investor. Researchers from Stanford Graduate School of Business, Carnegie Mellon University and the University of Iowa have concluded that people with brain damage that caused them to suppress emotions significantly outperform those with fully functioning feelings. They say that emotions can make 'normal' investors play it too safe. In contrast they found that the emotionally impaired are more willing to gamble for high stakes.

Ethical investing

See Chapter 16, 'Ethical Money', for a full run-down of ethical savings and investment products.

Other investments

Your mortgage

Investing? In a mortgage? Surely some mistake! No, actually, if you have a mortgage right now, and it's one in which you can overpay at any time, the best and safest investment you can make is to pay it off as fast as possible. In fact, Warren Buffet, the second richest man in the world, has recommended it a few times to his fellow Americans.

There are several good reasons:

- When you pay off your mortgage quickly you reduce the amount of interest payments you waste over the long term. Mortgage rates have been relatively low in the last few years but the long-term average mortgage rate is 8 per cent (averaged out over the last 50 years). If you have a repayment mortgage of £100,000 at 8 per cent, that will cost you over £131,544.87 in interest payments alone over 25 years.

- Any interest you save is the same as *making* that amount of money. Except that you don't have to pay tax on it! So, in real terms, you make more money than you would do if you put that extra cash into a building society account or similar. So, if you pay off £1,000 of your mortgage at, say, 5 per cent, that will be like investing that money in something that gives you 6.25 per cent gross because you haven't had to pay tax on it.

- You really can save a lot of money. If you pay a £100,000 mortgage over 25 years with an average mortgage rate of, say, 6 per cent, the total amount you would pay would be £193,290.42. If you paid it over 15 years however, you would save £41,396.19.

- Overpaying your mortgage is a totally safe investment. If you pay off £1,000, you have paid it off and have saved on the interest you would have paid, so you will reap the rewards. If you *invest* £1,000 you are never quite sure how much money you will make on it or, if it's a riskier investment, whether you might even lose it all.

- Many argue that if your mortgage rate is low you would be better off paying the minimum each month and putting extra into an investment (say a stock market fund) that gives you higher returns. Good point, and, on paper, quite right, except that, as already mentioned, you can't be sure that the investment will give you higher returns, certainly in the short term. So, although you could make more money that way, you might not. In fact, it's that very approach that caused part of the problem with endowments. The main problem with these products was (and is) that the charges were too high, but the people who put them together also overestimated the future growth of the stock market. This is why so many mortgage holders are facing a shortfall in the amount of their mortgages that can be paid off by their endowments.

Property

See Chapter 8, 'A House or a Home?', for an overview on property as an investment. Property has certainly outdone shares over the last 30 years but over a longer time – the last 100 years – shares have performed better. In fact the average annual return for shares over that period is just over 11 per cent. For property (and there are figures for only the last 50 years) the average return has been 9 per cent.

The shares-versus-property argument

This argument rages across middle-class dinner tables and IFA desks and it's still not resolved.

Property pros and cons

- Land is a finite resource, so property should rise in value over the long term as the pressure on housing increases.

- Divorce and split-ups are still on the rise as more of us decide we can't live with another human being. The less we share, the more pressure is put on the housing stock and the more valuable it becomes.

- Immigration is supposed to continue to rise in the UK, which will also increase demand, particularly in cities.

- It's relatively easy to borrow against the value of a property, so when house prices rise we gain even more than we would if all the money were our own – although this also means that losses are greater if house prices fall, particularly if they fall below the amount of the mortgage (negative equity).

- It's a 'tangible asset' – you can see it, touch it, feel it. You know it's there and it feels solid.

- Its very solidity can cost you a lot of money – even the best-behaved property needs to be redecorated every few years but you're unlikely to get away without some major one-off expenses such as when the boiler needs to be replaced or the roof is leaking. Also, if you're renting it out, you can have expensive problems with tenants and long void periods.

- Property can be very interesting and creative if you enjoy building, DIY and/or interior decorating. It's also a 'people' product, since it's somewhere where people live and work, so you can deal with a lot of other people through your investment.

- Property is not a 'liquid' asset. It can take months to buy and sell it and there are several costs involved in both – thousands of pounds at a time. Property values go up and down, too, so you may find yourself having to take a hit on the price if you suddenly need the money.

Shares pros and cons

- Historically, shares have generally risen over the long term, although you either need to know what you're doing when investing in individual companies or invest in an index tracker, which just follows the curve of the stock market.

- Shares are pretty liquid on the whole. You can sell them in a day if you want to, although if you suddenly *have* to get rid of them you could lose money if their value has dipped at just that moment.

- If you invest in individual shares you need to spend a lot of time and effort learning about them and keeping an eye on how they are doing. It's still less effort than sorting out leaking pipes, though.

- Buying and selling shares is quite a cheap process, particularly if you do it through an online broker. However, you do have to pay annual charges – still quite low if you go for a cheap index-tracking fund.

- You can invest in shares with less than £100, which you can't do with property. In fact, as property prices stand at the moment, just to get a 15 per cent deposit (the minimum required for most buy-to-let mortgages) you will need tens of thousands.

Whatever you go for, the principle of spreading your risk still applies here. Why not invest in both shares and property – and a pension (see the next chapter) if you can. Start with shares, which are cheaper to invest in, then move into property, if you still want to, when you've amassed your thousands!

Pensions

Yes, pensions are another form of investment – the most obvious investment for your future in fact. Chapter 10 covers pensions in detail, but don't forget that they are a form of investment, just like any mentioned in *this* chapter, and should be thought of in those terms. The rules and pros and cons covering pensions are different from those of other investments, but they still have the same basic aim: to help your money grow over time to create a pot of money for your old age.

Collections

Time was when people bought paintings, wine, antiques or classic cars because they liked them. Now, though, all these things, and more, are seen as serious investments – a replacement for a pension in some cases. All the money sections in the serious newspapers now have regular collecting columns covering everything from high-end antiques and art to the offbeat and wacky.

Of course there are many pros and cons to using collections as an investment vehicle.

Pros

- This is an investment you can actually enjoy. Share certificates aren't much to look at but a Rembrandt or a classic Jaguar certainly is.

- Like property, collections are things you can actually feel and touch, which often makes you feel more secure about the investment.

- It's a great excuse to spend money on things you love.

- It's something you can control, unlike pension funds or equity funds. It's up to you what you buy, when and at what price.

- With some types of collecting – great art or sculpture, for example – there are a very limited number of certain items. This very rarity means they're likely to increase in value over time.

- Some collections that are popular now can be very cheap to start.

Cons

- Collections of all types are totally vulnerable to the whims of fashion. You could have a fabulous collection of silverware, for example, but, when you come to sell it, it could suddenly be *out* of fashion and, therefore, not as valuable as it was.

- Storage, maintenance and insurance costs can be steep, certainly a regular annual amount. In some cases these costs can be much greater than annual management costs levied by equity funds.

- As with any investment, there's no guarantee that the value of your collection won't go right down to the floor.

- It can be very hard to find, and afford, individual items for your collection, particularly if your passion is old masters or classic cars or Louis XIV furniture.

- Collections are vulnerable to burglary, fire and other forms of destruction.

- Unlike shares, cash or property, most collections don't produce any sort of income, only potential growth.

- You could love the items too much to sell them when you need the money.

That said, though, as part of a portfolio of investments, why not use one of your passions as a possible money earner? If you have decent investments in other things such as shares, pensions and property, there's no reason why you shouldn't add some artistic or historical investments too.

Thanks to TV programmes such as *Antiques Roadshow* and the phenomenal popularity of eBay, the craze for collecting – and collecting for investment purposes – has taken over the country. In fact, it's big news in several Western countries and increasingly in Asian countries, too, so, if you happen to pick the right items to buy, you can be confident of a growing, global market for them.

What you collect, of course, depends on your tastes and, importantly, your financial situation. People with lots of money will collect top-of-the-range classic cars, rare antiques and art, gold, rare stamps, top wines and first-edition books. Even if you have little money to play with, though, you could still develop a decent collection of slightly less rare first editions and stamps, more affordable art and perhaps a classic MG. Even collections of off-the-wall, cheaper items have been rising in value recently and, if you pick the right things, you can make money out of kitsch after just a few years. Barbie Dolls, Beatles memorabilia, Bakelite products, Ladybird books and electric guitars half-trashed by a rock star are just some of the more bizarre collectables that are finding a growing market.

If you don't have thousands to invest right now but you'd like to start a collection that could make money later on, the professionals' advice is to buy things that today's teenage boys want but can't afford, such as GameCubes or BMX bikes. The idea is that in twenty years' time, when they're old enough to afford these things, nostalgia will kick in and they'll pay over the odds for something they've yearned for since they were 13.

Main points to keep in mind when amassing your collection are these:

- Collect only things you love. You can't guarantee that it will be a good investment, but if you love them you'll have had all that enjoyment of them over the years anyway.

- Go for the best you can afford – quality is better than quantity.

- Study your subject thoroughly so that you know what is a good investment and what isn't.

- Unless you're passionate about underground train tickets or Smurf memorabilia, try to collect things that already have dealers and a decent group of other collectors interested and willing to pay good money for them.

- Make sure you have the physical space to store the items, keep them from danger and protect them from deterioration.

- Make sure you have enough money to cover maintenance and insurance costs.

More information

Sotheby's – **www.sothebys.com**
Christies – **www.christies.com**
Bonhams – **www.bonhams.com**
www.ebay.co.uk
BBC Antiques – **www.bbc.co.uk/antiques**

Books and periodicals

Superhobby Investing – Peter Temple (Harriman House, £14.99)
Antiques Magazine – **www.antiquesmagazine.com**

Ugh – tax!

Yes, you are going to be punished for daring to make money for yourself, and the more successful you are in your investing, the more you'll be whipped by the Revenue. Go to Chapter 14, 'Taxation', for a lowdown on the various ways you can and will be stung by the lovely tax office (now called HM Revenue and Customs). But there are various ways you can, and should, protect your investments from tax.

- Make sure you use up your annual ISA allowance.

- Try to share some of your gains with a spouse, as each individual has a capital gains tax allowance even if they are married.

- If your potential tax bill is very high, consider investing in a pension product rather than one of the investments above (see Chapter 10, 'Your Future', for ideas), because pensions have a great tax advantage.

- Consider investing in a venture capital trust or an AIM (alternative investment market) fund for the income tax relief and IHT (inheritance tax) relief respectively (but don't let the tax-relief argument sway you if you can't find a good version of either of these investments). Find out about AIM at **www.growthcompany.co.uk**.

- Make a will (see below).

More information

HM Revenue and Customs – **www.hmrc.gov.uk**
The IFA Association – **www.unbiased.co.uk** (the website includes lots of tax-saving ideas)

A word about inflation

Think about what you can buy with £100 today. A nice pair of shoes? A week's rent of a room in London? A good digital radio? But what would it have bought 100 years ago? At the start of the 20th century £100 could have paid a servant's wages for a year.

That's inflation. It's basically the buying power of any given amount of money and in general, over the years, it tends to go up. In other words, the buying power that each £1 in our pockets has becomes less and less as time goes on, as wages gradually go up and the price of pretty much everything goes inexorably upwards too.

This is something you have to keep in the back of your mind when thinking about investing for your future. Although right now you may like the look of the amount of money you expect to be able to retire on, according to your (or your financial adviser's) calculations, remember that the further away that day is, the less that money is likely to be able to buy.

This is another reason why it's imperative that you invest the majority of your money in products that should return a higher percentage. As you will have seen above, this means, essentially, investing in the stock market and, perhaps, property and collections.

Make a will

As soon as you have any investments, you need to make a will. As with the property you live in, investments are subject to tax by the government if you don't leave instructions as to who they should go to when you die. Remember, the government, sweetly, will take 40 per cent out of your investments before your nearest relative gets anything. Not only that but you may not *want* your nearest relative to get all or even any of your money, so that's another good reason to leave a will.

See the section 'Making a will' in Chapter 12 for advice on how to go about it quickly and painlessly.

More investing information

The Motley Fool – **www.fool.co.uk** (excellent website on all things to do with investment and personal finance)
BBC website – **www.bbc.co.uk** – check out their investing section.
The *Guardian* – **www.guardian.co.uk**
The *Financial Times* – **www.ft.com**
The *Independent* – **www.independent.co.uk**
The *Telegraph* – **www.telegraph.co.uk**
Global Investor – **www.global-investor.com**
Economy.com – **www.economy.com**
Investopedia.com – **www.investopedia.com**
Moneyfacts – **www.moneyfacts.co.uk**

Books

The Motley Fool UK Investment Handbook – David Berger and James Carlisle (Boxtree, £12.99)
The Intelligent Investor – Benjamin Graham (Harper Business, £12.99)
Winning the Loser's Game – Charles Ellis (McGraw-Hill, £16.99)
Extraordinary Popular Delusions and the Madness of Crowds – Charles Mackay (Harriman House, £11.00)
Common Stocks and Uncommon Profits – Philip Fisher (John Wiley, £13.95)

10

Your Future

'I don't plan to grow old gracefully. I plan to
have facelifts until my ears meet.'
                                        – **Rita Rudner**

When people talk about investing for retirement they
usually mean pensions. Lovely word. No wonder they're
unpopular at the moment. Quite apart from the fact that
recently we've seen pensions scandals, poor performance and
a whole load of hand-wringing from the government about the
future of the little beasts, frankly the very *word* is offputting.
'Pension' smacks of age and decrepitude, not glamour and fun,
which is what we're all aiming at for our golden years, of
course.

In fact, pensions are simply another form of investment to
add to the ones already covered in Chapter 9, 'Make Your
Money Make Money'. They're different in that they are specifically designed for your retirement, they offer tax breaks while
you're saving and they have strict rules as to when you can take
the money out and what you have to do with it. However, *you
don't have to have one*. What you *do* need to have is (cue fanfare
of trumpets and glitzy curtain!) a *retirement fund*.

Your retirement fund is exactly what it sounds like – a pot

of money you accumulate over the years to pay for your glorious, glamorous retirement. It can be made up of all kinds of different sorts of investment (including or not including a pension), but, whatever vehicle(s) you've used to amass the money, you need to end up with a pot of cash that you can then invest in something that will pay you enough interest for you to live on for the rest of your life.

The retirement fund

Now the bad news. In order to live decently off your investments you need to have a serious amount of cash stashed away. To give you an idea, the current average wage in this country is around £25,000. In order to make that amount in interest you would have to have (wait for it!) around £500,000 invested. The reason for this is that you need to live off the *interest* made on that money – you wouldn't want to use the capital itself. On average you're likely to make about 5 per cent (gross) on your investments. That's the amount you tend to get in safe investments (when you're retired, ideally you should have your money invested in something that's not going to swing wildly up and down). So, to get just £20,000 a year, you'll need £400,000.

When it comes to how to save this seemingly enormous amount of money you should keep in mind that, as with any form of investing, the earlier you start saving for your retirement fund, the better. And, because of the joy and wonder of compound interest, even small amounts of money invested early on will more than match quite large contributions that you may have to make later in life. So, even if you're a low earner in your twenties and thirties, it's still worth putting away a little each month – at the same time as saving for more short-term goals such as a deposit for a flat. Even if you are a low earner and in your forties or fifties, don't let it stop you. A small amount saved at that stage is miles better than nothing saved at all. It's also worth going through some of the ideas in Chapter 2 ('Control Your Finances, Control Your Life'), Chapter 3 ('Dump Your Debt, Live Cheaper, Make Money') and Chapter 5 ('Financial One-upmanship Day to Day') to free up some more money to invest. If that doesn't work, increase your income with ideas from Chapter 6 ('Making That Bit Extra').

What you put that money into, though, should be decided by you. Your retirement fund could include various different investments including a pension, ISAs, cash, perhaps some property and even your stamp collection. *How* you make up that retirement fund is also up to you. Just make sure that you *do* it. However, as I've already covered the other investments in Chapter 9, let's have a look at the various types of pension you can have.

The glorious, glamorous, Technicolor world of pensions

There are various types of pension – the state pension, which everyone currently gets (although there's a big question mark over how long it will be around) and different company and personal pension schemes (see below for the list).

Once you actually retire you'll be allowed to take out a quarter of the money in your own pension funds tax-free, with which to do what you like – blow it on the dogs, have a cruise or invest it for income. By the time you're 75 you will either have to buy an annuity with the rest or you can take an 'alternatively secured income' instead that offers a lower monthly income but which lets you pass on any unused pension at your death to a loved one, subject to an inheritance tax charge.

The best way to think of your pension is as a kind of insurance plan for your old age. If you buy an annuity (or the 'alternatively secured income') with most of the money you save in your pension fund, it will guarantee you a certain amount of money each year until you die. That may not be an enormous amount but it's something and it's guaranteed not to run out. If you're undisciplined with money it's also a useful tool, because you're not allowed to touch the money until you retire, so it saves you from yourself!

The amount you're allowed to put into your pension scheme each year used to depend on how much you earned and how old you were. That's now been changed so you can put the whole of your earned income into your pension if you so choose, up to a limit of £215,000. This maximum limit will be increased by £10,000 each year until it reaches £255,000 in 2010–11. Check on the Revenue website at **www.hmrc.gov.uk** for more details. You can also build up a pension fund up to a lifetime limit (currently £1.5 million) before you get taxed on it.

Pensions for all

The state pension

As far as pensions go, your retirement income starts (and only *starts*) with the basic retirement ('state') pension. You will get this only if you've paid enough National Insurance contributions (NICs) over your working life (unless you've taken time off to care for someone or to have a baby). Otherwise, you'll receive a tapered amount of state pension, and possibly nothing.

Just to depress you, by the way, the current basic retirement pension for a single person is barely over £5,000 a year. Could you live on that? It's not likely to go up by very much in the future, either. However, anyone whose only income is the state pension has their money topped up by a pension credit (more information in Chapter 15, 'Mature Finances') and that is likely to continue for a while at least. If you'd like to, you can find out how much you're likely to get in your state pension (dependent on the NI contributions you've paid so far) by applying for a pension forecast. This will give you an idea of how much of the state and *second* state pension (see below) you'll be entitled to when you retire and will also let you know whether you have any missing years of National Insurance (NI) contributions and whether you can make them up. Go to **www.thepensionservice.gov.uk** for an online report or ring 0845 601 80 40.

There's a lot of uncertainty over the continued existence of the state pension, mainly because we're all living a lot longer and having fewer children. This means that the state will need to pay out more for longer but will have fewer people of working age, paying National Insurance contributions, to pay for it. Currently, pensioners are paid with money that comes from the NI contributions of people who are actually working. To keep that going you have to have at least the same number of people working as drawing state pension. Come 2020 the balance is set to start tipping. That's why there's been so much fuss about whether we should be forced to work until we're 70.

Whatever happens (and something has to, both in this country and in all other Western countries that have similar problems), the message coming over loud and clear from the government and financial observers is that we as individuals need, more than ever, to invest for our own future.

The state second pension

You may have heard of SERPS – the state earnings-related pension scheme – which was a kind of top-up to the basic pension and (remarkably) was related to the amount you earn (see the box explaining SERPS on page 180). Well, now it's been replaced by the state second pension, which has widened the net and provides a more generous additional state pension for low and moderate earners, and to certain carers and people with a long-term illness or disability.

The state second pension gives employees earning a low amount (check **www.dwp.gov.uk** for the current level) a better pension than SERPS, with the most help going to those on the lowest earnings.

Actually, if you're on a really low income it may not be worth your while bothering with SERPS or the state second pension at all, because it's all subject to means testing. So if you're able to save only a smallish amount in this secondary pension you could lose out, because if you didn't have anything in it you would get social security benefit payments anyway. It's worth it only if you're going to save a large amount – larger than the benefits threshold. Frankly, it's all a bit of a mess, and no one really knows what's going on – including the Treasury – so it may be better to save any money you're going to save in an ISA or other savings vehicle rather than trust your luck to the vagaries of the pensions fairies.

What was SERPS?

The state earnings-related pension scheme (SERPS) was designed to top up your income depending on how much you've earned over the years. It was 'earnings-related' because the more you earned, the more you'd pay in National Insurance contributions, so the more you'd get – up to a maximum of £500 per annum.

This has now been replaced by the state second pension, but anyone who contributed to SERPS up to 2002 will benefit from those contributions for years to come, which is why I'm mentioning it now!

Pensions for some

After the state provision (or not, as the case may be), there are a number of different types of pension that you could have, depending on your circumstances. The minimum age at which you can start taking your private or company pension will be raised from 50 to 55 by April 2010.

Company pension schemes

Company pensions have often been a pretty good proposition, because some of your payments are paid by your employer – hey, free money! Mind you, there are company pensions and company pensions. Bear these points in mind:

- Although it is a good thing to have someone else paying into your pension for you, it's quite possible that the fund they've chosen will perform badly. You generally have no control over the choice of fund – you're just stuck with it.

- The pensions to have in former times were the *defined-benefit* variety, because you knew how much you would get when you retired and it was generally a pretty decent amount. These are increasingly impossible for companies to sustain and they've been all but phased out. You're now highly likely just to have a *defined-contribution* pension, which means you'll get what you're given at the end of your working life. There's more on this under 'Defined-benefit and defined-contribution pensions' below.

- Having a company pension sometimes means you're tied to a job you really don't want to do but feel you can't leave because the benefits are so useful.

- In theory, you should be able to take your pension with you when you move jobs, but in practice they're not very portable (stakeholder pensions *are* very portable, though, so if you have one of those you're all right). This could leave you with a number of small pensions, each paying out rather little.

- If your pension is portable, you're still likely to lose out to some extent on the 'transfer value'. This is basically an exit charge whereby the pension fund retains a percentage of your accumulated savings in return for letting you take your money elsewhere.

- There is now a safety net for employees who contribute to a company pension that goes bust (and a few have done exactly that recently). It's called the Pensions Protection Fund (**www.pensionsprotectionfund.org.uk**) – and about time too!

However, given that a company pension involves someone else (your employer) putting money in as well as you, generally speaking they are 'a good thing'. As with other pensions, how much you can pay into your company pension depends on how old you are and how much you earn. If you're a member of a company pension scheme and you think it's a damned good one, you can top up your pension contributions to the maximum amount allowed using *additional voluntary contributions* (AVCs). Your employer's pensions department will be able to give you a form to fill in to do this.

If you change jobs you should be able to take your pension with you if you wish to. Under an occupational scheme, if you've worked for an employer for two years you get to keep the value of any pensions benefits that have built up if you change jobs. Either you can keep the 'preserved benefits' in the old scheme, or you can get that old scheme to transfer enough money (called the *transfer value*) to the new scheme to give you the same benefits as you had already built up in the old scheme.

Whether you're better to keep your preserved benefit or transfer to a new scheme is always a tricky question. In theory there should be no difference, because you should be able to invest the transfer value elsewhere and get the same final pension pot. But it's very difficult to check whether this is the case. The trouble with transferring is that it often costs you money to do it and that would make the transfer value less than what you'd have if you left the preserved benefits alone. So decide for yourself (or talk to a *fee*-based independent financial adviser) whether you would make more money in another vehicle and, if so, go for it!

With people changing jobs more frequently these days, some

are ending up with lots of little pension policies scattered around. So if you've flitted among a number of jobs and think you may have bits of pensions sitting around unclaimed, you can search them out through one of a few pension-finding services. Try the Unclaimed Assets Register (www.unclaimed-assets.com, 0870 241 1713) or the Pension Schemes Registry (0191 225 6393) or the AMP Pension Find Service (0800 068 5456). You might as well – there could be some very helpful extra bits of money just lying around, waiting for you to use them.

Defined-benefit and defined-contribution pensions

Defined-benefit

If you have a defined-benefit pension, this means that the monthly income you'll get when you retire is guaranteed. These are generally considered to be the better option, and are also becoming rarer than interesting celebrity TV programmes, due to the risks they represent to employers.

Even if you're currently paying into a company pension scheme that is defined-benefit, it can be changed into a defined-contribution (or money-purchase) scheme at any time before you retire, and this is happening to many employees right now. This could have the effect of increasing your risk, although it does give you more control over your pension contributions.

Defined-contribution

This means that the amount you pay in is defined (that is, you know that, if you pay in £100 per month, then you've paid in £100 per month), but how much you get when you retire depends heavily on the performance of the fund's investments, the level of charges, the whims of the pension fairies and so on.

Fringe benefits

Some company pension schemes include 'death-in-service' benefits. It's worth taking a good look at these, because they may save you having to pay life assurance premiums. Check the small print regarding spouses and children. Should you or your partner die, what will the survivor get? Does this include same-sex partners, if that is your situation? If you die just after retirement, what will your surviving spouse get? How long will these payments be made for? If you are relying on your spouse's company pension, what will happen if he/she predeceases you? Do you need an extra fund? If you're not married, can an unmarried partner benefit?

Personal pensions

Personal pensions give self-employed people, or those working for businesses without occupational schemes, a crack of the pensions whip. They're not nearly as good as company pensions because:

- only you pay into them (unless you can get Mummy and Daddy to contribute);

- they tend to charge high management fees and, therefore, do very little for the money you've invested in them.

Essentially, they're defined-contribution schemes into which you pay a percentage of your income. As with company pensions, your contributions have the tax you would have paid added to them by the Revenue, which means that if you're a higher-rate taxpayer they are still worth considering. That said, though, as the charges are so high with most personal pensions and the performance so abysmal, if you need a personal pension I would say the only types worth considering are a stakeholder pension and a self-invested personal pension (SIPP).

Stakeholder pensions

A few years ago, in a bid to make personal pensions a little more useful and exciting (as if they could be any more exciting than they already, thrillingly, are), the government changed some of the rules and introduced stakeholder pensions.

- The main change was that you no longer had to be earning an income to contribute to a personal pension. This means, basically, that most people are able to contribute up to £2,808 per annum to a personal pension, even if they have no earnings of their own. On top of this, the government adds a contribution calculated using basic-rate tax, making a total of £3,600 per year (check at **www.dwp.gov.uk** for the current rates). This is particularly useful for people going through career breaks or those on low incomes, because it means they can keep their pension contributions going.

- However, it's usually precisely these people who *cannot* contribute at this time because they don't earn enough to put anything aside. But if you are, say, taking a break from work to look after children and you're lucky enough to have a generous partner, they can make contributions on your behalf. Another advantage to this is that, under these rulings, you (or the grandparents) can also make pension contributions for your children (see Chapter 13, 'Family Matters').

- Stakeholder pensions have strict rules for fund managers too. The rules are that stakeholder pension providers can charge you a maximum of only 1.5 per cent of the value of your pension fund each year to manage it. If you choose to transfer into or out of a stakeholder pension, or you stop paying your contributions for a time, the stakeholder pension scheme provider will not charge you extra. All stakeholder schemes must accept contributions of as little as £20, which you can pay each week, each month or at less frequent intervals. Finally, the scheme must be run by trustees or by an authorised stakeholder manager, whose responsibility will be to make sure that the scheme meets the various legal requirements.

• You can get stakeholder pensions from all sorts of financial-services companies such as insurance companies, banks, investment companies and building societies. On the whole, stakeholder pensions are pensions based on tracker funds – they have to be, because very few other types of fund have such low charges.

• Some stakeholders charge less than others so look at the lower charging ones first.

If you're employed, your employer must provide you with access to a stakeholder pension scheme unless they have fewer than five employees or they already offer an occupational scheme. This can be useful for employees but it is nowhere near as good as a traditional company pension because the employer is not likely to contribute to the pot.

Self-invested personal pensions

Speaking of 'pensions' and 'excitement', probably the biggest news in the pensions world recently has been the expansion of products you can include in a self-invested personal pension. SIPPs are a bit like ISAs in that they're not an investment in themselves, just a sort of bag into which you can put various different investments.

The pros of SIPPs are that:

- you get to control what you invest in and not some faceless, obscure, high-charging bunch of fund managers;

- you can put actually interesting things into a SIPP, including property and art collections if you want;

- the charges for running a SIPP have dropped with the introduction of online SIPP providers;

- as with other pensions, you get the tax invested during the life of the investment.

As opposed to this, though:

- most of us can't even run our bank accounts properly, so, unless we increase our financial knowledge very quickly, we're not going to run our SIPPs at all well;

- many SIPP providers still levy comparatively high charges, so to get the most out of it ideally you need to have a lot of money invested;

- although the rules for SIPPs have been set (more or less), what various providers will actually accept within the SIPP vary enormously – for example, some will allow you to include foreign property, some won't;

- the rules governing putting collections into a SIPP are still pretty muddy and the government hasn't helped with its indecision over whether property could be included or not. You'll need good advice on how to run yours;

- as with other pensions, usually you have to buy an annuity with what's left of the fund when you are 75.

If you like to do your investments yourself, SIPPs are certainly worth a look. However, they are very much an advanced option – a good idea, really, only for people who are very experienced and confident in stock market investing.

The rules are still being clarified, but currently SIPP holders have several options as to what their pension fund can buy – in other words, what goes into the 'bag':

- commercial property;

- stocks and shares;

- investment trusts;

- unit trusts;

- OEICS;

- gilts.

So, think carefully before transferring other pension pots, especially from guaranteed final-salary plans, into a SIPP.

For a lot more information on the ins and outs of SIPPS (and really do read and study as much as you can if you're seriously considering investing in one), look at the Motley Fool's 'Pension Centre' at **www.fool.co.uk** and the money section on the BBC website (**www.bbc.co.uk**). Also download the free SIPPs guide from Hargreaves Lansdown (**www.hargreaveslansdown.co.uk**).

Is my pension any good?

Jolly good question and, as with most things pension-wise, one that's quite difficult to answer simply. However, here are some ways to find out.

- When you get your delightful annual review of your pension you will thrill at the obscure and befuddling prose, the strange terminology and even stranger figures. However, do your best to scour the pages to find out just how much you are being charged each year for the management of your fund. If it is higher than 1.5 per cent (and, if you can't see it in the literature, phone the company and nag them until they tell you), then it's probably time you froze this particular product and set up something better performing somewhere else.

- Have a look at the bottom line – how much you actually have in your pension pot right now. Have a look at last year's figure, and the year before that, and the year before that. Has it been keeping up with the stock market (or, ideally, beating the market) or would you have done better putting the money in your local building society?

- It's really not too easy to tell whether you have a good pension fund, other than checking the charges and the actual amount by which your fund is growing each year, but at least those two things will give you an idea of where you're at and whether it's all worth it.

- To keep a proper check on how your fund is doing for your future you can order a pension forecast from your fund managers. In a roundabout, confusing and long-winded way they will let you know what sort of amount of money you can look forward to having when you retire if you continue to contribute the same amount each month until that date. They'll give you two figures – the actual amount of money they expect you to have and the 'real' value of that money. That is, how much that money will actually buy you in real terms, taking inflation into account. Obviously, the second figure is the important one because we want around £400,000 in 'real' terms, not just in numbers. Add that to the other money you have invested and you'll get an idea of how much you will have once you hang up your briefcase for the last time.

- Luckily, you can actually transfer a pension, just as you can transfer a PEP or ISA. But you may be charged for it. If you are a member of the company pension scheme, provided you've been paying in for more than two years, you can leave the pension fund 'frozen' and start paying into a new one. If you've been paying into the company scheme for less than two years, you'll get your contributions back, minus tax and National Insurance. If you 'freeze' your pension, you'll get your retirement benefits when you retire, as usual.

- You can also transfer a private personal pension fund from one pension scheme to another. There are charges associated with this – surprise, surprise! – but if your pension is really awful it may be worthwhile.

- Bear in mind that when you transfer money from a pension scheme, the money cannot go into your own bank account and sit there for six months while you make up your mind about what to do next.

- Moving pension providers can be complicated and costly and in this case it may be worth seeking (fee-based) professional advice.

So, should I have a pension or not?

That's entirely up to you (there, that's helpful!). Here are a few points to consider.

- Given the fundamental principle that you should spread your investments where possible, it probably is useful to have a pension as one of them – even if it's a small one.

- If you're very undisciplined with money, a pension should form a large part of your retirement fund because you're not allowed to touch the money until you reach a certain age.

- If you pay higher-rate tax, it's definitely worth considering putting a decent amount into a pension because the government puts into your pension pot the extra 40 per cent that you would have paid in tax.

- If your company offers a generous pension provision, don't look a gift horse in the mouth.

- If you just hate the idea of pensions, and particularly being forced to buy an annuity with much of it once you reach 75, don't touch them. Go for the alternatives.

Alternatives

As mentioned at the top of the chapter, pensions are not the only way to invest for your future. In fact it's perfectly possible and acceptable to invest in anything *but* a pension and end up with a good pot of money for your later years. Look again at Chapter 9, 'Make Your Money Make Money', for various investment ideas. Here are just a few points to keep in mind.

- Pensions are the only investment where your tax is paid into the fund, although you do have to pay tax on any money you get through an annuity once you actually retire.

- ISAs can be a useful alternative to pensions (or addition). The tax situation is the opposite here. The investments you make come out of your net income (you've paid tax on it and you don't get it back), but the money you take out at the end is tax-free.

- Pensions are generally very unpopular at the moment – understandably so – but don't be swept along with the people who invest in property instead of a pension. There are many downsides to investing in property (see Chapters 8 and 9 for some of the pros and cons) and one of the biggest is that it's far too popular at the moment (remember: when everyone else is investing in something, that's the time to sell).

- You need quite a lot of money to start off with to invest in property, which means that some people are able to invest in only that one product – risky. Make sure you don't invest in property until you have a cushion of other investments first, possibly including a pension, even if it's a small one.

- Your collections of stamps, art, antiques, wine or gold coins could make up a useful part of your retirement fund but, again, they shouldn't be the only part of it. They're too much of an unknown quantity and cost too much to keep.

Useful contacts

Occupational Pensions Regulatory Authority (OPRA) – www.opra.org
Department of Work and Pensions – www.dwp.gov.uk
Direct Gov – www.direct.gov.uk
Pensions Service – www.thepensionservice.gov.uk
Stakeholder pensions – www.stakeholderpensions.gov.uk
Association of British Insurers – www.abi.org.uk
Age Concern – www.ageconcern.org.uk
Help the Aged – www.helptheaged.org.uk
Treasury – www.hm-treasury.gov.uk
Age Positive – www.agepositive.gov.uk

11

Stop *Them* Taking *Your* Money

'Business is the art of extracting money from another man's pocket without resorting to violence.'

– Max Amsterdam

You **don't have to** be mugged in the street to have your money taken off you. We're ripped off every day in all areas of life, mostly because of our own ignorance and inertia, but we can stop it by:

- getting clued-up about money;

- keeping informed about rip-offs and frauds;

- shopping around;

- not believing that shops, banks and service companies are our friends – they're not.

Sadly it's getting easier to extract money from us now, thanks to increased modes of communication and the fact that we use actual cash so much less.

Liars, fraudsters and a bunch of bankers

Here are just a few of the ways that, legally and illegally, you can be parted from your money, together with some tips and mantras on how to stop this happening.

- Don't immediately trust people in suits or in posh offices. This is part of the unspoken sales pitch to make you buy from them.

- To protect yourself against losing a lot of money in any situation, use this as a mantra: 'If it sounds too good to be true, it probably is.' Any time you are faced with a money-making proposition that sounds so fabulous you can't believe it's true, let that suspicion stop you putting any money into the venture right there.

- Always check any financial product or business venture thoroughly and never part with large sums of cash on the promise that you will be making a fortune in no time at all. Ask yourself why they want to make *you* rich rather than keeping the idea to themselves.

- Check your 'greed' level every now and then. If there's one thing that can make you vulnerable to really bad scams it's greed.

- Taking a big deep breath and not allowing yourself to sign on the dotted line then and there to an alleged 'money maker' can save you from big losses.

- If someone, or an organisation, promises to give you the secret to great wealth for a fee, ask yourself, 'If they know this secret, why aren't they just doing it themselves rather than selling it to others?'

Legal ways

As pointed out in Chapter 5, 'Financial One-upmanship Day to Day', there are many ways in which we have money taken off us, quite legally, because we allow it. Here are some of the main things you need to watch out for in the high street banks and established financial companies:

- excessive fees and minuscule interest payments in bank accounts – if that's what you're getting from your bank, vote with your feet and move;

- store cards and credit cards that charge exorbitant interest – cut them up and close them down;

- expensive personal loans that tie you in – don't go for them if they won't let you pay it back early;

- finance and insurance deals sold by car salesmen – *never* fall for these.

- any type of insurance from a bank;

- any mortgage that tries to tie you in after the fixed period;

- any investments that charge more than 1.5 per cent in management fees – not all bad, but question high charges.

Let's look at some of the other particularly wasteful and expensive products/practices you need to watch out for.

Payment-protection insurance

PPI is a particularly lucrative little scam that financial companies run. It's usually sold to people on the backs of loans, mortgages or store credit and the idea is that it'll cover the monthly repayments if you lose your job or can't work because of accident or ill health. *However*:

- it protects the lender, not you (in other words, they get the money, not you, if you're ill);

- it's far too expensive for what it is: often it can add as much as a third to the cost of the loan overall;

- much of the time it doesn't pay out if you run into problems, because it's full of get-out clauses, particularly for the self-employed.

Since they bring in a lot of cash to banks and other lenders (billions each year), they're sold pretty aggressively, so you have to be tough to withstand the barrage. The Financial Services Authority (FSA) has already implemented new rules to ensure that sales staff are clear about the information they give customers before getting them to sign up for PPI, but it's not enough. Just say no!

Really, a general income-protection policy would be better than PPI if you want the much-vaunted peace-of-mind factor.

Retail warranties

The competition in technological hardware such as white goods (washing machines, fridges and so forth) and brown goods (such as TVs, computers, DVDs) is so fierce now that the profit margins on most of the things we buy for the home are pretty small. This is why many shops, particularly the big chains, have been pushing add-ons such as retail warranties at the point of sale (the cash register). They're insurance products – like PPI above – and are supposed to extend the number of years for which you're covered for repairs and breakdowns.

The problem is that they're expensive (compared with the amount you would pay in repairs in that time and they're pointless because, (a) on the whole, electrical goods don't go wrong in the first few years of life now and (b) your items are covered for a good six years, anyway, by the Sale of Goods Act

1979, which states that the item should be 'fit for purpose' and that you could claim for damages after purchase.

Much better simply to set up a savings account (as mentioned in Chapter 4 'Saving and Borrowing') into which you put a small amount each month to cover repairs. That way you get to keep the money if you don't use it mending the washing machine.

From a former television and stereo salesperson

For quite a while, I worked for a major retailer in their television and stereo department. Continued employment was based on the ability to sell service contracts which are warranty extensions offered by the retailer . . .

A customer had the opportunity to buy from one to three years' worth of service contract coverage at the time of the sale, although the credit I got was the same regardless of the length of coverage. Realising that most people would not be willing to buy three years' worth of coverage, initially, I would advocate to the customer the longest and most expensive plan. This gave me an excellent opportunity later, after being rejected in my sincere attempt to sell the three-year plan, to retreat to the one-year extension and its relatively small price, which I was thrilled to get. This technique proved highly effective, as I sold sales contracts to an average of 70 per cent of my customers . . .

– from *Influence – Science and Practice*, by Robert B Cialdini

Secured loans

Those ads on the TV with 'happy' borrowers telling you how nice their lender is should be switched off immediately for your own good. Even if your favourite celebrity is advocating the loan, don't be taken in. Many of these lenders charge sky-high interest rates and will only lend against your home plus impose punitive penalties if a borrower is in arrears for just a month. In the last housing crash the majority of repossessions were due to these kinds of lender and these kinds of loan, or second mortgages that the borrowers couldn't manage. Sadly, lending in these areas has risen greatly during the recent housing boom. Don't be one of those borrowers – you could easily lose your house.

Human error

Another way that money is just taken out of your hands is through basic human error at the banks. Because, since the 1980s, banks have become 'money shops' rather than dependable institutions, they've cut back on staff to increase profits. This means that mistakes are often made in everyone's bank account – usually not to their benefit – so claw back money you may have lost by scouring your bank statement each month. So many mistakes are made by understaffed banks every day that it's more important than ever to keep an eye on what they're doing with your account. So hang on to all your receipts and ATM slips and check every statement carefully.

Mortgages are much harder to keep an eye on, but, if you think you're being overcharged, make a fuss with your lender. Ask to see their calculations. You could find they've made expensive mistakes when they are forced to check them.

Even dodgier

The banks may be bad but there are some institutions and individuals who are even worse!

Dodgy – but legal – loan methods

Even if you badly need some cash, try to avoid the following if you possibly can.

Cheque cashers

These are those booths you sometimes find on the high streets of big cities. They are rip-off merchants who prey on the cash-strapped and desperate (or very lazy). They provide credit on cheques cashed at a later date and their charges are typically 10 per cent of a cheque's value. So a £40 cheque held for one month would cost you £4.

Home credit companies

These companies are getting more and more successful as our debt-ridden society produces more people with poor credit records. Companies such as the highly lucrative Provident Financial run 'home-collection' loans. They're doorstep lenders, often using agents who live in the area to do the lending and collecting. The APR they generally charge is utterly shocking – for example, a Provident loan of £500 repaid at £25 a week over 31 weeks (a fairly typical loan) tends to be lent at an APR of around 365 per cent!

Pawnbrokers (or buyback stores)

It used to be that pawnbrokers inhabited the backstreets and dark alleys of big cities, but now they're out and proud and often to be found prominently in posh areas of town. Basically, they operate by using your goods as surety for a loan of some sort. The property you leave with them can be redeemed on repayment of the loan, plus any outstanding interest. Charges typically range from 5 per cent to 12 per cent a month (you would normally expect to pay that for a whole year with normal loans), which equates to an average of 85 per cent a year.

After six months, items that have not been collected and on which less than £75 has been lent are deemed to belong to the pawnbroker. If the loan exceeds £75, the item is still technically owned by whoever brought it in, but it can be sold by the pawnbroker. After deductions for debt, interest and charges, any surplus should belong to the customer. But, in practice, low sale prices mean that they usually receive nothing.

They lend up to only half the value of an item and they have a nasty tendency to undervalue (sometimes massively) the thing you take in.

Absolute money losers

Then there are all those schemes and ideas for making money that actually lose money for you. They generally work by promising you great wealth for little effort – always a suspicious concept! Here is just a selection of them.

The Lottery (or Lotto)

Since it launched in 1994, the Lottery has taken more than £50 billion from us. Camelot, the company that runs it, has paid back only half this sum in prizes, which makes it Britain's worst gamble. So, next time you're tempted to take a fiver out of your purse to buy five Lottery tickets, take another fiver out and set fire to it – that should give you an idea of what is really happening to your money.

However, it's really worse than that. Your chance of winning any prize whatsoever, let alone the jackpot, is around one in

54, which is a little under 2 per cent. The odds against hitting the jackpot are even worse – 13,983,816 to one!

The EuroMillions draw is even worse. Tickets cost €2 each and can be bought by anyone in the UK, France or Spain. Incredibly, though, the odds on your winning this jackpot are even worse than for the silly old Lotto. They're 76,275,360 to one! You are more likely to die buying the ticket than you are to win it!

Free lotteries

These are supposedly a legitimate, fair and harmless form of gambling. However, most are linked to other 'gaming opportunities' where money is taken from you and seldom seen again. Take part in these only if you're bored and you know they are entirely free – oh, and don't use your real email address. *Never* part with money to take part in online games, competitions or lotteries.

Gambling generally

'There are two times in a man's life when he should not speculate: when he can't afford it, and when he can,' said Mark Twain, and he should know. Gambling in whatever form is a mug's game. Odds on winning anything, whether from scratch cards or horses, the dogs or football, are extremely bad. Always remember that, on the whole, gambling is a way of whisking your money away into a bookmaker's pockets.

In fact, the only sure way to make money out of gambling is to run a racket yourself. Gaming companies make hundreds of millions every year and all those millions came out of punters' pockets – *your* pockets if you gamble at all. This is doubly true of online casinos, which collectively now siphon off more cash than Las Vegas, despite being located in obscure offshore hideaways and monitored by no one you've ever heard of.

Be-a-'millionaire' courses

These take different forms depending on what the current belief is about what is making money. At the moment it's property, so that's what's being plugged.

Certainly, any ads you see or hear for seminars on becoming a property millionaire within two years should be regarded with the same level of horror and incredulity as those awful time-share meetings that used to be on offer all the time. Most of the 'trainee property developers' come away £2,000 or more worse off, and that's just from the fees they are conned into paying to learn these so-called secrets.

Other companies are selling 'special' stock market software that will make you millions in shares for thousands of pounds. Again, the makers are getting rich quickly on the gullibility of punters who will stump up this money for software that doesn't – and can't – deliver.

Pyramid schemes

You are bound to have a seen a few of these either on cheaply produced posters by the side of the road or leaflets stuck on your car window or in classified ads in your local paper. Whatever the 'product' these schemes offer, they are mainly based on a chain letter. Statistically speaking, it is impossible to reach the levels and amount of money promised, because this would mean the number of people that would have to be involved would be as much as the entire world's population.

In recent years, women have been targeted by an unscrupulous group of people setting up so-called 'Women Empowering Women' and 'Hearts' schemes. Again, these work on a chain-letter principle, although there is no letter, and not even any product. The idea is for a woman to give £3,000 to someone down the chain, and then she has to find eight more women to do the same, who each have to find another eight women and so on. The theory is that you will make £24,000 but this is true only for the few who start the scam. For most of the others there is no chance.

Homeworking schemes

Advertisements for homework schemes frequently appear in situations-vacant or recruitment columns in newspapers, rather than the business-opportunities section, and tend to appeal to people who are most in need of legitimate work from home, such as the unemployed, single parents and the disabled. They are often simply exploitative and should be regarded with the greatest of caution.

If you are tempted by an ad like this, visit the Advertising Standards Authority's site, **www.asa.org.uk**, to see if they are aware of the business and what they know about it. There are genuine homeworking jobs but many are bogus. You can know that they are dodgy if they make you pay to get the work in the first place.

SMS and 09011 competitions

If you have a mobile phone you have probably had at least one irritating SMS telling you about a fabulous moneymaking scheme or a message waiting for you at a premium-rate phone number or a hot babe waiting to hear from you on another premium-rate phone number. There are also competitions you can go in for just by using your mobile phone, but these are also expensive and the odds on your winning anything are so remote you might as well stick the price of the call down the toilet.

All scratch-card competitions should be binned immediately, particularly if you have to call a premium-rate number to find out whether you've won. Those are obvious scams.

Similarly, TV competitions that ask you to call an 09011 number are largely a waste of money. Not all the results are checked and they tell you you've got another 10 minutes to phone, when in reality the producer already knows the winners. The questions are kept laughably simple to guarantee a high callout, so make sure you're not one of the callers.

Fiendishly, the whole premium-rate scam has now shifted to the Web, in the form of 'dialler programs'. These are tiny 'cookies' downloaded by accident that instruct your modem to dial a premium-rate number rather than your usual ISP. So, if you use the Web, either buy yourself some anti-virus software and a decent firewall or remember *never* to install any program file unless you know exactly what it is.

And that's just for starters ...

Internet scams

The Internet is a joy and a fabulous tool for saving and making money in all sorts of ways, but it has also spawned scam after scam and, incredibly, hordes of people are falling for them.

The sorts of things you should watch out for include promises of instant wealth, free gifts and incredible discounts and bargains, stories from people claiming 'astounding results' and a lack of verifiable contact details (no phone number is an instant giveaway).

Keep your eyes peeled for 'Matrix' or 'MML' schemes (they're like pyramid schemes, only bigger), chain letters, registers and bureaux that ask for subscription in exchange for finding you work, and, of course, anything containing the phrases 'make money fast' and 'risk free'.

You can usually spot scams by the fact that they charge registration fees or demand credit-card authorisation (for instance on the grounds of confirming your age). Whatever you do, never divulge personal or financial information except over a secure Internet connection (a little yellow padlock symbol will appear at the bottom of your screen when you're in one!).

Many websites now use 'tracking cookies' to see which pages you visit. This is a form of spyware, which can be installed on your PC without your knowing and compromise your PC security and your identity. Adult sites are mined with these, and some go further by hijacking your browser or installing a 'dialler program' that replaces your real ISP number with a premium-rate number. Always have anti-spyware software installed to spot and remove these cookies as they appear.

For more information on online scams check out these: **www.scambusters.org**, **www.crimes-of-persuasion.com**.

Financial fraud

Financial fraud is definitely on the rise, partly because there are so many new ways to do it, thanks to the Internet, mobile phones and the speed of information. One main way you can protect yourself from dodgy scams is to be informed about what to look out for. Here are a few of the typical methods used to take money out of your pocket without your even noticing it.

Identity theft

The fraud: Fraudsters act by stealing your personal information in any way they can – going through your rubbish looking for bank and credit-card statements, for example, or contacting you for information and claiming to be from a legitimate organisation.

They then apply for loans and credits cards in your name and run up bills that can not only cost you but also damage your credit rating. Often, you don't find out about it for months until a lender contacts you demanding payment for debts you know nothing about.

The solution: Be on your guard for signs that you might have had your identity stolen. Look out for:

- items appearing on your bank or credit-card statements that you do not recognise;

- applying for a state benefit and being told that you are already claiming;

- receiving bills, invoices or receipts addressed to you for goods or services you haven't asked for;

- being refused a financial service, such as a credit card or loan, despite having a good credit history;

- receiving letters from solicitors or debt collectors for debts that aren't yours.

Apart from shredding documents, the best way to keep an eye on things is to check your credit files on a regular basis for strange loans and credit cards that you've never applied for (see below for contact details for Experian and Equifax, which are the main credit agencies). This is particularly important if you've recently moved, since that's when the majority of identity theft happens.

Don't bother with special insurance for it, though. This new product – offered by insurance companies with an eye for the main chance – is largely useless and expensive (as ever). There's nothing they offer that you can't do yourself.

Skimming

The fraud: This is where your credit card is double-swiped – often in restaurants or petrol stations – when you're not watching. The magnetic strip is read and used to produce a new card or buy goods online.

The solution: Never let your credit card out of your sight in shops, restaurants or anywhere where you have to use it.

Phishing

The fraud: This is where you get an email that looks exactly like the kind you might get from your bank. It will ask you to reveal your security details, which then gives them access to your bank accounts. Click on a link and you'll be taken to an identical – but fake – copy of your bank's website.

The solution: Don't respond to *any* emails from financial organisations unless you're certain that they're the real McCoy.

Ponzi schemes

The fraud: These fake investment schemes are named after Charles Ponzi, who, in 1920, swindled millions of dollars from American 'investors'. Ponzi promised to turn $100 into $150 within 45 days by trading in 'postal coupons'. In fact, the 'income' he paid to investors was simply money provided by new victims. Schemes like this work by sucking in more and more punters, whose capital goes towards providing pretend 'returns' to the first investors. With these and other pyramid schemes, there's no obvious explanation of how this 'extra' money's made.

The solution: Avoid all schemes that offer 'guaranteed' returns of, say, more than 10 per cent a year, because these so-called guarantees are likely to be worthless. If it isn't obvious how the returns are being made and you can't see goods or other items being bought and sold, then you can be pretty sure you've fallen for a scam. In particular, watch out for betting syndicates and the like, since the only guarantee in the gambling business is that bookmakers always get richer!

Boiler rooms

The fraud: If you want chapter and verse on how a 'boiler room', works watch the film *Boiler Room* (with Ben Affleck and Vin Diesel). People who work in 'boiler rooms' are well-trained, smooth-talking salespeople who sell worthless – or non-existent – shares at top prices over the phone to people they know have money. Boiler-room salesmen flatter their victims and play on their fear and greed, causing many to abandon common sense.

The solution: The best thing to do is to hang up immediately! Boiler-room operators are renowned for their persuasive sales techniques, and even experienced, hardened investors have been taken in. What's more, if a boiler-room salesperson thinks you may be the slightest bit interested, they will phone you repeatedly until they make a sale.

Also, look in Chapter 5, 'Financial One-upmanship Day to Day', for ways to deal with annoying cold callers. That should give you some ideas.

What to do if the worst happens

The main thing to do is not to panic. If, for example, you have been the victim of some banking fraud and you have let the bank know as soon as you found out, you will usually get all your money back from the bank. However, it's in your best interests to act quickly, in order to minimise the damage. Some of the signs that you've been a victim of fraud are more obvious than others, but to protect yourself effectively, you need to make sure you're on top of all of your financial issues. That means keeping an eye on bank accounts and checking those statements each month!

What to do

- If any of your cards (be they credit, debit, store or whatever) or cheques have been lost or stolen, tell the providers as soon as possible. Take notes during all telephone conversations, in particular the name of the person you speak to. Follow up your telephone call with a letter confirming what was said and keep copies of all correspondence (print out any emails) sent, or received.

- If you receive bills or statements that are addressed to you but you know don't belong to you, contact the organisations concerned as soon as possible to alert them to the fraud.

- If any transactions appear on your statements that aren't yours, immediately tell the organisation concerned.

- Request a copy of your credit file/report from one of the credit reference agencies: Experian, Equifax or Callcredit. You can obtain a copy for as little as £2.

- If you spot an account or credit application on your credit report that you don't recognise, contact the company involved immediately to request they remove the data from your file.

- Consider closing your current accounts, and opening new ones with different numbers and details.

- Change all passwords for your online bank accounts.

- Report the identity theft to the police as a crime and obtain a crime number.

- If you've experienced some form of identity crime, you may find it useful to register for protective registration with the UK's Fraud Prevention Service (CIFAS). It costs, but it means that a CIFAS warning can be placed against your address so that, when a CIFAS member tries to search against your address, it will see the following message: 'CIFAS – DO NOT REJECT – REFER FOR VALIDATION', at which point it must contact Equifax directly.

Useful contacts

UK's Fraud Prevention Service (CIFAS) – **www.cifas.org.uk**
Experian – **www.experian.co.uk**
Equifax – **www.equifax.co.uk**
Callcredit – **www.mycallcredit.com**
Office of Fair Trading – **www.oft.gov.uk**
Serious Fraud Office – **www.sfo.gov.uk**

Experian's top ten tips to avoid becoming a victim of ID fraud

1. Take care of your personal information by keeping any documents containing personal information, including transaction slips and proofs of identity, secure.

2. Never throw away whole receipts, bank statements, utility bills or other documents that can be used by a fraudster to assume your identity. Your rubbish bin is a target for fraudsters. Always thoroughly destroy personal information before throwing it away, preferably by using a personal shredder.

3. Check your receipts against your card and bank statements carefully. If you find an unfamiliar transaction, contact your card issuer or bank immediately. If you bank online, use this facility to keep a constant eye on any transactions occurring on your accounts.

4. Monitor the information on your credit report. The fact that it takes most people nearly a year and a half to discover they are victims of identity fraud vividly demonstrates that most of us make life far too easy for the criminals. People who regularly monitor their credit reports typically spot whether someone is attempting identity fraud in their name within a matter of weeks.

5. Never disclose personal or financial details to anyone 'cold-calling', even if they claim to be from your bank, the police or another official organisation. It's always a good idea to phone them back on the number you have for them, not the one they may give you.

continues ➤

6. Use different passwords for different accounts. If a fraudster accesses one, they are less likely to be able to access all accounts.

7. If you have documents stolen, there is a strong chance these will be used to commit fraud in your name. If this does happen, Experian can help prevent a repetition by adding security features to your credit report. If a fraudster opens an account in your name, this will show up on your credit report and you can ask Experian to help you liaise with the lender(s) involved and make sure you're not affected by the fraud.

8. If you move home, redirect your post from day one. The new occupants might at best just throw letters in the bin instead of forwarding them to your new address; at worst, they might use the information to steal your identity.

9. Provide personal information and credit card details *only on secure sites* displaying bona fide logos of secure payment systems, such as Verisign or Worldpay.

10. Try to keep your personal information in different places around the house so a thief will find it more difficult to obtain complete information. Keep as much as possible locked up.

How to run your own scam

'If you sent a letter to enough people, say 500,000, saying that you could give them the secret to great riches, or a lucky number, or similar, and they just needed to send you a cheque for £20 to get it, I'm convinced you'd get enough response to make a tidy profit,' says Doug Carnegie, former editor of BBC's

Watchdog. 'Time and again we've seen these scams and they always work because there are enough people to fall for them. Most people take things at face value and sadly something as simple as that kind of scam could keep you in caviar for life.'

12

Being Together

> 'Wealth – any income that is at least one
> hundred dollars more a year than the income of
> one's wife's sister's husband.'
>
> **– H L Mencken**

Living with another person is where the rubber of romantic idealism hits the tarmac of reality, and the slipperiest patch on the road is money. Get that bit right – at least to the point where you can both come to some sort of agreement as to how you're going to organise it – and you're well on the way to a successful life partnership. Ignore it and you're setting up years of misery and probably poverty for yourselves, culminating in an acrimonious split.

Couples

It's rare that you gaze mistily into your beloved's eyes at the start of a big romance and think, 'I wonder how we'd organise the paying of our bills together.' In fact, I'd be worried if this has ever happened to you, but at some point *before* you tie the knot/move in together/have children (not necessarily in that order for many people) you *need* to 'have the discussion' – about money and how you're going to organise it. Seriously, it's an essential. According to the UK relationship charity, Relate, the number-one cause of rows that lead to separation in relationships is money – even more than arguments about the in-laws or performance in the bedroom.

The important things you need to agree on (or at least come to some sort of compromise on) are:

- whether you will have a joint account, separate accounts or a mixture of the two;

- how the bills will be paid and from what account – particularly the mortgage;

- who will pay more towards the bills – it's generally fairest to work on a percentage of each partner's income;

- what your individual attitude to money is (very important – you each need to know if the other is a spendthrift, a miser or just isn't that interested in money generally);

- what you each think it's important to spend money on – whether you love to splurge on travelling or parties or entertaining all the time, or whether you want to invest everything apart from increasing your collection of Chinese pottery.

In all seriousness, if you do the above properly, you could even avoid a bad marriage/cohabitation. People's attitude to money and spending says a lot about their character and, also, should tell you a lot about what it would be like to live with them day in, day out. It could show that you're really not suited to each other because you have fundamentally different values and interests. A big disappointment in the short term but a huge bonus (and serious money saver!) in the long term.

Marriage

So, you've 'had the discussion' and you've decided you *can* bear each other after all. In fact, you're going to get married (if you've decided just to live together, skip the next bit and see 'Living Together' on page 218). Great, now another thoroughly unromantic suggestion: a prenuptial agreement.

I never thought I'd advocate these, but, having seen and heard of so much financial misery surrounding divorce, and knowing that more than two in five marriages now end this way, it does seem that a prenuptial agreement could be sensible and practical, particularly if one of you has a lot of money or if either of you is marrying for the second time.

In the USA 'prenups' are far more common than here, but then they're also legally recognised. Here, premarital agreements (as they are known in this country) are not legally binding but, with the number of divorces increasing, they're often used as a basis for a settlement. In fact, there have been hints from the government that such agreements should be given more credence – not least because of the potential cut in the legal aid bill.

At the moment, in some cases it could prove persuasive to a court when divorcing couples are arguing about who promised what to whom – but it's usually only when the marriage has been comparatively short and there are no children involved. It's up to you but it might be worth thinking about before you take that walk down the aisle or drive to the register office if you're the wealthier partner in the relationship. Actually, it could be essential if you're about to enter a second marriage (they have an even higher divorce rate than first marriages) and want to safeguard inherited family money, your business, or your children from a previous relationship.

The wedding

Now back to the romantic stuff. The wedding – ahh!

We may be in the 21st century but the majority of weddings are still mostly paid for by one or both sets of parents. However, more and more of us are paying for our own weddings as people get married later. Couples may have more money behind them at that stage but if you're paying your own way, the price of all things matrimonial will be of more interest to you than they might have been if Mum and Dad were paying.

So, first the bad news. The average cost of a UK wedding is around £18,000 – interestingly, about the same as the average cost of a divorce. Some weird irony there! However, *you* don't have to splurge that amount of money on your wedding. In fact, unless you really are wealthy, I would actively urge you not to. There's nothing romantic about starting your life together heavily in debt. If rows about money are the number-one cause of divorce in this country you're setting yourself up to fail by doing that.

It's such an important day, though, so why shouldn't you have a good one? Well, the good news is, you can and you really don't have to take out a mortgage in order to do so. Here are some tips.

- The basic wedding doesn't need to cost more than £100 – that's the price of marrying in a register office. If you're more interested in the reception than the service itself, think about saving on the ceremony in order to have more money for the fun afterwards.

- Make sure that everyone who is paying for the wedding is happy with the budget.

- Try deciding what you really want and then seeing how inexpensively you can get it.

- Be realistic and remember that there's no such thing as a

physically perfect wedding. The 'perfect' side depends on you and the people who are there. If you rip something or the photographer pulls the plug on the organ while you're signing the register it's no big deal. Similarly, the flowers don't have to cost an arm and a leg to make a lovely show.

- Shop around for everything.

- Try deciding who you really want to have at the wedding and then working on the invitations, rather than deciding on 100 guests and then inviting people just to make up the numbers.

- Hotels with wedding licences will often offer a discount for your room hire if you have both the ceremony and reception there. They will also often lend you a cake stand and knife, print place cards and so on, but if they charge for this then check against prices elsewhere. Hotels may also offer a free room to the bride and groom.

- With the reception (and any other aspect of the wedding if you can manage it) try not to let them know that it's a wedding. The moment you mention the 'W' word in certain circles the price doubles. If you just describe your upcoming reception as a private party, you can cut the costs right down. Also, if you can get married on a weekday rather than a Saturday that's cheaper too.

- Beware of 'tie-ins', such as when the wedding-car people insist on supplying their own flowers.

- The less 'traditional' your wedding, the more freedom you have to use your own imagination and creativity and it'll probably work out cheaper, too.

- Be critical and bargain hard.

- Keep a poker face – beware of high-pressure sales tactics. Those wedding-dress saleswomen may look sweet but they're tough sellers!

Living together

Moving in together is so common in Britain now that it has become pretty much the norm for most people. Sometimes couples then go on to get married but more often they either split up or just carry on as a couple. Actually, the *most* common thing is that they just split up. In fact, sorry to rain on your hearts and flowers, but, statistically, the future isn't that rosy for cohabitees. Only 18 per cent of cohabiting relationships last a decade or more, compared with 75 per cent of marriages. One recent survey found that the average length of a cohabitation was just 18 months.

So, while you may feel you don't need a piece of paper to prove how much you love each other, you do need one if you're going to get the same financial security given to married couples. Apparently, most people still believe that living together gives you the same rights as getting married. They are wrong. There's no such thing as a common-law marriage or a common-law wife or husband, at least not in the eyes of the law.

It's very important to be aware of this when you're pooling your wealth and setting up house together. For example, no matter how long you've been living together, if one of you dies, the other will not automatically inherit their assets. If you split up, men will not have any automatic right to see their children, and women will not be entitled to any kind of financial support for themselves (although children are).

Cohabitation agreements

Short of rushing to the altar or register office, there is something you can do to make things clearer when you move in together: set up a 'cohabitation agreement'. This is seen by courts as a binding contract between unrelated parties, and can therefore be enforced if the court so chooses. They can set out who owns what and how the loot will be divided if you do break up, and they can be particularly useful if one of you is much more wealthy than the other. You might even be able to negotiate yourself a decent deal if you're the less wealthy party. See **www.advicenow.org.uk/livingtogether** for more information, and a sample cohabitation agreement.

Property ownership

The biggest possible loss, if it does all go horribly wrong, is the loss of the property – or part of the property – you've been living in. If you're married and you get divorced, both parties have a right to a share of the former marital home. If you've just been cohabiting, however, there's no such automatic right. This is why if you buy a house or flat, or move into your partner's place and start contributing to the mortgage or the bills or you buy furniture for it, you need to protect your interests.

There are two ways you can be entitled to a share of your house: (a) if the home is in both your names (more of that later); (b) if the house isn't in your name, but you can prove you have contributed directly to buying or substantially improving it in some way. For example, if you paid the deposit or have contributed directly towards the mortgage instalments, this would constitute a beneficial interest. You've actually 'bought' a little bit of the house even though the title deeds don't say you have.

This second way is much trickier than the first, particularly when it comes to proving your contributions. Say, for example, one partner has paid the mortgage while the other has covered all the household bills. This might have been convenient – and even felt as if you were sharing things out nicely – but it leaves you unequal in the eyes of the law. The non-mortgage-payer would somehow have to prove that the arrangement was based on an understanding or agreement that you were effectively making contributions towards the purchase of the house itself by freeing up the other partner's income.

If you live in your partner's house, therefore, it makes sense to have a joint account for the household bills and the mortgage. Keep the bank statements as evidence of your contributions. That brings me back to the other option: joint ownership. If you decide to co-own your home then you need to think about how you want to divide it up in legal terms. There are two ways of doing it: either jointly or on the basis of 'tenants-in-common'.

Joint owners

This is the more common option when married couples buy a house together: you both own the house between you and there's no technical division of the property. If one of you dies, the surviving partner automatically owns the house, regardless of whether a will has been drawn up. This means you can't 'gift' your share of the property to anyone else. Because lots of people don't bother to make wills, this at least covers the problem of dying intestate, since there'll be no arguments about who subsequently owns the whole house.

If you split up, though, it's worth bearing in mind that you might end up feeling short-changed if you've put more money into the house than your partner. It may be that you each paid half of the deposit and then split everything, from the mortgage payments down to the decorating bills, right down the middle. Or, alternatively, you might have paid most of the deposit and then forked out far more towards the mortgage payments than your partner did. It doesn't matter either way – in the eyes of the law you still share the home equally. You could contest this in court, but that would be time-consuming and costly, and might not end up the way you wanted, anyway.

You can sell the house only if both of you agree – this may cause problems if one of you wants to sell and the other doesn't but can't afford to buy out the remaining share.

Tenants-in-common

With tenants-in-common each member of the couple owns a share of the house (could be half each or different proportions, depending on who has put more money into it from the start). The difference between this and joint ownership is that there's a technical division of the property, so each owner can leave their share of the house to anyone they like. This can work well in certain circumstances – it gives each partner an element of control – although it can be tricky if one dies and leaves their share to someone else.

In the case of friends or siblings who share ownership of a property, being tenants-in-common is probably a good thing. If you and your brother inherit your parents' house together, the chances are you'd rather leave your half-share to your spouse or your children rather than pass it on to him. However, as well as being the most common option for couples, joint ownership does also seem the easiest and the best choice. Unless you've got such a valuable house that planning for Inheritance Tax through the generations is a necessity, it doesn't really seem fair to inadvertently shackle, or be shackled by, someone you've loved.

Renting

If you move in with your partner into their rented flat you won't have any right to stay there if you break up – even if you've contributed to the rent. If you'd like to safeguard your position there (perhaps to give yourself time to find somewhere else if it all goes pear-shaped), get yourself on the rental agreement as a joint tenant – if the landlord agrees.

Pensions and life insurance

Couples who live together, unlike married couples, are not entitled to receive the state pension or bereavement allowance for deceased partners. Some occupational and personal pensions will pay out to partners but many won't. You should check with your provider to find out what they will do. Personal pensions can be arranged to cover whoever the pension holder wants, although if you want special provisions you often have to pay a lot more. If you're worried about your partner not having enough money to cope if you shuffled off this mortal coil first, take out a life-insurance policy to provide for them.

Day-to-day practicalities

Who holds the purse strings?

So, you're married or cohabiting. Whatever you're doing you're living in the same house and sharing bills – or you should be sharing in some way. The first question to ask yourself is who should manage the money in a relationship and how should it be divided. Well, sadly, there are no easy answers. The catch-all response is 'whatever works for you both' – easy to say. But, in order to find out what actually does work for you both, you have to communicate with each other. This is obvious to most couples but not all. It's amazing how many couples live in the same home for years without ever tackling the issue of money. Many couples now will be open from the start about every sexual partner and position they've ever had, but will clam up the moment money is mentioned.

Really, though, money management in a relationship is of paramount importance, so you need to talk early on about a number of financial matters. If your current arrangement isn't working, then you need to talk about it again.

- Ideally, you should talk about your individual attitudes to money, whether you're a spender or a saver, what tips you picked up from your parents and what kind of spending patterns of theirs you think you copy.

- Discuss how you both think your money should be managed (if you have any idea at all – many don't) and which of you would be better at it (you may have to do it together if neither of you has the confidence to do it).

- Talk about what's important to you both as a couple. Is it future security? Would you like to take a year off in a few years' time to make a trip round the world together? Are you saving for a house, and how much would you need for a deposit?

- Importantly, let each other know how much you earn and what savings you have. Then you can work out how much each should contribute to the shared expenses.

When it comes to shared expenses and savings, talk through some specifics.

- It makes sense to agree from the start about what should be considered a joint household expense. The roof over your head, the gas, electricity and council tax, for example, are shared expenses.

- But what about things such as clothes, CDs and books? Is he going to get angry if you regularly spend a fortune on fashion items when you know the boiler needs replacing? Are you going to get angry if he has a passion for collecting DVDs when he knows that you have no interest in them?

- Savings: do you both have ISAs and pensions that you regularly pay into, and should these be considered joint expenses that will enable you to enjoy financial independence when you retire?

- There's also the tricky question of what to do if one of you is earning more than the other. Should you both contribute equal amounts to the joint expenses or work out a percentage based on your separate earning power?

- If you can work out what your agreed joint monthly outgoings are and who's going to contribute what, then open a joint household account and make sure your agreed contributions are direct-debited into it. Ensure that all bills are paid from it (use standing orders or direct debits to cut costs and avoid time-wasting). Then keep personal accounts for yourselves for your own money so that you can retain a modicum of privacy and independence.

Financial matters can run fairly smoothly while you are just a couple, so long as these basic issues are addressed and both sides are generous with each other and curb their tendency to criticise and complain. However, everything changes when the first child is born and one partner (usually the woman) gives up work for a period. Of course, many women go back to work quite quickly, but this isn't always the best for her or the family. Even so, however long one partner is out of work, unless they have a private income the issue of how one person's income is to be shared between the two has to be agreed from the start.

In the past, women have often been virtually imprisoned by their husbands' total control of the money – reduced to asking for money every time they wanted to buy a lipstick or similar and then left helpless and ignorant when faced with bills and household finances if their husband suddenly died. Things have moved on for many, though by no means all, in this country. However, it can still be a problem to know how to divide up money that one partner is earning so that the other partner not only gets bills paid but has their own money to spend on more frivolous things. There are two possible ways of doing it (although you may have worked out something of your own that is quite different, so fair enough!). As the child-caring partner:

- you could have a monthly 'salary' from the partner who's working, which you would agree between you; this money would be transferred into your personal bank account each month to spend on yourself or others or even to save as you wish;

- you could agree between you that you would access your partner's account whenever you liked as a joint account; this would mean that it would be hard to surprise each other with presents or trips out, but at least you would both know how much money you had at any point.

Whatever you decide to do is entirely up to you as a couple and should suit both of you. There is no 'right' way to do it other than making sure that both sides are considered and that they know where they stand. If one system doesn't work after a while, discuss it again and change it. Just make sure you keep talking!

Dealing with a spendthrift partner

When you're married, even more than when you cohabit, you can be put in a very vulnerable position by a partner who spends all and more of their income. Any loans in both your names (including the mortgage) that are not paid are the responsibility of both spouses, so, even if you're doing your bit and paying what you should each month, if your partner isn't you could lose your house, or at least your peace of mind.

If you (or they) realise things are getting dangerous, the rule is, again, to communicate with each other about it. It's harder if they don't recognise the problem but there are ways to tackle it.

- First, talk about why they spend so much and how they view money and borrowing. Sometimes people take on the spending habits and the fears of money or poverty that their parents had without even realising it. Talking about it can sometimes open their eyes to thoughts and attitudes that aren't really their own and don't make sense.

- If you're dangerously in debt, work out the numbers for yourself first. Try to have a calm conversation, using your figures to illustrate the financial position you're both in. Use whatever tactics you know think work – after all, you know your partner better than anyone.

- Show them how much money is being wasted on interest payments every month.

- If they hate their job, point out how many hours of work they're putting in just to service the debts. It might annoy them enough to want to pay them off as soon as possible.

- Try to get them to suggest ways of tackling certain debts. Show them your own plan of action and ask if they think it would work and what they think could be done to improve it.

- Try to sell the idea that the two of you are a team fighting the rest of the world and that, if you both work together, you will be able to have that new car, gadget or holiday. If you can agree that action needs to be taken, then start talking about how you're going to do it. Get them involved, even if it's just in a minor way.

- If your finances are really dire, consider the prospect of one or both of you getting a second job. While it may sound painful at first, there's almost always time in the day or night when you can find a few hours for part-time work. The income you bring in can make an incredible difference to your debts.

- Above all, communicate, communicate, communicate. Share the successes and failures so that you keep each other motivated.

Gay couples

Civil partnerships, which came into force in December 2005, give legal recognition to a same-sex relationship. This means that gay couples who register get the same rights as married couples when it comes to tax, social security, inheritance and workplace benefits. See **www.womenandequalityunit. gov.uk/civilpartnership.htm** for more information.

If you don't want to register your relationship, however, you'll have no more legal entitlement to each other's loot than a heterosexual couple do. Just as there's no such thing as a common-law marriage, there's no such thing as a common-law gay marriage. Since the 2005 legislation there are a few other things for gay couples to be aware of.

Will

Make a will! It's been said before, but why not say it again? If you don't, everything you own will go to your closest relatives, leaving your partner with nothing. It also wouldn't hurt to find a gay-friendly lawyer who will understand the issues involved for a gay couple in making a will – look out for adverts in the gay press. (There's more on making a will below.)

Pension rights

If you die before retirement, many pension schemes will pay out a lump sum and/or the whole of the accumulated pension fund to a relative or dependant or a different 'nominated ben-eficiary'. If you want the money to go to your partner, make sure that a nomination form (sometimes called an *expression-of-wishes* form) has been completed.

- Check with your pension scheme what will happen about the payment of benefits in the event of your death.

- Check whether you can nominate a beneficiary for any

lump-sum payout. If so, check that you've nominated the person you want to benefit – your partner, a charity, your neighbour's goldfish, or whoever.

- Check whether the scheme provides a pension for a spouse or dependant. If so, does this include an unmarried or same-sex partner? Can you nominate a beneficiary for the dependant's pension? If so, check that your nomination is up to date. Seek financial advice if your scheme doesn't provide benefits for an unmarried, same-sex partner: can the rules be changed, or can you change to a scheme that does?

Property

If you do own a property with a partner, it's worth checking that you have joint ownership – a solicitor may have assumed that a same-sex couple would rather own their property as tenants-in-common. As described above, if this is the case, and you die without a will, then your partner won't get your share of the property. Fine if you want it that way, but worth being aware of.

Useful contacts

The Gay Business Association: **www.gba.org.uk** lists companies offering gay-friendly financial services.
www.gayfinance.info
www.gaytimes.co.uk
www.pinkfinance.com
www.pinkmortgage.co.uk
www.fresh-finance.co.uk

Making a will

Don't skip this bit! It's important – really.

As soon as you have anything of value to your name, and certainly as soon as you get married, you should make a will, however simple it is. More than half of us die 'intestate', that is, without a will, and even more do nothing about avoiding inheritance tax before shuffling off this mortal coil. This causes a load of nuisance – and potential expense – to the loved ones who survive us and it also means they can lose out on a lot of the money they might have inherited. Even worse, if you don't specify who should get what when you go, the authorities divvy out the cash according to their rules. This can mean that your hated ex who went off with your best friend *and* the boxed set of Abba CDs could potentially end up with your money too.

The tax office love people who leave no will because they pour serious cash into their coffers each year. If you die intestate they take 40 per cent of your worth before anyone else gets a sniff of it. Now, however much you might love and admire the Inland Revenue (and, given the amount of tax money we give them each year, you'd think we adore them), surely you don't want to give them all that cash.

Making a will doesn't have to take long and can be pretty painless. At least you can take pleasure in mentally giving things to people you love – or sticking it to those you don't.

- You can make your own will using one of the will packs from W H Smith, Tesco or Office World (about £15) or one of the many on the Net. Go to **www.tenminutewill.co.uk**, **www.lawpack.co.uk** among others.

- If you prefer – and certainly if you have a complicated set of possessions or family situation – you can get a solicitor to draw one up for you. Go to **www.solicitors-online.com** for a list of local lawyers, or **www.searchwill.co.uk** for a qualified will writer in your area. Also, you could contact the Society of Trust and Estate Practitioners (STEP) for will-writing specialists (**www.step.org** or phone 020 7838 48850).

- Or do it for charity. Once a year the Law Society of England and Wales runs a Make a Will Week, when solicitors write wills for a one-off donation to charity. Another scheme is Will Aid, whereby thousands of solicitors donate the fees they make for will writing to charity for one month. Keep an eye on the media and on the Internet for when these events come up in the year.

- Before you write the will, work out who should inherit what you own, how much each and at what age they should have it.

- If you're married, don't think that everything you own will go to your spouse. It depends on the total value of what you own, what it is, how you own it and which other relatives also survive you. Make sure you remember your spouse in the will!

- If you just cohabit – whether your relationship is heterosexual or same sex – you certainly have to name your partner in your will, otherwise they could get nothing.

- You will also need to say who will deal with your affairs after you've gone – who will be your executors.

- Don't forget charities you'd like to give to and also put in what kind of funeral – if any – you would like.

- Don't forget your debts. Most people have debts, at least during their working life, and, on your death, creditors have to be paid before any money can be distributed. If your debts are bigger than your assets, consider taking out a life-insurance policy to ensure that your family at least get something.

- With mortgages held under joint tenancy (which is the norm with married couples) and any loans in both names, the surviving spouse will be liable for paying off the debt. If you have only cohabited you won't be liable for any debts your former partner incurred unless they were taken out in both your names.

Useful contacts

www.tenminutewill.co.uk
www.lawpack.co.uk
www.step.org
www.lawsociety.org.uk
www.lawscot.org.uk
www.lawsoc-ni.org (the Law Society of Northern Ireland)

Book

Wills, Probate and Inheritance Tax for Dummies – Julian Knight (Wiley, £12.99)

Divorce and separation

> *'A divorce is like an amputation: you survive it, but there's less of you.'*
> **– Margaret Atwood**

We hear a lot about rising divorce rates, even though the number of marriages is falling. In fact, there are far more separations for cohabitees but it's harder to quantify them. Whether you've been married or cohabiting, though, splitting up is never pleasant and it always costs – particularly if you've been married and even more if you have children.

Divorce

The main things that are considered by the courts when a couple divorce are how the assets (property, investments, furniture and so forth) will be divided up and how the spouse on a lesser income, or caring for the children, will be paid (maintenance).

In theory, all joint and individual assets are added up, the debts deducted and then the remainder is split 50–50, although it doesn't always work like that of course. Whether you get anything at all from the split depends on which one of you has the most income and assets. Your age also matters, because the court will want to know how much of a working life you have ahead of you to support yourself. The length of the marriage is also important. The other very important factor is the children, if you have any – who will look after them, what their financial needs are, how old they are and therefore how long the absentee parent will have to pay towards their keep, if at all.

Here are some of the elements you'll have to deal with.

Maintenance

The spouse with the lower, or no, income (usually the woman) is entitled to apply for maintenance for herself (and her children if she has some). If it's for herself she should apply to the County Court or High Court, and can ask either for regular payments for a given period of time, or for what's called a *clean-break* settlement (where you have a one-off lump sum in full and final settlement). This is useful if you think you may cohabit and/or remarry later. Maintenance payments are lost once you remarry and frequently if you cohabit for more than six months, so a lump sum is often the most sensible route to take.

Assets

The main asset is generally the family home but you will usually be entitled to a portion of any assets that are connected with the marriage. If you have young children who need a roof over their heads, and you're looking after them, then the court will often give you the right to live in the family home until they reach 18 or have finished full-time education. While this may seem a good solution, remember that it means your ex still owns a share of your home and he'll want his portion when the last child is no longer dependent. If you go for this option you could find yourself having to sell up to pay him his share many years down the line when you've practically forgotten you were ever married to him in the first place.

This is one of the reasons why women (and increasingly men) often opt for the clean-break settlement. It's worth noting that if you and your partner can come to an amicable arrangement over the finances, a break-up needn't involve huge legal fees and a fight in the courts. However, it is always sensible to get any kind of amicable agreement officially approved by the court so that you can enforce the terms should there be problems later.

Pension

The spouse on the lesser income also has the right to transfer some of his or her former spouse's pension fund into one of her own. Previously, you could claim some of it only once they had actually retired. If you don't have much of a pension scheme in operation for your own needs because you've spent years at home bringing up children, this is very good news. However, your entitlement is to only 50 per cent of the value of the pension built up during the course of the marriage. If you have been married 10 years and he or she has built up their pension over 20 years, only 10 years is technically available to you. There is also the fact that, as it is part of a pension fund, it will have to remain as part of a pension fund. Perhaps this is why so few exes have taken up this right since it was introduced a few years ago.

Separation

Maintenance

If you have been cohabiting, for whatever period of time, neither of you will have the right to maintenance from the other if you separate.

Assets

You will both be entitled to take from the relationship any property that you can prove is yours. If you've bought a property together, it can be sold and the money split according to the law if you've bought as joint tenants or tenants-in-common. However, if the property is in the name of just one of you, on the whole, the other partner will have no right to any of it. However, if you can show that you've contributed directly to buying it or improving it in some substantial way, you may be able to claim a 'beneficial interest' in it. You do need to prove this, though, such as with bank statements that show how much of the mortgage you have paid or with receipts for redecoration and furniture.

If you have children together, the courts may allow the partner caring for the children to live in the home you used to share while the children are growing up. However, this doesn't always happen and they may have to find somewhere else to live to which the absentee parent would have to contribute.

Pensions

If you're splitting from a partner you have never married, you have no right to any of their pensions or investments, however long you have been together. On the plus side, though, you will also not be liable for any of their debts, unless it's a loan that is in your joint names.

Useful contact

Relate – **www.relate.org.uk**

13

Family Matters

'Never lend your car to anyone to whom you have given birth.'

– Erma Bombeck

This is where your attitude to money, and life generally, will really have to change. When you're a couple you can pretty much carry on with life as before – apart from keeping each other informed about your whereabouts! Once just one little baby turns up, though, your whole approach to life will change. Suddenly a Volvo estate looks like a cool car to have, you take an interest in life assurance and pensions and sleeping is one of your favourite activities.

Budgeting for a baby

They say that funding a child through to adulthood will cost you the same as the average house in the UK, but ultimately it's up to you how much you actually end up spending. You can save a lot by doing your own childcare (or getting grandparents to chip in), by sending them to state school and by living outside major cities. But it's worth putting aside as much money as you can for a couple of years – or a year if you can't wait that long – before *really* trying for a baby. Basically the more money you have in your savings, the less stress you will have and the easier life will be, even when you go back to work, if that is what you want to do.

Only you know how much money you might need and how much you can afford to put by right now, but the things that you (and your partner) will need to consider are:

- your loss of earnings for the length of time you stay off work once you have had the baby; also loss of earnings if you decide to go part-time if and when you return to work;

- the various costs associated with babies and children (see later in this chapter);

- how your pension and savings contributions are going to be paid while you are not earning;

- the cost of moving house – probably to a bigger place to accommodate the new baby – if that is something you are considering.

Of course, many babies are not planned and you may be reading this now emitting short bitter laughs as you flip through Mothercare catalogues. But, even if you do suddenly find yourself about to be a parent, you have nine months to save and set aside as much money as you can to make things easier for yourself later on. You can put quite a bit away in that time if you concentrate. Happily, there are also other ways of boosting your income once you have had a child, and you should get every penny that it's your right to have from your employers and from the government. You'll need it.

Costs of having a baby

Let's just start with the first year of a child's life (a particularly expensive one for you, since your household income will probably be lower too). If you have the money, and don't mind spending it, there are lots of delightful and expensive things you can buy for a new baby; but, if money *is* an issue, try the many ways of cutting costs and even doing without things that won't deprive either yourself or your baby. You can find lists of items you should have and those you might like but could happily do without on one of the many baby websites such as **www.babycentre.co.uk**, **www.babyworld.co.uk**, **www.ukmumsnet.com** and **www.thinkbaby.co.uk**.

Many department stores and specialist baby shops have handy lists for parents-to-be, of course, but many items in these lists are not strictly necessary. For example, midwives say that just a plain washing-up bowl will do to bath baby in the first few months of its life and many parents do perfectly well without a Moses basket and changing bag. A lot of clothes can be bought second-hand and, if you have friends, relatives or neighbours who have recently had babies, they will often hand over clothes that are now too small but still have a lot of wear in them. If you breastfeed, not only will you ensure the best nutrition for your baby (and lose weight gained during pregnancy yourself) but you could save yourself the best part of £1,000 in powdered milk and sterilisers.

Probably the biggest cost you'll face is the loss of your earnings (or those of your partner). Unless you can get family to help, someone will have to care for your child. If you are employed you will be able to get help through maternity pay, but that lasts for only a few months. After that you will have to choose between work (and paying for childcare) and staying at home. Again, the government is helping more now with tax credits and childcare vouchers (see below), among other benefits, so make full use of those (even if it does mean filling in tedious forms and trying to understand government-speak).

Day-to-day family finances

So many families are in debt now – partly because of over-spending and partly because of the increasing cost of living – that, even if you never bothered to watch the pennies before, now is the time when you really have to. There's a ton of help on the Internet for this. For a start, just have a look at **www.moneysavingexpert.com**, **www.fool.co.uk**, **www. ivillage.co.uk, www.icircle.co.uk** and look at the many and various American family and budgeting sites for ideas. Go back to Chapter 2, 'Control Your Finances, Control Your Life', Chapter 3, 'Dump Your Debt, Live Cheaper, Make Money', and Chapter 5, 'Financial One-upmanship Day to Day', for a lot more ideas for cutting costs and getting the most for your money.

The important things to keep in mind, though, are these.

- You need to keep a balance between living and saving for the future. Don't be stingy (life is always smaller for stingy people), but remind yourself that, by saving now and investing for your children's (and your own) future, you're doing them more good than you would by spending all your money and more on toys, gifts and so on.

- *Really*, the best things you can give your children are the free things. It's not a trite saying: it's the truth. No amount of expensive gifts and posh holidays can come close to the value of your love, security, interest, time and unselfish care.

- With babies, most clothes and equipment can be second-hand. Make the most of hand-me-downs from friends and relatives. Check that items are clean and in good working order, for example, that the brakes on a pushchair work efficiently. But never have second-hand cot mattresses for your baby. They always need to be new. And avoid buying a second-hand infant car seat, unless you are sure it hasn't been in an accident, and it still has its fitting instructions.

- If you have the time, grow and make as much as you can. Food that's homemade tends to taste better, anyway, and it's certainly a lot cheaper than the ready-made stuff.

- Keep children's TV watching to a minimum. In particular, try to keep them away from the ads. Join campaigns to cut down on this pernicious child-focused advertising.

- Don't waste money on lots of new toys. You can borrow a toy for a fortnight for a small sum when you join a toy library (ask your local council for details). If your little one already has more toys than she knows what to do with, pack half of them up and store them away for a few months, then take them out and swap them with the old ones – immediately she will have a new set of toys.

- Keep and use all the coupons and tokens you get free, but only if they're for items you would buy anyway.

- Join mystery-shopping agencies that give you free children's or household items (see Chapter 6 'Making That Bit Extra' for contacts). Try www.cosmeticresearchonline.co.uk for free trials of family products.

- Don't spend what you don't have, even if the children are insisting that 'everyone else has got one'. If you need to be really strict with yourself, take cash (not cheques or credit cards) to shops so you can't spend more than you'd planned to.

- Teach your children early on the value of money (see below for ideas) and they'll be less likely to throw tantrums if you say you can't afford to buy something.

Find more tips in books such as *Mr Thrifty*, by Jane Furnival (Michael O'Mara, £4.99) and the American *Miserly Moms*, by Jonni McCoy (Bethany House, $12.99).

Childcare

This is where the costs really start mounting up. If you think you could manage on one salary, or you have parents who are willing to sacrifice their lives for your childcare needs, or you just can't bear the idea of someone else looking after your child, then skip this section. But, if you would like to go back to work after having your baby, you may find that the cost of paying someone to look after the little one may be the same as, if not more than, your salary or your partner's. Once you've looked at the options and done the sums, don't be surprised if you decide that you or your partner (whoever is earning less and would be the better childcarer) would do better to stay at home and bring your child up full-time, rather than pay someone else to do it.

There are various childcare options around and all of them, apart from blackmailing the grandparents to do it, will really cost. You can't put childcare costs against tax, either – something for which several organisations are campaigning, so far in vain. Parents in this country tend to pay about three-quarters of the costs of childcare (one of the worst proportions in Western Europe) with the government paying most of the rest plus a contribution by employers. In order of affordability, here are the current childcare options.

- The cheapest option is a childminder. The disadvantages of childminders is that they look after children in their own homes, so you have to get your children to them and pick them up in the evening. Also, childminders could look after more than one child at a time, including their own, so you cannot be sure that your child will get the attention he or she deserves. However, childminders are regulated and (supposed to be) checked by the local authority, so they are, on the whole, safe, although the level of checking varies from authority to authority and some are far more lax than others. Find out more from the National

Childminders Association at **www.ncma.org.uk** or from your local council.

- Nursery places are more expensive – much more if you live in London. Again, you have the disadvantage of having to take the child to and from the nursery, which may not fit in with your working hours. It is also hard to monitor what goes on inside a nursery while you are not there. However, nurseries are very good for socialising children and can be particularly beneficial for an only child who might otherwise miss out on playmates. For more information about nurseries and how to find one in your area, check out the National Daycare Trust's website at **www.daycaretrust.org.uk**, the National Day Nurseries Association at **www.ndna.org.uk**, the government's website **www.everychildmatters.gov.uk** and the comprehensive information on the BBC website **www.bbc.co.uk/parenting/childcare**.

- The most expensive full-time childcare option is to have a live-in or live-out nanny. Again, prices vary, depending on where you live, but remember that being a nanny is a proper job and they will need an annual salary of between £18,000 and £30,000 (including tax and National Insurance which must be paid), depending on their qualifications and experience, what the job entails and where it is. You can cut these costs in half, almost, by doing a 'nanny share', whereby your child and your neighbour's child are both cared for by one nanny and you share the cost. The advantage of nannies is that they look after your child in your house and they are devoted solely to the care of your child and will not be spending time looking after others instead. However, to afford a full-time nanny you will need to be earning £27,000 to £40,000 per year. In fact, if you are just earning that you will effectively be going out to work purely to pay for the nanny, so realistically you would want your salary to be some way above that. For help in hiring a nanny look at *The Good Nanny Guide* by Charlotte Breese and Hilaire Gomer (Vermilion, £14.99) or check out one of the many parenting websites (including the BBC one **www.bbc.co.uk/parenting/childcare www.nannytax.co.uk**, which offers payroll services for parents with nannies.

If your child is under three years old, you should not have an au pair, unless they're there just to help you. Au pairs are not proper childcarers and should not be employed as such. Au pairs, unlike nannies, are not trained or qualified to look after children. Au pairs are not paid a salary, but are given weekly 'pocket money' as well as room and board with you, the chance to speak English and soak up some British culture (if that's what it can be called) in return for some *light* housework and help with the kids.

Childcare vouchers

If you are employed by a company that is registered with the Childcare Vouchers scheme then you could get some help with the cost of childcare. However, make sure you get advice on it because it's possible that the vouchers could stop you getting tax credits (see below).

The way it works is that your employer can grant you childcare vouchers worth up to £50 a week on which they won't pay tax or NI, and nor will you. If you're in a higher tax bracket, this weekly help can really make a difference. There is a list of different types of childcare (and childcare qualifications) that are allowed, so check you are happy with the choice of childcare available. For more information go to **www.childcarevouchers.co.uk**.

Life assurance

Once you have even one child you need to think about taking out life assurance. In order to work out what level of cover you need, decide who is totally dependent on you for income. If you've got a fair bit of equity in your home, you can always take a gamble that property prices will remain high enough for your family to sell the property if you die, and move some-where smaller. It's likely that they will need some sort of an income as well, though, and your spouse might not be able to cope on their own, so think about how your children's needs would be met if you weren't around.

Decide how much of a lump sum would be needed to pay off the mortgage and how many years' worth of your annual income they will need to keep them financially comfortable for as long as necessary. Perhaps you've got children who will need to be seen through school and university, or a partner who can't take your place as the breadwinner.

Work out how much your own family actually needs as a lump sum if you go. The best way is to multiply your net annual income by the total number of years you think your family will need support and there you have a DIY formula for life insurance.

The basic rule about buying life insurance is to go for the deal that offers the cover you believe you need at the best rate. All the companies are offering pretty much the same thing (although do check the small print because some have clever ways of wriggling out of paying), so there's no reason to pay over the odds.

Consider sickness cover, too, if your employer doesn't already offer it. If you were to have an accident or become dis-abled or ill for a long time – but you didn't die – would your family be able to manage? If not, think about buying some kind of cover so that you'd have a guaranteed income. This is espe-cially important if you're self-employed, although, again, check the small print because you need to make sure that the policy is watertight. Look around at what's on offer.

Making a will

I know I go on about it but, really, if you have any property or investments and, certainly, if you have any children, you should make a will and update it as your circumstances change. See Chapter 12 for information on how to make a will and see Chapter 14, 'Taxation', for ideas on how to avoid as much Inheritance Tax as possible.

The good news

It's not all money going out when you have children. There are more benefits than ever for those with children, and particularly those on low incomes. Just make sure you get whatever you should have.

Benefits – maternity, paternity

The government is planning to boost both maternity and paternity rights by an extra £1,400 from 2007. Currently, working mothers can claim statutory maternity pay for six months. It is proposed to increase this to nine months from April 2007. Your employer is supposed to pay statutory maternity pay, provided you are employed for the six months prior to your leave and earn at least £79 a week (check on **www.dwp.gov.uk** for the current figures).

You can claim 90 per cent of your average earnings for the first six weeks, with no upper limit, but this falls to a small amount for the remaining 20 weeks. Payouts count as earnings, so, frustratingly, you pay tax and make National Insurance contributions on any money you receive. However, don't worry if you decide not to go back to work at the end of your maternity leave. If you don't return you can still keep the cash.

Fathers can currently take one or two weeks' consecutive paid paternity leave and claim a maximum £106 a week. Adopting couples can claim statutory adoption pay.

Visit the Department for Work and Pensions at **www.dwp.gov.uk** or **www.entitledto.co.uk** or speak to your employer to find out what the situation is now.

Finally, as an aside, there are some benefits now that allow *both* parents to take 13 weeks' unpaid leave each for each child. This new 'parental' leave can be taken at any time until the child reaches five years old, so it doesn't strictly come under maternity rights. However, you could use them to extend your time off work without losing your right to return to your job.

Tax credits

Tax credits keep changing, not only in what they offer but even what they're called, so don't feel bad if it all seems too confusing to understand. The system's not run very well, either (*there's* a surprise!), so things can go wrong with your payments through no fault of yours. The idea of tax credits is that parents (and even non-parents) are rewarded for working rather than perpetuating the old system where many found they were better off being on benefits than getting a job.

Child tax credit

You don't have to be on a low income to claim tax credits. Check at **www.hrmc.gov.uk/taxcredits** for the current rules, but even if your combined earnings are £66,000 you can still claim if your child is under a year old. You don't have to be actually working to claim, either.

You can get support for children up to age 18, although beyond age 16 claims will be considered only if they are in full-time education or working less than 24 hours a week. Child tax credit comes in two parts: the 'family element', a single, flat-rate payment each year for every family earning less than a fixed amount a year (check the government website for the current figure); and the 'child element', which is paid for each child you have, depending on your income. The less you earn and the more children you have, the more you get. You can also claim extra if your child is disabled.

Working tax credit

Working tax credit is designed to top up the incomes of lower earners, including those without children. You must work at least 16 hours a week to claim if you are single; if you're part of a couple you must work 30 hours between you. The amount you get depends on your income, but there are lone-parent, disability and over-50 payments on top. Parents can also claim up to 70 per cent of childcare costs.

Tax credits and child benefit generally go to the main carer, which means that, when parents are separated, it will generally be the mother who can apply. For information on tax credits, call the Inland Revenue tax credit helpline on 0845 300 3900 or claim online at **www.hrmc.gov.uk/taxcredits**. You can also find out more at **www.direct.gov.uk**.

Child benefit

Every child up to the age of 16 (and then up to the 19th birthday for those in full-time non-advanced further education) is entitled to weekly child benefit to be paid to the parent(s). The benefit is usually paid to the mother. Lone parents can claim a little more per week. Call 0845 302 1444 or claim online at Revenue and Customs (**www.hmrc.gov.uk**).

Children and money

Investing for your kids

This is something that is becoming much more popular, particularly among the chattering classes. The introduction of the Child Trust Fund is proof that the government is trying to get all other parents interested in the concept too. Of course, years ago (and even now in the developing world) it was the other way around: you had children so that they could help to keep you going in your old age. Now the older ones are having to provide for the younger ones in their old age (and even middle years).

Of course, one of the best ongoing presents that you could give to your children is to invest some money for them that can be left undisturbed until they are adults. This will enable them to benefit from the miracle of compound returns. Imagine what would have happened if, when you were born, your parents had had the foresight (and financial ability) to invest some money in the stock market on your behalf. In fact, I have coined the term GLUTIMs (Grandparents Leaving Utter Tat Instead of Money) to describe forebears without financial foresight (like mine, bless them!).

The Child Trust Fund

You would think that everyone would have embraced the *free money* given to new parents since 2005. But no. As usual, the government has come up with a good, reasonably generous idea and then ruined it by making it seem complicated, unattractive and even frightening for many people. But, honestly, it's not a worrying thing. It's pretty straightforward. Here are the facts.

- Child Trust Funds are like ISAs for children – they are a tax-free investment for their future.

- The government starts it off with a £250 cheque – free money! – and then a second one when the child turns seven.

- If you don't use that cheque within 12 months the government will invest it for you, although you can move it later on if you want to.

- Parents, relatives and friends can add to the fund up to £1,200 a year altogether. The children themselves can add to it later on if they're in a position to do so.

- Children won't be taxed on any income or increased value from the investments, even when they take the money out at the end.

- The child cannot touch the money – and neither can anyone else – until the child is 18. From that point they can do what they like with the money.

- Parents have to choose what type of investment vehicle they put the money into. There are three basic types:

  - a cash savings account (like a cash ISA);

  - a stakeholder account, which invests in an equities fund for the first 13 years – after that the money is shifted gradually into lower-risk investments for the next five years;

  - a shares account through which you can buy shares in individual companies.

So far the vast majority of parents have put the money into the first option – cash. I assume this is because more people understand cash accounts than equities investments, but it's a shame. Remember that 18 years is a long time for money to grow and for the ups and downs of companies to be smoothed out. If you want to make sensible money for your child, the second two options are the most lucrative, even if they are riskier. Look at **www.fool.co.uk**, **www.moneysavingexpert.com** and

www.bbc.co.uk/money for good advice as to the pros and cons of the different types of investments.

Cash gifts

Bank and building society accounts are a good place to start with your investment plan for your children. Not that they're exactly fabulous investment vehicles on their own in the long term, but in the short term they're very useful for collecting up enough cash to plonk into a serious product later on. You might be able to put some or all of your child benefit in it each month plus any bits of cash from the relatives.

Shop around and remember that, for the purposes of collecting a decent amount of money for your child over a year or so, you don't need instant access, which is good, since you sometimes get higher interest rates on the 60- or 90-day-notice accounts.

Probably the best way to set up the account is to do it in your own name (and that of your partner if you like) but to designate your child as the beneficiary. That means that, while you have control of the account, the money is treated as hers and she will be able to take control of it when she reaches 18. But make sure you fill in the R85 Inland Revenue form when you do it, because that will mean that any interest is paid gross.

Once she gets old enough you could open an account in her name (see below for details on how to do that). One thing you will have to be careful of is that, if you make a gift to your child that earns the child income of more than £100 in any one tax year, the whole amount will count as your own income for tax purposes. With two parents there is a £200 limit (described by the Inland Revenue as £100 in respect of gifts from each parent, not £200 shared, if you see what they mean). This rule only applies to gifts from parents, directly or indirectly, not other relatives or friends, and on money given from other sources children have the same income tax allowance as adults. Admittedly, given the very small amounts of interest you can earn each year in bank or building society accounts, you would have to be depositing truly serious amounts of cash in the first place to earn that kind of money. So, frankly, this is unlikely to be something you will need to worry about when it comes to just savings accounts.

Money from grandparents, relatives or other adults is treated as the child's own. Like adults, children have their own personal tax allowance so any income they receive within that limit on this money will be free of tax. They also have their own capital gains tax allowance, which can be handy if, as a family, you have a lot of investments.

Doing your own fund

As explained above under 'The Child Trust Fund', the best vehicle for investing for your children is something that is shares-based. They have a long time to wait for the money to grow, so you can happily put money into something that would seem risky in the short term. If you go for shares in hand-picked companies, then it will be good-quality companies that you are looking for, ones that you think may still be around and doing well in 30 or 40 or even 50 or 60 years' time. Just think what kind of riches you would now be earning if your parents had had the foresight to buy you shares in, say, IBM, Coca-Cola or American Express when you were just a wee one.

Bare trusts

They sound rude but they're not at all. Bare trusts help you invest for your child without putting any extra tax on you. First of all, if you're buying shares, or units of a tracker fund, for your child, you buy them in your name. Normally you add the child's initials after yours to designate that the shares, or units, are held on your child's behalf. This is what is known as a 'bare trust'. It's easy to set up and needs no involvement from a solicitor. As parents you act as bare trustees, looking after the investment on behalf of the child until they can be registered in the child's name. This will be when he reaches 18 (16 in Scotland), and you, as trustees, have to hand over the assets of the trust. The bare trust essentially separates all the investments in it from your own investments (for taxation purposes) but gives you complete control over them. They offer the child no protection from irresponsible parents (although, if you are reading this, you could hardly be described as irresponsible, could you?), but this is the best way for you to handle the investments without incurring tax yourself. Another advantage is that there's no inheritance tax charged on it if you are unfortunate enough to shuffle off this mortal coil before your child reaches 18.

Other trusts

If you want to set up a trust for your child but don't want him to get his hands on it until he's at least 25 (understandable), you can set up an 'accumulation and maintenance' trust, where there are trustees who decide whether or not the child gets anything from it until he's 25. Even after that they could hold the money back if the now adult child doesn't seem capable of using it wisely. These kinds of trust involve a lot of effort and legal complications, though, so do it only if you're putting away significant sums and make sure you get legal advice (which will also cost).

Friendly societies

A lot of people go for the child savings products offered by friendly societies – they're understandable, tax-free and, well, friendly. However, they're also deceptively expensive in terms of charges and over time tend not to perform very well. If Granny or Auntie sets up a friendly account for your sprogling just smile and thank her, but don't bother with one yourself. Much better to look to shares for your investments. However, if you want to know more about friendly society products go to the website of the Association of Friendly Societies **www.afs.org.uk**.

Investing child benefit

You may think (and you may be right) that you don't have any money left over from your daily expenses with which to invest in your child's future. That's understandable and if you're struggling to pay debts then, as with investing for yourself, those debts need to be paid before you put money into anything else. However, if you are solvent and you think you could do without it, child benefit could be seen as investment money.

Don't think that, because it's a relatively small amount each month, it won't make a difference to your child's future. It will. Remember, even small amounts of money invested regularly and wisely and over a long period of time can grow significantly. Child benefit tends to go up a little each year, so check at **www.entitledto.co.uk** or **www.dwp.gov.uk** to see what the rate is now (if you don't know already). To give you an idea, at the time of writing, child benefit for the first child is £17 a week. If you invest that in a nice cheap index tracker, wrapped in an ISA to protect it from tax, for 18 years (the amount of time you get child benefit), it should leave a pot of money for your first-born of around £42,450. This could help her pay part of her way through university, put something towards a property or start her off on her own business.

Teaching the value of money

The most important influence on children is their family, and that applies to money matters at least as much as anything else. It may sound daunting, but the habits you encourage and the example you set in the way you deal with your finances will affect how your children deal with their own cash right up until they reach retirement age. And, even if you veer from cash crisis to cash crisis yourself, there are simple steps you can take to encourage your children to manage their own money better.

The first big lesson should be that money doesn't grow on trees – well, technically, bank notes start off that way, but you know what I mean. The earlier you start to give your children a basic idea of how much things cost and encourage them to weigh up the pros and cons of spending, the better.

- The best way to encourage them to save and spend wisely is to lead by example, and let them see you dealing with money well yourself.

- Talk to them about how much different items cost when you're out shopping. Use a trip to the supermarket to point out different prices and compare different brands – and hopefully keep them entertained enough to avoid tantrums while you're at it. Let them check the receipt when you get home, maybe even ticking off the items as you put them away.

- Encourage them to see further than just cash. Explain the different ways to pay for things, such as credit cards and cheques, and talk about how a piece of card like a train or theatre ticket can be worth a lot.

- Challenge their thinking. Instead of saying 'We can't afford that', ask 'How *could* we afford that?' They might even come up with some useful answers!

- Short of dragging them off to live in an Amish community, you can't really prevent your children being exposed to the lure of advertising. But you can encourage them to question the claims of the commercials, perhaps talking to them about the motives of the makers or getting them to try to 'sell' you a product to see how easy it is to exaggerate.

- Teach them to save. Start with a piggy bank and then, on a monthly basis, get them to pay the money into their own bank or building society savings account. They will grow up with a sense of achievement around money and a sense of play and reward. (See 'Children's bank accounts' below.)

- Teach them about compound interest. Children who can delay their desire for instant gratification have been shown to do better in all walks of career and financial future, so you could be giving them more than just a maths lesson.

- Think about what your parents taught you about money and whether you really want your children to have the same beliefs.

- Don't think that bailing them out is always the best or most loving thing to do. Sometimes you have to help them learn their own lessons in order to grow.

- Go to the website of the Personal Finance Education Group, **www.pfeg.org**, for actual teaching materials on personal finance.

Pocket money

Pocket money has gone up faster than earnings in the last decade or so, vastly outstripping inflation. It can be a very useful way of gradually giving children independence and teaching them about money management, or it can be a way of buying affection, replacing your time and interest or giving them the idea that money grows in Daddy's pocket. There are no right or wrong answers when it comes to how much pocket money you give – if at all – but, in these spendthrift, consumerist times, it's important to think through why you're doing it and what would be the best way to do it.

- Be clear with your child about what their pocket money needs to cover. You may also want to give them extra money from time to time for buying special things, such as birthday presents for other family members.

- Let your child choose whether they want their pocket money to be paid in weekly or monthly amounts.

- Talk to other parents about how much they give their children. Then work out how much you think is reasonable, given your income and what you pay for.

- Encourage them to think about when to spend their money, and what on. Let them decide whether they blow the lot on pocket money day, or spend a few weeks saving for something special.

- Play by the rules. Don't cave in and dole out more cash each time your child spends their pocket money early. Otherwise, they'll never learn about saving and going without.

- Keep pace with their growth by increasing pocket money by a certain amount each birthday.

Household chores?

A constant question on Internet parenting message boards is whether children should be paid for doing chores or whether it should be something they are expected to do anyway. Ultimately, what you decide depends on what you and your partner feel is acceptable. Be clear with your child about what you expect of them, and consider some of these options:

- Segregate chores into those that have to be done anyway, and those that can be paid for.

- Alternatively, split their pocket money, giving some of it whatever they do, and the rest of it once they have done their chores.

- Pay them for doing occasional extra jobs, such as washing the car or cleaning out the garden shed. This teaches them the basics of working and earning money.

Teenagers

Teenagers, by their nature, are likely to want more money than their younger siblings. The temptations of designer clothes, socialising and new technology start to tug as never before. Peer-group pressure can weigh heavily and they may feel like an outsider if they don't have the latest clothes. Be sensitive to this but try to help them think for themselves and develop their own style early on instead of slavishly following fashion.

- Encourage them to think about things such as how much designer labels cost, and the extra things you could buy if you forego the big names.

- This could also be a good time to substitute a monthly allowance for pocket money, giving them greater scope to practise budgeting. Don't be afraid to keep an eye on how things are going, especially at the start.

- Compromise – you may be prepared to pay for one premium item of clothing if they go for cheaper options elsewhere.

- Don't make them think that things have to cost money to be desirable. Show them the ideas in this book for cutting costs while still having a good life.

- If they still want more money, suggest a part-time job: 13–15-year-olds can work up to five hours on Saturdays (and weekdays in the summer holidays), to a maximum of 25 hours a week during school holidays. They can't work for more than two hours on schooldays and Sundays. Over-15s can work up to eight hours on Saturdays and school holiday weekdays, and up to 35 hours a week during the holidays.

Ideally, if you follow these rules, teach your kids the value of money and encourage them in the ways of earning, saving and spending wisely, you won't end up with that most dreaded of parental burdens, the KIPPER! What is a KIPPER? It stands for Kids In Parents' Pockets Eroding Retirement Savings. It's a growing phenomenon in the UK and in America and it involves 'kids' in their twenties, thirties and forties still living with Mummy and Daddy, eating their food, using their electricity, paying only a pittance towards their upkeep, using the house as a hotel and generally refusing to grow up and take responsibility for their own lives. The solution is simple really: just kick them out. But many parents, and mothers in particular, are loath to do this, making excuses for them and grinning and bearing it. This is costing them dear though – billions of pounds a year throughout the UK, and for many it means their retirement is set back by a few years. Think it through carefully – is it really love to cosset and pay for your big kid or should he spread his wings, take the knocks and start to grow properly? It's your call but don't just accept the status quo. Do something about it if you think you need to.

Mack's maxim

Next time your teenager asks for an advance just say "no". Consider giving them your budget for the weekly supermarket shop, tell them that they have to feed the family with it but that, if they succeed, they can have what's left over – if they've spent frugally and there is anything left over! Go on, I dare you! (You're allowed to supervise so don't panic.)'

– Jane Mack, the Motley Fool

Children's bank accounts

Banks, building societies, and even the Post Office are all vying for children's cash. Opening one of these accounts is a good opportunity to get children thinking about money as well as being a useful, and tax efficient, way of investing for them.

There are three main types of account for children:

- those for under-eights, which are usually in the name of the parent or guardian;

- those for 8–12-year-olds, where they can make deposits and withdrawals on their own and will have their own passbook;

- accounts for 13–18-year-olds, which are more like the adult version, with cashpoint cards and chequebooks for over-16s (however, children can't go into the red: overdrafts aren't given to under-18s).

When setting up children's bank accounts there are a few points to consider.

- It makes sense to shop around, because interest rates and incentives vary. Look at **www.moneysupermarket.com**, **www.moneyextra.co.uk**, **www.moneysavingexpert.com** for ideas. The 'Parenting Fools' and 'Investing for Children' discussion boards on the Motley Fool (**www.fool.co.uk**) also have up-to-date information on the best accounts.

- Check how often interest is paid into the account – most pay on an annual basis, which could seem like an age to a child.

- Freebies such as books, badges and birthday cards can mean a lot to children, but explain to them the value of interest rates. All other things being equal, though, go for the best freebies!

- Consider only those banks with a handy branch – Internet accounts are rarely open to children, although, if they are, they make a lot of sense because they tend to have the best rates and children are happy using the Internet from a very early age.

- Make sure you fill in a form R85, which stops any tax being taken out of the child's savings account.

- Children may have smaller incomes than adults, but they get the same annual income tax and capital gains allowances. Yippee!

- Make all investments for your child in their name. If it's in your name you will have a tax nightmare to deal with.

- There's a limit on the interest that a child can earn tax-free on money from their parents – currently it's £100 from each parent. After that, the income is taxed at the parents' rate. But the rule doesn't apply to money given by friends or other relatives.

For more information on setting up savings accounts for children, check out Leaflet IR110, A Guide for People with Savings, from (**www.hmrc.gov.uk**).

Stakeholder pensions for babies

Weird? Unnatural? Maybe, but, for a really long-term investment, setting up a stakeholder pension for your little one is a pretty good plan, although admittedly you may not be around to see it bear fruit. Stakeholder pensions were originally set up to give those on little or no wage (women taking a break from work to have children, people on low pay or the unemployed) the chance to contribute to a pension (and therefore take some of the burden off the government). What they hadn't bargained for was that a number of families with cash to spare saw that, since *anyone* could have a stakeholder pension, regardless of age or earnings status, that meant that even babies could have one. The scheme is tax-efficient for you and for your baby, which, of course, will mean a lot to him at this stage. It also gives you a chance to invest in something that he won't be able to get his chubby hands on and fritter away (*your* child? – surely not!) until he needs a pension, by which time there will probably be little or no state pension.

Another plus is that you can stop and start contributions as you wish, so, if you start a plan on behalf of a child and your financial circumstances change, you can stop without penalty. There is also the advantage for Granny and Grandpa, if they have some money to invest, of passing money that might otherwise be liable for inheritance tax to their grandchildren through a stakeholder.

Under the stakeholder rules, everyone can contribute up to a certain amount each year (check on **www.dwp.gov.uk** for the current amount) into a stakeholder with the Inland Revenue adding in the tax you would have paid. Even if you can't afford to invest the full allowable amount each year, putting child benefit in for a rather longer period can create a sizeable sum too. Research from HSBC shows that if you invest the allowance from birth to the age of 18 in a stakeholder pension then, assuming premiums increase in line with the retail price index, by the time he is 65 the total fund value will be worth over £500,000.

You can also console yourself with the fact that pension contributions, however small, made at this point in his life will be worth more than the equivalent contributions made during the 42 years from 18 to 60. The one big downside to it all, sadly, is that, by the time he comes to draw on the pension you lovingly provided for him, you probably won't be around for him to thank. More information at **www.stakeholderpensions. gov.uk**.

Investing for university

If you do manage to teach your kids the value of money and the importance of saving, they'll be streets ahead of everyone else when they come to take their place at one of the hallowed students' union bars somewhere in the country. Financially, life is not easy for students nowadays, and it can be just as tough, if not more so, for their increasingly impoverished parents.

See Chapter 7, 'Student Finances', for where to go for help and information on loans, grants and other financial assistance. When it comes to investing for university, the same rules apply as above. Again, you have a decent amount of time to allow your money to grow (if you start when they're toddlers), so the stock market is the best place to put your money. There are all sorts of special, glossy investment packages offered by financial advisers, apparently tailored to your parental needs. But in fact they tend to be endowment-based or, at the very least, invested in expensive managed funds. As with other areas of life, the rule here is that the more layers of packaging around a financial product, the more expensive it will be and the less good it will do you. As with food, the simpler and more raw the better!

Don't forget your future!

It may seem like a long way off but don't allow yourself to forget your own future while caring for your children. Women (and it is usually women) who take time off work to look after children, or carers looking after a sick or elderly relative, can protect their basic state pension by claiming benefits under the Home Responsibilities Protection Scheme. Go to **www.the pensionservice.gov.uk** or call 0845 60 60 265 for information. Make sure you get child benefit in your name, because that will automatically protect your pension qualification. Look at **www.entitledto.co.uk** for more information.

If you're working, this is the time to look into your company's pension scheme, if you haven't already. If not, try to put money into a stakeholder pension (see Chapter 10, 'Your Future', or go to **www.stakeholderpensions.gov.uk** for more information on that). If your partner can contribute to it then so much the better. Or put money into an ISA (equities-based for serious earning power).

Cohabiting couples

All of the above applies as much to cohabiting couples as it does to married ones. However, there are some differences you need to be aware of if you have children and are unmarried.

- Although unmarried fathers are required to pay maintenance for their children, they don't have the same rights over their children as married (or divorced) fathers do. They have to obtain a legally binding parental-responsibility agreement (with the mother's consent) or a parental-responsibility order (if she won't play fair).

- An unmarried father who jointly signs the birth register with the mother from 1 December 2003 now has parental responsibility. This does not apply to children born before the legislation was passed, although it is a common misconception.

- An unmarried father without parental responsibility has no right to act on the child's behalf (except in emergency) or to be consulted over which school the child attends, which religion, if any, he's brought up in, what medical treatment he receives, what name he's known by, or whether he's put up for adoption. An unmarried father can't get a passport for the child or access official documents or school/medical records. However, he still has to pay maintenance through the Child Support Agency which could have money deducted from his wages.

Similarly, though, an unmarried woman who has lived with a man for 20 years, has borne him four children and done everything that a wife would do has no right to the house they share (unless her name is on the title deeds) or any of his property if they split up. The children do, though, so she could stay in the family home until the youngest has reached 18. After that, she's on her own.

So, if you're serious about living together and having children together without a marriage contract, it's important to draw up some sort of cohabitation agreement. This isn't legally binding, but can be used as a starting point in a court of law if there's a dispute after separation. The father needs to gain a parental-responsibility order – either by applying for one or simply by signing the birth register when the baby is born. Both parents also need to work out who owns what and, ideally, have both names on the property deeds as tenants-in-common or joint tenants (see Chapter 8, 'A House or a Home?', for more information on that).

Divorce and separation

If divorce is hell then divorcing when you have children is the hottest part of hell. Not only do you have all the emotional misery attached to divorce – and divorce involving children, which is ten times worse misery – but it's appallingly expensive from start to finish. The only winners in divorce are the lawyers.

Even if you're unmarried it can be expensive, and certainly miserable, because maintenance has to be sorted out together with access, who owns what and who is entitled to make decisions about the children's future. Unmarried couples face rather more uncertainty during a relationship break-up because, much as the term 'common-law wife' or 'common-law husband' is bandied about, it's a myth that the courts recognise it. Either way there will be questions to resolve. Where will you live? Where will the children live? Who's going to pay for what?

If the father has obtained a parental-responsibility order, he will have a say in part of the child's life but, married or unmarried, the father (or mother if she doesn't have primary care of the children) will have to continue to pay maintenance. The Equal Parenting Council (**www.equalparenting.org**) campaigns for more shared care of children after divorce and separation. It argues that children with a relationship with both their separated parents do better on every measure. They do better socially and academically and have better life outcomes. They're also more likely to stay away from crime and drugs. Try to arrange this where possible – even though the primary carer of the children may try to block access – for the children's sake, even more than the parents'.

Overall, though, divorced parents agree that the more you can keep the lawyers out of the equation the better. Parents who are constantly applying to the courts for decisions on maintenance and so forth lose money every time. If you can agree contact and maintenance levels between you, so very much the better. In fact, it may be possible to use a mediation agency instead of expensive legal processes to do the job. Try National Family Mediation (**www.nfm.u-net.com**) or Family Mediation Scotland (**www.familymediationscotland.org.uk**). There's also the Family Mediators Association, which you can contact on 0117 946 7062.

Find more help online at:
www.divorce-resource.org
www.divorce.co.uk
Children and Family Court Advisory Service –
www.cafcass.gov.uk
Equal Parenting – **www.equalparenting.org**
Families Online – **www.familiesonline.co.uk**
Solicitors Family Law Association – **www.sfla.org.uk**

Single parents

Single parents need all the advice above and more, particularly the parts about saving money where possible. Women make up around 90 per cent of lone parents and because, on average, women earn around 80 per cent of what men earn and are more likely to take part-time work (which, per hour, is generally paid less than full-time employment), they struggle with money more than most. This is why more women than men file for personal bankruptcy. It's not that they spend more (in fact, on average, women have smaller debts than men), they just tend to be single parents more often – one of the poorest people to be in our society.

So, if you are a single parent, make sure you get all the maintenance, tax credits and benefits you can possibly get your hands on. Get as much information about these as you can, too. Scour the government websites such as **www.direct.gov.uk**, **www.dwp.gov.uk**, **www.csa.gov.uk** (Child Support Agency) and **www.hmrc.gov.uk** (the Revenue). For more help also go to the website of the National Council for One-Parent Families, **www.oneparentfamilies.org.uk** (their advice line is 0800 018 5026), Gingerbread, **www.gingerbread.org.uk** (their advice line is 0800 018 4318), **www.singleparents.org.uk** or **www.loneparents.org.uk**. Also, try the lifestyle sites **www.single-living.com** and **www.soyouvebeendumped.com**. Many of the general family websites have help for single parents or those on low incomes too. Have a look at **www.mumsnet.com**, **www.ukparents.co.uk**, **www.ivillage.com**, **www.handbag. com** and certainly the parenting sections of **www.fool.co.uk** and **www.moneysavingexpert.com**.

As with other areas of tax and benefits, the rules, amounts and even names of government schemes change each year, but there are some basic principles that you should know.

- If you are a mother with care of your children you should get maintenance from the father. The Child Support Agency (CSA) calculates and collects maintenance from the absent parent – the amount you get will depend on his income. The CSA usually collects payment if the mother is receiving income support or income-based jobseeker's allowance. Otherwise, the CSA will get involved only if either parent asks it to. You can get more information from the CSA on 0845 7133133, **www.csa.gov.uk**.

- Try to set up support systems where you can – discussion boards on websites are a very useful back-up to lone parents, as well as neighbours, friends and family.

- Get together with other single parents to support each other and even share childcare in order to help each other go out to work part of the time. With tax credits, it's now possible to make more money by working – even part-time – than just depending on benefits.

- Don't rush into another relationship out of loneliness or a desire to get a new parent for your child. Second marriages have a worse longevity record than first, and step-parenting is fraught with difficulties.

Useful contacts

Raising Kids – **www.raisingkids.co.uk**
BBC Parenting – **www.bbc.co.uk/parenting**
Better Homes and Gardens – **www.bhg.com**
Babyworld – **www.babyworld.co.uk**
Babycentre – **www.babycentre.co.uk**
iCircle – **www.icircle.co.uk**
iVillage – **www.ivillage.co.uk**
Handbag.com – **www.handbag.com**
Mumsnet – **www.mumsnet.com**
Motley Fool – **www.fool.co.uk**
Parents Centre – **www.parentscentre.gov.uk**
UK Parents – **www.ukparents.co.uk**
Parents.com – **www.parents.com**

14

Taxation

'If you make any money, the government shoves
you in the creek once a year with it in your
pockets, and all that don't get wet you can
keep.'

– Will Rogers

They pay for health, education, our infrastructure and
general running of the country, so you're not allowed to
whinge (too much) about paying taxes. *However,* that doesn't
mean to say that you have to pay any more than you *need* to
pay. Sounds obvious, I know, but billions of pounds are wasted
every year in this country through overpayment of tax. It's not
about tax evasion (which is illegal) but tax *avoidance* – big difference.

It doesn't take too much effort to save yourself a lot of
money in taxes (and in charges to avoid) each year, although
it does help to start off by knowing which taxes you are liable
for in the first place.

Mmm, delicious taxes!

You could be forgiven for thinking that we're being taxed more and more as time goes on because, frankly, you're right. Taxes have gone up and whatever new governments say they are likely to continue to go up.

Income tax

The Inland Revenue will allow you to earn a certain amount before you start getting taxed on your income. It's called a *personal allowance* and usually goes up a little each year to keep pace with inflation. It's only a few thousand a year, so don't get excited (check on **www.hmrc.gov.uk** to see what that allowance is for this tax year), although pensioners get a slightly higher personal allowance, depending on their age (look at **www.pensionservice.gov.uk** for more information on this).

Once your income exceeds the tax-free personal-allowance figure, a series of tax bands then come into play and it depends how much you earn over and above the personal allowance as to which tax band you fall into. The tax bands are essentially 10 per cent, 22 per cent and 40 per cent, although these could change at any time, so keep awake and try to take some sort of interest around Budget time (hard, I know, but at least read the main points in the newspapers the next day). The actual tax bands change each year (generally going upwards), so to find out the current bands just ask your local tax office or go to **www.hmrc.gov.uk** and look them up. But essentially it works like a tier system:

- The first few thousand pounds of your earnings is tax-free (personal allowance).

- The next band is a thin one of around a couple of thousand and is taxed at 10 per cent (starting rate).

- The next much larger band is taxed at 22 per cent (basic rate).

- Anything over that is taxed at 40 per cent (higher rate).

Note that the tax rates are marginal. In other words, they apply only to the band of income concerned and don't apply to the whole amount of money you get. So, if you earn £1,000 above the level for higher-rate tax you'll pay 40 per cent only on that £1,000.

Remember that you will also be taxed on your investment income, which is usually the interest you earn from your savings or the dividends you receive from holding shares. With dividend income there's a complicated system of tax credits involved, which I won't go into here, but you can find out what the current situation is on government websites such as **www.hmrc.gov.uk** and **www.direct.gov.uk**.

National Insurance (NI)

National Insurance is paid by both employers and employees and doesn't mean much to most people other than that they're the whopping great sums of money that get taken out of your salary every month before you see a penny of it.

Much as governments like to deny it, National Insurance is really a type of income tax. Broadly speaking, the principal difference between income tax and NI is that the income tax applies to income of all types (including investments, for example), but NI applies only to what might loosely be termed 'earned' income (your salary or your pay if you're freelance). It's a mind-numbingly complex concept, taxation-wise, and is used to pay for certain social security benefits such as sick pay, maternity pay and your state pension. It's also now used to prop up the National Health Service.

There are four 'classes' of National Insurance contributions (NICs) and it depends on how you're employed as to what type you'll pay. The single most important thing that NI contributions pay for is the state pension. Your NICs are mostly being used at the moment to pay the meagre pension that's being doled out to our pensioners – just as your state pension (if you ever get one) will be paid for by your children and grandchildren.

You will be entitled to the basic state pension only if you've made full NI contributions throughout your working life (although there are exceptions if you have to take time off work to have a child or care for a relative – see **www.dwp.gov.uk**, **www.direct.gov.uk** or **www.entitledto.co.uk** for more information). The government expects you to work for 44 years to qualify for the full pension. If you haven't worked for the full 44 years, your pension is reduced proportionately. And, if you've worked for less than 11 years, you get zilch!

Not many people make their own provision for old age, so it's important to check that you're up to date with your NI contributions to ensure that you'll get at least something when you hit retirement age. You can check this by asking for a pension forecast from the State Pension Forecasting Team on 0845 3000 168 or go online at **www.pensionservice.gov.uk** or **www.dwp.gov.uk**.

Capital gains tax

If you're in the happy position of having investments that appreciate through the year, you could find yourself being made *un*happy by the tax you have to pay on it. This is what is known as capital gains tax (CGT). As they say, 'A fine is a tax for doing wrong. A tax is a fine for doing well.'

Capital gains tax is a pretty punitive one (if you don't believe me, check it out at **www.hmrc.gov.uk**), so you want to avoid it where possible. Happily, there are ways. For a start, the government let you keep some of your profit before taxing you on the rest. Sweet of them! Again, the amount you are allowed tax-free changes each year but it is at least in four figures (find the current level at **www.hmrc.gov.uk**). The specific rules and regulations can be complicated and, if you end up with an extensive share and/or property portfolio, then you definitely need an accountant to sort out your tax liabilities. However, for most of us the basic rules are that if you sell some shares or property (not the house you live in) you will probably have to pay capital gains tax on it for that financial year.

Inheritance tax

It used to be the province of the rich and landed classes to worry about inheritance tax (IHT), but as property prices have risen *far* faster than the IHT tax bracket – and no governments have seen fit to alter this situation – you're likely to be over the limit even if you have just a two-bed semi in Croydon.

IHT is another punitive tax. Any wealth you own above the allowed amount, including the proceeds from selling your house, will be taxed at 40 per cent on death, with the main exception being gifts made to your spouse. Fortunately, there are ways of reducing your potential liability. One of the most effective, if you can afford it, is to make gifts during your lifetime. Another is to create a 'deed of variation', which enables you to alter a will to change a deceased's instructions.

Although inheritance tax may become payable on gifts made during your lifetime, in practice most gifts are free of tax, because you can take advantage of various exemptions that are available. These are divided into two categories: *immediately exempt transfers* and *potentially exempt transfers*.

Immediately exempt transfers

- Annual gifts of up to £3,000 (check **www.hmrc.gov.uk** to see that this amount hasn't changed). This amount can be given to one recipient or divided among several each year. If the allowance isn't used in one year, it can be carried forward to the next year only.

- Any number of gifts of up to £250 per recipient per year (again, check the website about this amount). It's important that a recipient shouldn't receive any more than this amount or else the exemption will be lost.

- Gifts of any amount that are funded out of your normal spending, provided they don't reduce your normal standard of living.

- Gifts for the maintenance of your family, such as for children under 18 or still in full-time education. There is no specific limit on these gifts.

- Gifts made on marriage. Parents and grandparents have their own limit. There's also a limit for financial gifts from friends (check the Inland Revenue website to find out what it is now).

Potentially exempt transfers

Any gifts exceeding the immediately exempt transfer limits would be counted as 'potentially exempt transfers'. This means that, if you live for seven years after the gift is made, they will not be liable to inheritance tax (IHT). If you die earlier, they will be counted against your tax-free allowance. If they exceed that amount, the tax payable will depend on how long you've lived since making the gift. For example, if you die within three years of making the gift, the full amount of any inheritance tax on the gift will be payable. If you die between three and four years later, only 80 per cent of that amount will be due and so on (check out **www.hmrc.gov.uk** for a list of the percentages). So keep healthy and don't let the taxman get your children's money!

The good news – avoiding tax

Income tax

There are various ways you can cut down your income-tax bill, although, if you're employed, there's relatively little you can do about the tax on your salary (other than get tax credits – see below). Here are some of the main ways to cut down.

ISAs

You don't have to pay tax on the interest from an ISA, nor do you have to pay capital gains tax on profits from investments in an ISA. Currently, everyone over the age of 16 can take out a mini cash ISA each year, to deposit up to £3,000 for tax-free interest. And everyone over 18 can have a mini share ISA, to invest a further £4,000 into equities (shares). Those with a bit more money can take out a maxi share ISA (instead of mini ISAs) to invest up to £7,000 into equities. Check on websites such as **www.direct.gov.uk** and **www.fool.co.uk** to see whether these are still the limits.

Contrary to popular belief, though, ISAs aren't actually investments in themselves. They're just 'wrappers' that protect your savings from tax. If you have a shares ISA, that means that you've invested in a company or in an equity-based fund and you have wrapped it in an ISA. Similarly, if you have a cash ISA, that means that you've invested in a cash product such as a building society account and you've wrapped it in an ISA so that you don't have to pay tax on the interest you make.

Couples

If you and your partner are in different tax bands (and you both trust each other!) make the most of it and keep more of your interest. If one partner is a lower-rate taxpayer, keep your savings in his/her name. For example, if you have £3,000 in an account paying 5 per cent, you will make £117 per year in interest, as opposed to £103.50 from a joint account. If he/she were a non-taxpayer, you would make £150.

Venture-capital trusts

A venture-capital trust (VCT) is a quoted investment company, similar to an investment trust, which offers income-tax incentives if you buy shares in it. The tax incentive is pretty good – currently you get 40 per cent tax relief even if you're not a higher-rate tax payer (check on **www.hmrc.gov.uk** to see what the current tax relief is). However, this tax incentive comes with a high degree of risk because VCTs can invest only in small private companies, plus those listed on the Alternative Investment Market (AIM) and OFEX (a market for small UK companies run by a broker, and not by the London Stock Exchange). Also, VCTs have picked up a rather poor reputation for making money. A large number haven't increased investors' income at all and many have lost a lot for them. Also, management charges for VCTs are much higher than for most funds. So, although the tax incentive is very pleasing you really need to consider what you're investing in if you do go for a VCT, and make sure you research your options carefully beforehand. There's more information about VCTs at **www.trustnet.com/vct** and **www.fool.co.uk**.

National Savings certificates

National Savings offers accounts that pay interest tax-free. But, although they offer the guarantee of at least getting your money back, the accounts are not particularly competitive and might not be worth investing in, even with the tax benefit. Check out **www.nsandi.com** for more information.

Premium Bonds

They're tax-free and, if you like to have a flutter without the worry of losing the shirt off your back, why not buy a few? The minimum investment is £100 and there's always the possibility that you could hit the jackpot. Go to **www.nsandi.com** to find out more.

Friendly societies

Friendly societies are like credit unions in that they were originally set up when local groups of people got together to form mutual savings societies. Everyone is entitled to hold one friendly-society savings plan, which is not taxable. However, friendly societies' charges tend to be rather high – about £2 per month quite often. Also, the investments are usually based on insurance products (a type of endowment), and their returns are traditionally very poor. Find out more about them at **www.afs.org.uk**, the website of the Association of Friendly Societies.

Form R85

If you're a non-taxpayer already, register to receive gross interest on your bank and building society accounts by completing an R85 form, which you can pick up at the bank. Similarly if your spouse is a non-taxpayer, or pays a lower rate of tax than you, transfer your money to their account and save up to 40 per cent in income tax.

Tax credits

Make sure you make the most of any tax credits you're entitled to. If you think the whole system is complicated and messed up, you're right. It is. And it doesn't help that even the names of the various types of credit you can get keep changing with each different Budget. However, it's worth persisting because there's money to be had in them there tax credits. There's *working tax credit* (which you can get even if you don't have children), *child tax credit* and *pension credits*. Tax credits can be paid to you through your wages or straight into your bank, building society or post office. It's a slightly complicated process to get the money recredited to you, and they've made some well-publicised mistakes over it in recent times, but to find out if you qualify, and how to get your hands on the money, go to **www.entitledto.co.uk**, **www.direct.gov.uk** or **www.hmrc.gov.uk**.

Capital gains tax

- Avoid CGT by sharing some of your investments with your spouse so that you take advantage of *both* your CGT allowances, because the government lets married couples transfer shares and property between each other without incurring any tax liabilities at all. There must be some trust involved, since it must be made as a 'gift without reservation' and the new owner has complete say over what happens to it! In a similar way, if you're paying tax on share dividends, you can reduce your tax bill by transferring this capital to the spouse in the lower tax bracket. This would serve to reduce your overall tax bill as a couple.

- You can't do this if you're cohabiting, though, as the transfer will be deemed a gift to your partner made at current market value. So you will be regarded as having realised any gains the moment you hand them over to him, even if you didn't get a penny.

- When it comes to investment property, the easiest way of protecting yourself from too much CGT is to put the property into joint names with your spouse or partner.

Since they get an annual allowance you'll be able to make a decent profit before either of you faces a CGT liability.

Inheritance tax

- First, make a will. That in itself stops the government from taking a big chunk of what's left of your money before anyone you love, or are just related to, gets a sniff of it. See 'Making a will' in Chapter 12 for more information on how to go about it and how to do your own will if you'd like to go that route.

- Transfers of assets between spouses are also exempt from inheritance tax. Anything your husband or wife inherits from you is tax-free, although this is not the case if you just cohabit. Your partner then has to pay tax on anything that didn't have his or her name on in the first place.

- Give as much away as you're allowed to while you're still alive. It's much nicer, anyway, to experience your children's (or your favourite charity's) gratitude while you can.

- Give as much of your surplus as possible to charity in your will. Better for them to have it than the taxman. Go to **www.rememberacharity.org.uk** for more information on how to do this.

- Invest in AIM-listed shares. AIM is the Alternative Investment Market and is like a FTSE index for small companies. Many small companies start on the AIM and then transfer to the FTSE when they 'grow up'. Some AIM-listed companies can do very well indeed, but, because the companies are small, it can be very volatile and you can lose a lot if you're unlucky with your investment. However, most AIM companies are what is called 'unquoted' and, since there's an odd little IHT rule that says that any assets held in an unquoted company qualify for 100 per cent IHT relief after the money's been there for over two years, tax planners have become rather excited about it. It isn't easy to work out which companies are unquoted and which aren't. The Revenue doesn't provide a list of them (helpful of them!), and just suggests that you seek advice from a tax accountant or financial adviser (and hope that they know – they don't always). Go to **www.unbiased.co.uk** for local financial advisers and the Chartered Institute of Taxation (**www.tax.org.uk**) for tax advisers.

- Set up a trust. This is a written arrangement whereby an appointed trustee is given money or assets to hold and manage on behalf of the person you want to benefit. They're a useful, if sometimes complex, way of giving money, property or shares to others while ensuring that someone you trust (hence the name) is overseeing them. You can create a trust while you're alive by a formal trust deed (or 'settlement') or you can create one in your will (a 'will trust'). You will need advice on this, so find out about local experts from the Society of Trust and Estate Practitioners (**www.step.org**, 020 7838 4890).

- Get expert advice. If you have a fair amount of assets or a complex personal situation, it's best to get proper advice on inheritance tax planning. If your accountant is a specialist in this, then speak to him or her, but most aren't, so it's best to ask around or look on **www.step.org** and **www.tax.org.uk**.

Mmm. Lovely! Filling in your tax return!

Filing a tax return falls somewhere between punching yourself in the face and unblocking a drain with your bare tongue on most people's lists of fun things to do. The tax people may try

Top tips for avoiding tax

- Use your ISA allowance. Check on **www.hmrc.gov.uk** for the current limit per financial year, and make the most of it!
- Make sure you send in your tax return by the 31 January deadline. Self-assessment forms received after that time incur penalties of at least £100.
- Use your personal tax allowance. If you're not sure what that is, ask your accountant or speak to your local tax office. Find them at **www.hmrc.gov.uk**.
- Make the most of your pension allowance. Optimise contributions to personal or company pension schemes and consider making additional voluntary contributions (AVCs) – although be careful of these, because they can be expensive and not worth the tax saving.
- Use your spouse. If you pay tax but your spouse doesn't, move some of your money to their name to use their tax allowance.
- Plan your inheritance. If you own your own home it's likely that your assets are already over the inheritance tax (IHT) threshold. Write life-assurance policies in trust, make use of all IHT allowances and, of course, make a will.
- Take advantage of any share plan your employer offers. These are tax-efficient and can be highly lucrative if the company is doing well.
- Give to charity through Gift Aid or payroll giving so that the charity benefits from the tax you would have been paying.
- If you're a non-taxpayer, make sure you're not being charged tax at source by banks and building societies. Go to **www.hmrc.gov.uk** to download a form, R85,

continues ➤

with which you can claim tax back on your savings.
- Make sure your child benefits from the Child Trust Fund – free money from the government and tax-free savings.
- For more tips on avoiding tax go to **www.unbiased.co.uk**. They even have an online calculator, which will show you how to maximise your tax savings.

their hardest to dress the whole thing up in informal language and shiny forms, but it's all too tempting to ignore the brown envelopes stuffed with forms of tedium. But just because filling in a tax return isn't much fun – some might say undergoing exploratory surgery without anaesthetic is more fun, and who am I to argue? – it doesn't mean it's not worth doing, and doing on time. You never know – you might even find you're due a refund on overpaid tax. And failure to return the forms can lead to fines and penalties, or getting stung with an unexpected tax bill plus interest a few years down the line.

Here are some basic pointers on how to do it.

- Getting organised will make things easier. Gather together all the documents you need – for example, bank statements, payslips, dividend vouchers, interest statements or tax deduction certificates, trust vouchers – before you begin.

- Pour yourself a glass, or mug, of something fortifying.

- Check you have the right forms – you may need extra pages and guide sheets if, for example, you're self-employed.

- Pour yourself another glass!

- Check the deadlines for returning the forms. There's an earlier deadline if you want the Inland Revenue to calculate how much tax you have to pay. If you prefer to do it yourself or want to file online, then you have longer. Of course, it doesn't hurt to get started earlier – returns can be done as soon as the tax year has finished. Get in quickly – a bit like buying Christmas cards in January!

- The process might be fiddly, but at least there's plenty of information on what to do. To get help and advice on filling in a self-assessment tax return, call the Inland Revenue Self-Assessment Helpline number on 0845 900444. It's even open at weekends and on bank holidays because these people don't have a life. They also provide general advice for self-assessment. Also, check out page 9 of the PDF guide for information on how to do it: **www.hmrc.gov.uk** (clink on the link for self-assessment tax return advice).

- If that all sounds too much like hard work, why not take the easy way out and pay an accountant to do the dirty work for you? If you don't have a friendly – and sharp – accountant to hand, try your best with the accountancy organisations (see below) to find a good one.

Problems with the Revenue?

If you think you've been overcharged, or wrongly fined by Her Majesty's Revenue and Customs (HMRC – what used to be the Inland Revenue), there are some things you can do to get satisfaction.

- First, talk to the person you have been dealing with directly to see if they can sort it out.

- Try the customer-relations or complaints manager in that person's office to see if they can put it right.

- Contact the director responsible for the office you are dealing with (find out who on **www.hmrc.gov.uk**).

- If you're still unhappy, try the independent adjudicator, whose services are free. You must normally apply to the adjudicator within six months of receiving a response from the Inland Revenue director who has dealt with your case. Ring the adjudicator's office on 020 7930 2292 or go to **www.adjudicatorsoffice.gov.uk**.

- You may be able to complain to the Parliamentary Ombudsman. Complaints to the ombudsman must be made through an MP within 12 months of the cause for complaint. Find out more at **www.ombudsman.org.uk**.

Useful contacts

Department for Work and Pensions – **www.dwp.gov.uk**
Directgov – **www.direct.gov.uk**
HM Revenue and Customs – **www.hmrc.gov.uk**
The Association of Chartered Certified Accountants – **www.acca.org.uk**
The Association of Taxation Technicians – **www.att.org.uk**
The Chartered Institute of Taxation – **www.tax.org.uk**
Low Incomes Tax Reform Group – **www.litrg.org.uk**
Tax Aid – **www.taxaid.org.uk**
www.janevass.net/tax (author of *The Daily Mail Tax Guide*)

Books

The Daily Mail Tax Guide – Jane Vass (Profile, £9.99)
The Daily Telegraph Tax Guide – David B Genders (Pan, £9.99)

Tax facts

- In ancient Egypt, tax collectors were known as 'scribes'. During one period, the scribes imposed a tax on cooking oil and they audited households to make sure the appropriate amounts of cooking oil were consumed and wives were not just using cheap alternatives.
- Ancient Athenians imposed a poll tax on foreigners – people whose parents were not both Athenians – of one drachma for men and a half-drachma for women.
- In 60 CE Queen Boadicea (or Boudicca) led a revolt against the Roman occupation primarily because of corrupt tax collectors. Her troops allegedly killed all Roman soldiers within 100 miles.
- Contacting your tax office for advice every now and then won't mean that they suddenly 'notice' you, put you on a register to watch and run regular inspections on you.
- Hard though it is to believe, tax inspectors are actually not from the planet Zorb, who have webbed feet and enjoy eating tarmac. However ...
- ... VAT inspectors are.

15

Finances for the Mature Type – That'll be You, Then

'Old age is fifteen years older than I am.'
– Oliver Wendell Holmes

Is it too late?

So you're in your fifties, or sixties, and you haven't saved anything like enough in your retirement pot. What do you do? Good question, glad you asked. There are a few things you can do, but don't expect to make pots of money in just a few years – unless you're willing to sell body parts, guns, drugs or your top secret recipe for chilli strawberry muffins. Here are some ideas you could follow.

- If there is a pension scheme at your workplace to which your employer contributes, start putting money into that.

- If you don't have that, start your own stakeholder plan (see Chapter 10, 'Your Future', or **www.stakeholderpensions.co.uk** for information).

- Start putting money into a tracker fund (see page 162 for details on how to do this) if you would like to retire in five years' time or more.

- Start a business on the side to make extra cash (see Chapter 6, 'Making That Bit Extra', and other ideas later in this chapter), but check with an IFA first to make sure that you won't make too much money to stop yourself qualifying for pension credits.

- Look into freeing up money from your property to live on (see 'Equity release' later in this chapter).

- Make sure you're getting all the benefits and tax credits you are entitled to. See **www.entitledto.co.uk** and **www.direct.gov.uk** for a checklist of what you should get.

- Move your current investments to better-performing ones. See the advice in most of this book and speak to an IFA (make sure they're fee-based so that they're genuinely independent) about how you could maximise what you have.

- Decide to work for longer before you actually retire and put the maximum amount you possibly can into investments for your retirement.

Making the most of your pension

Up until recently, pensions legislation allowed you to take up to 25 per cent only of your cash pot as a one-off, tax-free lump sum. Recent changes, though, mean that anyone retiring from now on can take up to 1 per cent of their 'lifetime allowance' in cash. Currently that allowance is £1.5 million (although it will grow over time), so, as 1 per cent of £1.5 million is £15,000, if your pension pot is less than £15,000 you can take it all out in cash and spend it as you will. You have to pay tax on most of it but you get to have 25 per cent of it tax-free.

The rest should be used to buy an annuity by the time you are 75 (see 'Guide to annuities' below for more information) although you could instead opt for an 'alternatively secured income' that offers a lower monthly income but which lets you pass on any unused pension at your death to a loved one, subject to an inheritance tax charge.

The few people in this country (and it is only a few) who have very large pension pots may be penalised under the new pension laws. If you have more than the current 'lifetime allowance' (£1.5 million at the moment) you will be taxed heavily on what's over that. If you are lucky enough to have this kind of money stashed away you should get independent financial advice on how to avoid too much of a tax headache.

By the way, if you think you're owed pensions from past employers or you had private pensions in the past that you've forgotten or lost, you can find them through the pension-tracing service at the Department of Work and Pensions. Call them on 0845 6002 537 or check out the website **www.thepensionservice.gov.uk**.

Income drawdown

If you have a bulging pension pot and a pension scheme that allows it, it might be worth putting off buying an annuity until you're much older by using an option called 'income drawdown', or 'income withdrawal'. This way, you can take income directly from the fund for your first few years of retirement and leave the rest of it invested, rather than having to buy an annuity straight away.

The amount you can take out each year is subject to a maximum based upon annuity rates provided by the government's Actuary's Department (**www.gad.gov.uk**) – it can't be more than you would have got if you'd bought an annuity.

The point of doing this is that you can take the income you need (subject to the limits) while keeping the fund invested in the stock market for longer. Although there are no guarantees, this is likely to be the best way of letting your money grow, but it's only really cost-effective if you've got a large pension fund.

If you die while you're using income drawdown, your pension fund can be passed on to your spouse or another nominated beneficiary. A spouse or dependant can use the whole lot to buy an annuity or provide an income through income withdrawal. Otherwise, a spouse, dependant or another nominated beneficiary can get the cash value of the fund, minus 35 per cent, which goes to the government.

Phased retirement

This is similar to income drawdown, but not quite the same. If you have an eligible pension plan, phased retirement allows you to put off drawing all of your pension benefits at the same time. Your fund is instead split into, say, 1,000 different segments, so you can take a certain number each year rather than having to cash in the whole lot at once. As with non-phased retirement, you must still use 75 per cent of each segment to buy an annuity, but this way you could end up with lots of little annuities, rather than having to invest in just one. This allows you to be more flexible in your choice of annuity, and also lets you leave the rest of your pension fund in investments, hopefully giving it the potential to grow.

Guide to annuities

> 'I advise you to go on living solely to enrage those who are paying your annuities. It is the only pleasure I have left.'
>
> – Voltaire

The government – and you won't be surprised to hear this – doesn't trust us a great deal. It doesn't trust us not to blow the entire amount of our retirement fund on a world cruise or on

Pretty Boy in the 3.30 at Sandown. If the government did trust us not to do any of these things and we let it down, then it would end up having to feed and house us, and that's why it makes us buy an annuity with the money we have accrued in our pension fund.

Annuities are basically a kind of insurance payment that we get every month for the rest of our lives. The company that pays out this annuity (and we can and should shop around for the highest rate possible) promises to pay a certain amount every month for as long as we live – whether that be another two, 12, 20 or 200 years (unlikely but you never know). Naturally, they don't want to lose money, so, the longer they *think* you will live, the less they want to pay each month because, the longer you live, the more they will end up shelling out. This is why women tend to get worse annuity rates than men, and the older you are when you retire, the better your annuity rate will be.

With the basic annuity, an insurance company effectively takes your money and uses it to buy some low-risk assets such as gilts. It has to do that because it has to guarantee your income (and be confident of making a profit itself). But you may be looking at 20, 30 or even more years of retirement (let's hope so), and that sort of investment tends to be awful over that long a period.

Annuity rules have recently changed, along with various pension regulations. It used to be that you had to take an annuity by age 75, but that no longer exists. Instead you have the option of taking what is called an *alternative secured income*. This could mean that you can pass on any unused pension after your death. However, you will still have to take an annual income from your fund, which will be taxed (as annuities are, anyway).

There are also, now, two new types of annuity – the *limited-period annuity* and the *value-protected annuity*.

- The limited-period annuity lasts for five years, after which you can buy either another one or a normal lifetime annuity.

- The value-protected annuity will give you a lower amount each month than a normal annuity but it will pay out any unused amount to your heirs, so it's useful if you want to pass on money to a partner or children on your death.

With any type of annuity, though, there are some basic rules you need to follow in order to get the most from them.

- There are no two ways about it: you need to shop around. Don't just take the annuity offered by your pension provider – what are the chances this will also just happen to be the best value? It's possible, but highly unlikely. Sadly, this is what most people do and they miss out on extra money for years.

- It's worth looking for index-linked annuities, which will rise according to inflation. Although your starting payout will be smaller, you'll get more each year to keep up with the changing value of money.

- The two most influential factors on the size of your annuity are your age and current interest rates. The older you are, and the higher interest rates are, when you buy, the bigger your annuity will be. This can be worth bearing in mind if you're considering using income drawdown or phased retirement to delay purchasing your annuity.

- Although your pension savings were tax-free, you have to pay tax on the income you get from the annuity. Keep that in mind when working out your budget.

Pension credit

Pension credit was brought in by the government to help people with very small pensions. You have to be over 60 to qualify and, as with so many helpful government benefits, the system is more complicated than it needs to be. For a start, it's made up of two parts: the *guarantee credit* and the *savings credit*.

- The guarantee credit guarantees a minimum income if you're on a low income and if you're either single and your weekly income is below a certain amount (check on **www.dwp.gov.uk** or **www.direct.gov.uk** or **www.entitledto.co.uk** for the current limit) or you have a partner and your joint weekly income is below a certain amount (check the websites above for the current limit).

- The savings credit is only for those over 65 whose total weekly income from pensions, savings and investments is very small (check the websites above for the current amount).

If you're getting pension credit, you could also qualify for:

- housing benefit;

- council tax benefit;

- cold-weather payment;

- funeral payments;

- community-care grant;

- budgeting loans;

- crisis loans;

- winter-fuel payments;

- Sure Start maternity grant (although – how likely is that?);

- free school meals.

So check with your local benefits office or **www.entitledto. co.uk** or **www.direct.gov.uk** to see if you could get any of these. There is the possibility that some of the above benefits could be reduced if you get pension credit, but you would still be better off with the pension credit anyway.

Useful contacts

Call the Pension Credit helpline on 0800 99 1234
www.dwp.gov.uk
www.entitledto.co.uk
www.direct.gov.uk

Investing for income

Once you've stopped working you will need to use the investments you have to boost your income. This means investing in products that will give you a monthly or annual return rather than just going for growth. However, if you're planning on living a good long time (and you are, aren't you?), you should keep at least half an eye on growth while you take your income from one or more products.

As with investing for growth, the rule of spreading your risk still stands when investing for income. You will, naturally, go for products that are less risky anyway because we're talking short-term benefit here, and, if you go for something that will swing wildly up and down, you will be very unhappy when you hit one of the lows. But why not mix it up a little – invest in some good, solid, stable income-providers and then take a punt on some riskier ones with a smaller amount of your money? It's up to you and your feeling about risk, but look at the various options.

You may like to put your money into one or all of the following.

Cash

Probably the safest investment you can make, if you want a stable income, is to put it in the bank or building society and live off the interest. Make sure you go for the highest rate you can find and keep an eye on the rates so that you can move your money if they go down. Don't put all your money in cash, though, because (a) the Bank of England often brings interest rates down, which will mean that your rate will go down with it and, (b) it being a safe investment, the returns are not terribly good on even the best savings account.

National Savings

Being tax-free, National Savings products (**www.nsandi.com**) are of particular interest to pensioners. They have various savings schemes, including a guaranteed monthly-income bond specifically for retired people. Again, their rates are not spectacular, but it is a good, safe investment for some of your money and worth looking into if only for the tax break!

Bonds

It's when you retire that bonds really come into their own. They're pretty safe and secure and tend to give you more than the basic savings account. One disadvantage is that the rates (which are fixed for a few years at a time) can look pretty sad if interest rates rise while you have your bond; and another is that, if the rate is good, it will end at the fixed period and you'll have to adjust your budget to cope with a new, lesser rate.

Property

If you know what you're doing, property can yield a very useful monthly income while, hopefully, increasing in value at the same time. However, it all depends when you buy, what you buy and where you buy. Get it wrong and it will end up costing you money. Even the best of properties tend to cost money, too, so it's possible that any income you get from it will be cancelled out by the costs of repairing and maintaining it. Also, there are no guarantees that you will have your rent paid each month. You could have months with no tenants and, even when you get them, rents could go down as well as up in your area.

So do consider property, particularly if you have found a low-maintenance place nearby that is popular with tenants and you're a bit of a DIY whiz yourself. Don't put all your money into it, though, because property is risky and you will need a safety net of a nice, secure investment at the same time.

High-yield shares

'Invest in shares for a stable income!' you exclaim. Well, yes, actually. If you know what you're doing (and that's the key) you can get a decent income, *and* see your capital grow, by investing in high-yield shares. It's particularly useful if you're in your early retirement and planning on sticking around for a good few years yet, thank you very much.

High-yield shares are those that give a good dividend each year, or twice a year, as usually happens, compared with the price of the share. The 'yield' on a share is the dividend divided by the share price. Not all companies give dividends, but large, well-established ones generally do. Even the large companies sometimes cut their dividends every now and then but on the whole they're pretty reliable.

In order to spread your risk you should invest in a number of shares from different sectors, say 15 to 20 different companies that you have investigated and believe to be stable and regular earners. Either that or you could pay a stockbroker to invest for you if you trust him or her and don't mind paying their charges.

Stephen Bland at the Motley Fool (**www.fool.co.uk**) is an expert on high-yield portfolios (HYPs, as he calls them) and if you would like to go down this route – even with a small percentage of your money – read one of the many articles he's written on the subject on the website. You could also follow the portfolio he set up a few years ago, which has consistently beaten the stock market. Many Motley Fool readers who have been bitterly disappointed by the performance of their pensions and insurance products have run portfolios according to Stephen's advice and haven't looked back.

Equity release

Many older people find themselves to be asset-rich, but cash-poor. Finally mortgage-free, they own a nice big house but have little money to spend while living in it. One way around this is equity release, which frees up some of the cash for you to spend here and now. There are two main ways to do it.

Reversion or part-reversion

You sell your home, or at least part of it, to a reversion company, which then allows you and your partner to stay there for the rest of your lives. You can receive the money in a lump sum, or as an income, or both. You won't get the market value of the property, however – more like 20–50 per cent – in exchange for the company letting you continue to live there. When you do die (or move out for some other reason) the proportion that you sold becomes the property of the reversion company, and the rest goes to your children or whoever you wished to benefit.

Mortgages

This is like taking out a loan (usually called a lifetime mortgage) against your home that doesn't have to be repaid until after you die. You can get the money either as a lump sum or as a fixed income, and you continue to own your home.

There are two main types of lifetime mortgage, interest-only and rolled-up interest.

Interest-only

You take out a loan, which will be repaid by the sale of your house when you die. In the meantime, you just have to pay the interest on the loan. This may be at a fixed or variable rate of interest, but you need to be sure you have enough money from your pension or other income to be able to meet the repayments.

Rolled-up interest

You don't have to repay the loan, or the interest on it, until you die. Interest payments are calculated and 'rolled up' into the value of the loan. Depending on how long you live, these interest payments could end up pushing the value of the loan above the value of your house, but most lenders will offer a *no-negative-equity guarantee* to stop more money being owed once the house is sold.

Most schemes set a minimum age at which you can take out the policy (usually 60) and a minimum amount you can borrow. You must normally have no or very little mortgage outstanding on your home.

Is equity release right for you?

- It's a very complex issue, and one where it really is essential to seek independent financial advice. You can also get more information from the Council of Mortgage Lenders (**www.cml.org.uk**) and it's probably a good idea to talk to a (fee-based) independent financial adviser, although don't necessarily take their advice as the final word. Surveys by newspapers and the Consumers' Association have found that their advice can be misleading or just plain wrong on this subject.

- The main benefit is that you don't have to leave your

home. You can continue living there for as long as you need to, and also get some extra cash in the meantime.

- Equity release may also remove or reduce the amount of inheritance tax your descendants have to pay, as your house will not, effectively, be worth as much.

- Depending on the scheme you sign up for, interest might build up so much that it swallows all or most of the equity in your home.

- If you invest the cash you receive, you're likely to have to pay tax on the income, which means you would get less than you expected.

- There could be penalties if you want to move home in future.

- Most schemes involve legal and valuation fees.

- Any means-tested social security benefits you're getting might be reduced because of any extra income from an equity-release plan.

- There have been many scandals in the past surrounding various equity-release schemes and although many loopholes have been closed and the sector has been tightened up generally, you still have to be very careful. The industry is largely self-regulated by SHIP (Safe Home Income Plans – see **www.ship-ltd.org**) and if you're interested in going for one of these plans make sure you do it with one of the companies that are members of SHIP.

Useful contacts

SHIP – **www.ship-ltd.org**
Age Concern – **www.ageconcern.org.uk**
Help the Aged – **www.helptheaged.org.uk**
IFA Promotion – **www.unbiased.co.uk**
Council of Mortgage Lenders – **www.cml.org.uk**

Third-age businesses and ways of making extra cash

Third-agers are known to be better than other 'agers' at running businesses. The success rate of businesses set up by those who are 50+ is far higher than those started by people in their 30s and 40s, for example. It just shows that experience does count in some areas. Go to Chapter 6, 'Making That Bit Extra', for advice on running your own business. The chapter also has various ways to make cash on the side, which can be useful for retired folk. There are many other ways of boosting your income, though, particularly if you have more time or space to spare. Here are just a few of them.

Run a B&B

Many people around retirement age find themselves with a property that has spare rooms. You could rent them out or you could go further and turn it into a B&B. The British Tourist Authority has a booklet on setting yourself up as a B&B. Call them on 020 8846 9000 for the 'Pink Booklet', which costs £7.99 + p&p. Or look at their website at **www.visit britain.com**.

Once you get the house ready for visitors, register your business with local tourist authorities to attract custom. Aim to get into guide books, but remember that competition is tough and you will need to offer something special to make a living. You could make anything from a few hundred pounds a month to a few thousand a month, depending on the type of property, where you're located and how many guests you have staying with you.

Boarding pets in your home

If you have animals already and you're at home a lot, why not charge to look after other people's. You can usually do this through word of mouth, but advertising in local shops could also bring in customers. You can charge between £100 and £250 per animal per week with the owners providing food and pet equipment.

Propagating seedlings

If you are nicely green-fingered you can make regular money at car-boot sales, local shops and garages by selling plants in pots that you've propagated from seed yourself. Without too much effort you can make £100 a month and with more time and push you could go up to £1,000 or so.

House sitting

Increasingly in demand as more people are worried about burglaries as they're away. Probably best to register with a house-sitting agency such as **www.safehandssitters.co.uk**.

Doulas

If you're a mother you are pretty much qualified to be a doula. Doulas are birth partners and post-birth partners – like surrogate mothers to new mothers – and any woman who has had a baby and wants to help other women get through it happily could become a doula. You will need to take a doula course with British Doulas (**www.britishdoulas.co.uk**), who run four-day courses for women who want to become birth partners and post-birth partners. As a birth partner you can make £200–500 for a birth or as a post-birth helper you can make around £10 an hour.

Poll clerk

Election Day polling stations have to be staffed in order for a government to be elected! Apply to your local authority expressing your interest and they will put your name on a list. If you're successful, you will be sworn in the day before the election. The pay is an impressive £230 for the day.

E-commerce

Basically, e-commerce is the buying and selling of goods and services through the World Wide Web. Although it's a hugely complicated subject, the basic model is simple enough: you sell – either products or a service – and the customer pays; you send and that's it. The secret is to make this process as swift, user-friendly and secure as possible; and naturally there are a thousand ways to do it. The possibilities are endless. You could sell food, T-shirts, lawnmowers, CDs, designer bras among others. Services you offer could be Christian dating, Muslim matches, tarot-card reading, song-critiquing, parental advice and many others.

These are just a few of the possible money earners you could go into now you are older and wiser. But you may have other ideas – you may have another kind of career that has always been in the back of your mind as something you'd love to do. So why not go for it? This is the time to try!

Watch out for KIPPERS

'By the time I have money to burn, my fire will have burnt out.'

Anon

As I mentioned in Chapter 13, 'Family Matters', KIPPERS are the bane of older parents' lives. The acronym stands for Kids in Parents' Pockets Eroding Retirement Savings and, together, KIPPERS in this country are costing their parents at least £2 billion a year! Of course you love them, of course you want to help. And of course, when they've split up with their partner and need support bringing up their children, you should help where you can. But please take a deep breath, stand back and remind yourself that you don't want to be a burden to them later on and you're going to need a decent amount of money to retain your independence for as long as you can.

Sometimes even older children (and I'm talking those in their 30s and 40s) need to learn lessons and be forced to stand on their own two feet. It's up to you, but if you are at least aware of what's going on – and the fact that you're not the only one being leaned on – you can make a more informed decision about how to deal with your KIPPER.

A place in the sun?

More and more people are retiring abroad – or at least they spend a lot of time thinking about it while they're working. Currently around 200,000 Britons a year move abroad, the majority being retired people or those about to retire. It's understandable that you would think of moving to a warmer, sunnier climate for your later years.

- When you've had decades of the marvellous British summer you naturally hanker after the real thing – for rather longer than two days a year.

- Life is so much easier in the sun – you don't have to wear so much, you tend to feel happier and lighter and it's cheaper to run a home when you don't have to heat it.

- Many of the warmer countries are often cheaper as well. One's retirement fund can stretch further with their prices.

- More and more countries now have reciprocal arrangements with Britain for health and pension provision (see below for more detail).

On the other hand ...

- It's estimated that around a fifth of people who move abroad regret it for some reason – quite often because they're simply homesick and miss friends and family. They also often find that the paradise in the sun they thought they'd found has all sorts of hidden horrors that only living there uncovers.

- Although many warmer countries are generally cheaper to live in, a lot of expats find it hard to curb their spending and often end up finding their cost of living is as high as it was back home.

- Many retirees abroad miss the infrastructure they had back home – knowing their doctor, dentist, lawyer and so forth, and having them close to hand. They often find it takes a long time to develop this support network abroad.

However, if you do decide to move abroad when you retire, arming yourself with information beforehand will make it a much smoother, happier and wealthier time.

Your pension and investments

Pension

The good news: you can still get your state pension if you live abroad. The (potentially) bad news: you will qualify for pension increases only if you live in a country with which the UK has a reciprocal agreement. This includes all the European Economic Area (EEA) countries and the USA, plus a few other countries around the world. Among those not covered, however, are Australia, Canada and South Africa. Get full details from the Pension Service (**www.thepensionservice.gov.uk**, 0845 6060265).

To get your state pension paid abroad, you need to let your local authority know where you're going and give them the details of a bank or post office abroad where you want to get your cash. You'll need to make similar arrangements if you're hoping to receive any personal or occupational pensions. The Pensions Advisory Service on 0845 601 2923 should be able to help with any queries. Also try the International Payments Office on 0191 218 7777 or see **www.directgov.uk.**

- You can get a forecast of how much state pension you'll be entitled to if you live abroad by filling in form BR19 (see **www.hmrc.gov.uk**).

- If you're sent abroad by your employer, you can stay in your UK company pension scheme. Expats can carry on paying into a UK personal pension for up to five years.

- Consider continuing to pay voluntary National Insurance contributions in order to get your state pension.

- People who move abroad are allowed to pay into a British pension and get tax relief on their contributions for up to five years after leaving the country.

- You may have to pay tax on your state pension, although that's unlikely if this is your only source of income from Britain. However, if you also have an occupational pension, that and the state pension will probably put you over the limit for paying tax.

Investments

Many people who decide to retire to foreign climes have a nice fat lump sum from their pension and/or savings to invest. See Chapter 9 for more information on investing. If you move abroad, you can either invest your money in the UK, where tax will be taken off automatically, or put it into an offshore fund. If you take the latter option, any income on the investment will be paid gross. You're expected to declare it either in the UK or in the country where you live. The charges on offshore funds are usually higher, but they can end up making you more money if you time things right. The Revenue has recently tightened up loopholes for British investors trying to avoid tax by investing in offshore funds, but expats can sometimes use their non-residential status to pay less tax on these funds.

See **www.expatinvestor.com** for more information.

Tax

There are two joys to consider here: the taxes you might have to pay in the UK and the taxes you might have to pay abroad.

UK tax

- You have to tell the Revenue when you go abroad, and usually need to fill in a P85 form so that they can keep tabs on you.

- To be classed as non-resident, you aren't allowed to spend more than 182 days in the UK in any single tax year, or to spend more than an average of 90 days a year in the UK over a maximum of four tax years.

- You normally have to live abroad for up to three years to get unconditional non-resident status, though you might get conditional and/or retrospective non-resident status for this time.

- Overseas income is not liable for UK tax. Yippee!

- However, you have to pay tax on most income from UK sources. There are a few exceptions, such as certain government securities and some former colonial pensions. You should also be able to get interest on bank and building society savings accounts paid gross if you fill in a tax exemption form.

- If you earn income from UK investments (such as shares) while you are living abroad, tax will be deducted at source.

- If you keep your house and rent it out, you'll have to pay tax if the rental income comes to more than your expenses (including agent's fees and mortgage interest) each tax year.

- Things are different if your new country has a double tax agreement with the UK. The conditions of these vary from country to country, but it usually means you are taxed on income in your new country of residence rather than in the UK.

- Don't forget to tell your local council that you're off – their council tax and electoral registration departments should be informed.

- Leaflet IR20, 'Residents and Non-Residents – Liability to Tax in the UK', is available from your tax office or from **www.hmrc.gov.uk**.

- For details of UK income tax while abroad contact Inland Revenue, Centre for Non-Residents – UK 0845 070 0040, abroad +00 44 (0)151 210 2222.

Inheritance tax

Think that just because you've set up home abroad you'll avoid the pesky business of having to pay inheritance tax to the British government? Think again!

- You will have to pay UK inheritance tax if your 'domicile' is still the UK, even if you've been living abroad as a non-resident for many years. If you die abroad, you (or at least your estate) may well end up having to pay tax charges in both the UK and the new country you've been living in.

- To get out of paying inheritance tax, you have to be domiciled abroad for at least three years just before you die and have all your assets overseas.

- If you'd like to make it easier on yourself by changing your domicile to the country you've moved to, seek professional advice, because it's more complicated than it would seem on the outside. Specialist lawyers could help. Contact the Law Society (**www.lawsociety.org.uk**), who could point you in the direction of lawyers who deal in this kind of thing.

Tax abroad

There's lots of the lovely stuff. Don't assume that taxes abroad will be the same as, or even similar to, those that you're used to back home. Rates of taxes, such as VAT, vary from country to country. Other parts of the world might impose a wealth tax or estate duty between husbands and wives. There may also be another, special, tax slapped on foreign residents. Now doesn't that make you feel lucky?

Even so-called tax havens have other ways of getting your money, perhaps by demanding that you buy expensive property in order to live there or deposit a certain amount of money with the government, just in case you need to be repatriated.

Wherever you're going, make sure you thoroughly research the local tax situation before you head off, and seek legal advice when buying property abroad.

Property

Buying your own little place in the sun is the stuff of many people's dreams. If you've decided to make a faraway place your retirement home, then getting your own property there can make sense. House prices in many popular locations are far lower than those in the UK. If you sell your property in Britain, it shouldn't be too hard to use the money to buy an affordable house abroad instead, particularly if you've paid off all or most of your mortgage. There, are, however, some things to be aware of.

- You're looking for somewhere to see out the rest of your days, not just for a two-week holiday. Find out what the area is like out of season. Does the house have heating and insulation? How much will it cost to run air conditioning in the summer?

- Location, location, location is, supposedly, the most important thing to look at when choosing property. But, while you may have sorted the million-dollar views, it doesn't mean the bricks and mortar aren't important. Be as vigilant about the state of your foreign home as you would be a property in the UK.

- Find out about the land the house is built on – is the title guaranteed, and does the property have all the necessary planning permissions?

- Also, look at the materials the house is made from – do they comply with building-safety regulations?

- Research housing-market trends in that country. There's no guarantee the property will increase in value just because the housing market did well for a while in Britain.

- Check the taxes and charges. Property may be cheaper than in the UK, but stamp duty and/or estate agents' fees could cost a lot more.

Healthcare

This is a tricky one because the situation varies greatly from country to country. However, access to good healthcare is very important once you reach your later years, so check exactly what you are and aren't entitled to before you go.

- The UK has mutual healthcare agreements with many countries. However, these may not cover all your medical expenses – you may be entitled to only reduced-cost, rather than free, healthcare. Your entitlement may also be different depending on whether you are classed as a visitor or a resident of that country. Get expert advice before you go (**www.direct.gov.uk** is a good starting point).

- UK pensioners resident in another EU country are entitled to the same healthcare as a national of that country. However, check exactly what this entails – it may not be the same as the treatment you'd get in the UK. For example, certain medications are not available in certain countries. Services, such as district nursing, may be rare or non-existent. Privately run alternatives may be costly, and the UK government won't be able to help you pay for them.

- The government strongly advises us not to scrimp on health insurance – check you have a comprehensive policy that covers private medical and dental treatment, plus medical repatriation to the UK.

- Also, be aware that you won't automatically be allowed to come back and use the NHS for free. Non-residents are not entitled to free NHS treatment, unless you can show evidence that you're coming to live in the UK as your permanent home. NHS regulations are subject to change, so check for the most up-to-date information at **www.nhs.uk**.

- If you retire to another EC country before state retirement age, you can apply to DWP Overseas Contributions (**www.dwp.gov.uk**) for a form E106, which will give you access to local healthcare for up to two and a half years. After that, however, you'll have to get private insurance to cover you until state retirement age. Once you're a UK pensioner, you and your dependants can get local healthcare by filling in a form E121.

- See **www.dwp.gov.uk** or **www.thepensionservice.gov.uk**, or get in touch with the medical benefits unit of the

International Pensions Centre, 0191 218 7777, or medical benefits unit, 0191 218 7547 for forms and queries.

- See **www.retirement-matters.co.uk** for lots of useful advice on healthcare abroad.

- Leaflet SA29, 'Your Social Security Insurance, Benefits and Health Care Rights in the European Community', should be essential reading if you're looking to retire to another EC country. Get it from your social security office or **www.dwp.gov.uk**.

Practicalities

Registrations

Register with the local authorities in order to get access to any local welfare services to which you're entitled – ask them if you're in doubt. Also, register with the local British Consulate – this will help them keep in touch with you if you're in difficulty or, say, there's a national disaster. If you're moving to a country in the European Economic Area (EEA) – that is, anywhere in the European Union plus Iceland, Liechtenstein and Norway – you need to apply for a residence permit within three months of arriving.

Voting

You're entitled to vote in general and EU elections (though not UK local government elections) for up to 15 years after leaving the country. To do this, you need to contact the electoral registration office at the local council where you registered to vote, and get a bunch of forms to fill in. See **www.electoralcommission.gov.uk** for more.

Friends and support

The local British consulate is a good place to go to get started. See www.fco.gov.uk for a list of consulates abroad. They should have details of any expat or English-speaking organisations in the area such as clubs, associations and charities. These are worth contacting, even if you feel you've moved to get away from it all – they're likely to be a good source of practical advice and a good basis for a support network while you're getting on your feet.

Lawyers

There are lawyers in the UK who have, say, knowledge of French or Spanish law. However, it's likely to be far cheaper to get a lawyer in the place to which you've moved. The local British consulate should have a list of local English-speaking lawyers to help you with any legal matters. And, if you still haven't made a will, then see one and do it!

Driving

Check local driving laws and traffic regulations – they're unlikely to be identical to those that you're used to in the UK. Not everywhere will accept your UK driving licence. If you're moving to a country outside the EEA, you'll need to get an International Driving Permit (IDP) before leaving the UK, and take it with you. In most EEA countries, you can drive on your UK licence, but will then have to get a local driving licence if you become a resident.

Useful contacts

www.direct.gov.uk – loads of useful information on moving abroad

www.ageconcern.org.uk – has a very helpful 'Retiring Abroad' leaflet

International Pensions Centre, 0191 218 7777, or medical benefits unit, 0191 218 7547

Foreign and Commonwealth Office, **www.fco.gov.uk** – service for Britons overseas, 020 7008 0117

Book

The Daily Telegraph Guide to Living Abroad – Michael Furnell and Philip Jones (Kogan Page, £9.99)

Making provision for care

We're living a lot longer in the West, which is good news, for the most part. What it does mean for many, though, is that a fair amount of this extra time is likely to be spent in some kind of care home – whether just a basic residential home for the elderly or an actual full-blown nursing home with constant or partial medical care. As more and more people are having to go this route the question of who will pay for it has been the subject of much wrangling in recent years. It's not going to get any better, either, because the ageing population creates an increasing burden on the state.

Rules are likely to change in the next few years, so keep an eye out for new legislation that could materially affect you. But, right now, here is the way it currently works.

- In England and Wales you're expected to pay all or part of your fees for care (either at your home or in a care establishment) unless your savings – including the value of your home – are less than a certain amount set by the government (currently £20,000, but check **www.dwp.gov.uk** or **www.direct.gov.uk** to see if it has changed). If your home is your only asset it will usually have to be sold to pay the bills (though not necessarily immediately – see below).

- However, the good news is that there are things that can be done to avoid your losing your house provided that you don't already know that you need nursing care – in other words, you haven't already been diagnosed with a degenerative illness that you will need care for later on. If you get rid of your assets after you've been told that you're ill, you will be treated by the authorities as having made a 'deprivation' and your family or your estate will have to pay.

- You can raise the money with an equity-release plan (see above for details of those), with what's left of the value of the house going to loved ones. Some advisers recommend putting the house in trust for the benefit of beneficiaries before the problem arises. However, this may not be watertight.

- You can also get insurance to pay for nursing care (see below) but policies can be expensive and it may be too late for you to start one now. It's probably best to get independent financial advice about it.

Being cared for at home

Given the choice, most people would prefer to be cared for at home for as long as possible. Care is provided by social services or you can go direct to private agencies. Whichever one you go to, you can have some help from the state but only if you have practically no savings or assets.

- As a general rule of thumb, if you've got more than £20,000 capital and/or savings (for the current figure, check on **www.dwp.gov.uk** or **www.entitledto.co.uk**), you will get little or no help with the cost of your carer. This doesn't include your home as long as you continue to live in it. And it is only your assets and income that are assessed – anything your spouse personally owns is irrelevant.

- However, if you need some sort of personal care and you're over 65, then you may be able to claim attendance allowance from social security. It's tax-free and is not means-tested but is based on the level of care you need and whether it's daytime or night-time care, or both.

- If you're under 65 you can sometimes claim disability living allowance if you think you qualify. This offers similar rates to attendance allowance, depending on how mobile you are and how much care you need. Go to **www.dwp.gov.uk** for more explanation of these allowances and how much money they represent right now.

Being cared for in a home

Should you need to go into residential or nursing care, the rules for working out how much of the fees you have to pay yourself are again based on your assets and your income.

- If you have more than £20,000 in capital (currently), you'll have to pay the full cost of residential care before the local authority will chip in and help. (In Scotland and Wales the limits are slightly different – see **www.dwp.gov.uk** for the correct amount.)

- You can't be forced to sell your house but, since you're not living in it, it will be considered an asset that is taken into account when they work out how much you're worth. If you don't sell it, but you can't pay the fees either, then the local authority will claim it all back from your estate after your death. However, if you've got a partner or relative over 60 still living in the home then your share of the house won't be taken into account.

- But your local authority can approach your spouse to see if they are willing and able to contribute towards the cost of your care. In theory, this is a voluntary contribution, but, if your spouse can afford to make a contribution without hardship but doesn't want to, local authorities can make them!

- Once you're down to your last £20,000, how much you pay then works on a sliding scale of contributions until you're finally left with a very small amount of assets and savings (currently £12,250 but check on **www.dwp.gov.uk**), at which point social services will pay for the lot.

The whole thing is confused by the fact that, in England and Wales, you are expected to pay only for the 'personal care' part of your stay. The medical part is supposed to be paid for by the NHS, but health authorities are interpreting government guidelines so differently across the country that families often have a fight on their hands to persuade the authorities to pay up.

Immediate-care annuity

This can be a useful way of paying for long-term care without eroding the value of your estate – and therefore depriving your children and grandchildren on your death. It's also something you buy only when you know you need it, which is particularly helpful.

It works in a similar way to a pension annuity in that you pay a lump sum to the annuity company and they pay a guaranteed amount *directly to the care home* for as long as you live. Interestingly, the Revenue has agreed to pay this *gross* – in other words, there's no tax on the income.

The amount paid out has to be exactly what the care home is charging – so you can't make anything on it – and if the care home charges go down (unlikely, let's face it!), or you go back home to look after yourself, you won't benefit from the money not being paid to the home.

The amount you pay over in the lump sum will vary depending on your age, your health and your medical needs, and, as with normal annuities, whether you want the income to be index-linked. The older and more unwell you are, the cheaper it will be, of course.

Long-term-care insurance

As the name suggests, this is insurance that you can take out to help pay for long-term care later on. The problem with this – as with most insurance policies – is that you're paying for something that may or may not happen. Also, you need to start the policy some time before you're in a position to need care. With immediate-care annuities you buy them only when you need them, which does seem a better idea all round.

Clearly, quite a few people have thought along these lines and the policies are not particularly popular. Only one organisation provides them, the Pensions Annuity Friendly Society (contact below). The idea is that you pay into the policy with a one-off premium or by making regular payments. If you need to make a claim you will have meet certain criteria laid out in the policy to benefit at all. If you stay in good health until you die, you won't need to claim at all and the money will have been wasted – but that's insurance for you!

Useful contacts

Department of Work and Pensions – **www.dwp.gov.uk**
Care Funding Bureau – **www.carefundingbureau.co.uk**
Sharing Pensions – **www.sharingpensions.co.uk**
Pensions Annuity Friendly Society –
www.friendlysocieties.co.uk/pensionannuity

Making a will

I've said it before, but I'll say it again anyway: if you have any assets, you need to make a will! See 'Making a will' in Chapter 12 for more details on how to draw one up. However, when you get to a certain age it's worth considering making a 'living will'. This is to cover you if, for any reason, you can't make your wishes known while you're still alive.

The living will

It's not – yet – possible to make people live for ever, but the leaps and bounds in medical science mean that we can be kept alive for longer and longer. However, although our life expectancy is increasing, it doesn't necessarily mean our quality of life will be preserved until the end. It's becoming more and more common, therefore, to draw up a document – known as a living will – letting your loved ones and doctors know what you would like to happen if you get so ill that communication is an impossibility.

As yet, living wills don't have the legal standing of a traditional will. Doctors are obliged to do the best for their patients, which usually means keeping them alive for as long as possible. However, moves are being made to give living wills more legal weight, and many doctors are of the opinion that, if a patient has bothered to draw up a living will, their wishes shouldn't be ignored.

- If you do want to draw one up, it's worth doing it sooner rather than later. Making it while you're still in good health will be seen as a strong indication of your feelings.

- Keep your living will clear and concise, and include your full name and address. Get it witnessed by two people.

- Include the circumstances in which you want it to apply – for instance, if you are terminally ill and unable to communicate or if you lose your mental facilities.

- You can include advance directives, which state treatments that you do not want to receive, and advance statements, which describe treatments that you would prefer to receive. Advance directives have more weight than advance statements.

- Keep the living will with your standard will, and let your loved ones know where it is. Also, keep a card in your wallet saying where it is.

- If your living will comes into force while you are pregnant, the doctors are obliged to do whatever they can to keep the baby alive, regardless of what your living will says.

- Get more information from the Terrence Higgins Trust at **www.tht.org.uk** (they also provide a sample living-will form in exchange for a donation), the British Medical Association at **www.bma.org.uk**, or the Law Society at **www.lawsociety.org.uk**.

Fun funerals and other joys

It's now possible to arrange and pay for your funeral long before you pop your clogs. Planning your own funeral might seem a bit morbid, but it can make things a lot easier for the people you leave behind. First, you can decide how the ceremony will pan out.

If black garb and staid processions aren't really your thing, you can always request something a bit different. The explosion-loving cult writer Hunter S Thompson requested that his ashes be fired from a cannon. An Essex-based company, **www.heavensabovefireworks.com**, will make your ashes into a firework, if that's what you desire.

For humanists and atheists the British Humanist Association has a list of people who can do non-religious funeral ceremonies. Their website is **www.humanism.org.uk**. If you'd like a 'green' funeral with a coffin made of biodegradable material such as willow or chipboard and even the use of horses to pull the cortège rather than mucky cars, you can ask for one in your will. There's lots of information about these on the Web particularly at the Natural Death Centre (**www.naturaldeath.org.uk**) and the general funerals site (**www.ifishoulddie.co.uk**).

It also makes good financial sense to pay for it nice and early:

- This will stop your descendants or executors getting burdened with the cost. Funerals are rarely cheap – currently £1,800 to £4,000 or more, depending on the part of the country and how many bells and whistles you opt for. Cremations are usually slightly cheaper, but prices are on the up and the average still comes in at about £1,600. This can be a big hit when they're still reeling (or at least they still should be reeling) at the sadness of losing you.

- Even better, you'll get a bargain by paying today's price. If you shop around, you should be able to find a company that will guarantee that neither you nor your estate will have to shell out extra in the event of your death whenever you pop your clogs.

- There can be problems if the company that gave the guarantee goes out of business, though. Luckily, the government has introduced new regulations to safeguard customers' money, but it's still worth checking out the situation when you sign on the dotted line.

- A lot of companies offer funeral insurance, but this can be riskier, because you're insuring yourself for an unknown sum in the future. There's no saying that funeral costs won't soar in the years before your death, meaning even the priciest policy won't pay out enough to cover the costs.

Top 10 funeral songs (if you're feeling cheeky!)

'Another One Bites the Dust'
'Stairway to Heaven'
'The Only Way is Up'
'Who Wants to Live Forever?'
'Tears in Heaven'
'Always Look on the Bright Side of Life'
'Simply the Best'
'I Will Always Love You'
'Angels'
'Time to Say Goodbye'
... and anything by Stiff Little Fingers, the Dead Kennedys or the Grateful Dead

Probably not a good idea ...

'I Will Survive'
'Good to be Back'
'Start Me Up'
'Never Gonna Give You Up'
'Look Back in Anger'
'Killing Me Softly'
'Ring of Fire'
'Highway to Hell'
'Firestarter'
'Drop Kick Me Jesus Through the Goalpost of Life'
'I'm So Miserable Without You, it's Almost Like Having You Here'

Useful contacts

Age Concern – **www.ageconcern.org.uk**
Help the Aged – **www.helptheaged.org.uk**
www.50connect.co.uk (very useful website for the 50+)
www.retirement-matters.co.uk
www.direct.gov.uk
www.dwp.gov.uk
www.nhs.uk
www.entitledto.co.uk
www.hmrc.gov.uk

Books

The Good Non-Retirement Guide – Rosemary Brown (Kogan Page, £15.99)
Wills, Probate & Inheritance Tax for Dummies – Julian Knight (Wiley, £12.99)

16

Ethical Money

*'When a fellow says it hain't the money but the
principle o' the thing, it's th' money.'*
– Frank McKinney 'Kin' Hubbard

Ethical living equals money saving – it really does! Most
environmentally friendly and socially responsible practices
actually work out cheaper. Even ethical investments – laughed
at by the City when they first came on to the market – are now
proving themselves to be money earners (or they're not losing
any more than the established funds). In fact, increasingly
now, high-net-worth individuals are being more careful where
they invest their money, which means that ethical investment
products are becoming more popular and, therefore, could
become more lucrative than the usual investments in the
future.

So do your bit for the environment, and for society generally, and you'll find your costs go down and your investments
look healthier.

Ethical money day to day

Transport

Running a car is, on average, more expensive than paying for accommodation or food in this country. Most people pay between £2,500 and £3,800 a year to own a car, including depreciation, interest lost, insurance, breakdown cover, MOT, tax, spares, servicing, parking, fuel and fines. Obviously, driving a car is not good for the environment but many of us have to (or really want to). If you do, here are some ways you can cut costs and limit the damage you do.

- Service your car often and check tyre pressure. It can actually cut fuel costs.

- Drive smoothly and consistently and cut your speed. Driving at 50mph is 25 per cent more fuel-efficient than driving at 70mph.

- Before buying a car, consider joining a car-sharing scheme or car club, which is a lot cheaper than owning your own. Look at www.carclubs.org.uk, www.liftshare.com and www.nationalcarshare.co.uk. Also, www.gumtree.co.uk often has lift-sharing opportunities.

- Smaller, cheaper cars tend to use far less fuel than big gas guzzlers such as four-wheel-drive vehicles.

- Investigate alternative fuels such as electricity, biodiesel and LPG (liquid petroleum gas). Check out www.lpga.co.uk, www.biodiesel.co.uk, www.plugitin.co.uk and www.evuk.co.uk.

- Find more tips at Transport Energy (part of the Energy Saving Trust) at www.transportenergy.org.uk.

- Using a bicycle to get around is not only better for the environment but keeps you fit and healthy (so long as you're careful on the roads) and costs next to nothing. You might get into cycling as a hobby and go on cycle tours. Contact the Cyclists' Touring Club at **www.ctc.org.uk**, 0870 873 0060.

Travel

Once upon a time, a holiday could simply mean a nice day out by the seaside. But times are changing, and 1998 became the first year in which more Britons jetted off to foreign climes (29 million) than stayed at home (27 million). Half the population now flies once a year, and the industry is expected to grow by three times in the next 30 years. It's no wonder: while rail and bus fares rise, air travel has, recently, been getting cheaper, with fares dropping by 10 per cent over the past decade.

However, there are hidden costs associated with the flying boom. Airport parking is rarely a bargain, and transport to airports can add up to as much as a cheap plane ticket, with the cheapest airlines often using those that are further out of main cities. There's also the effect on the environment: travelling by air can create three times the emissions for each passenger as a car journey of the same length.

Even cheaper holidays cost money – ask yourself whether you can really afford, and really want, to go away. And, whether you're going abroad or staying further afield in the UK, consider the costs of the different ways to get there, and what you are doing with your money once you arrive.

- When away, try to avoid hiring a car wherever possible – not only can cycling, walking or public transport save you money better on holiday, the environment will thank you. Sadly, damage to the Yosemite Valley and southern rim of the Grand Canyon has been caused by cars.

- See **www.seat61.com** for rail and ship alternatives to air travel.

- It can be cheaper to travel independently to a destination than going through a big multinational tour company.

- If you do go for a tour operator, look for a member of the Association of Independent Tour Operators (**www.aito.co.uk**). Some tour companies, such as ATG Oxford (**www.atg-oxford.co.uk**), set aside part of their pretax profits for community projects in the host country.

- Eat and drink local produce rather than imported food – it's likely to be cheaper, as well as keeping money in the local economy.

- Get away and do some good with a volunteering holiday. Willing Workers on Organic Farms has a wide range of placements on small and large farms and in countryside businesses – workers are usually expected to do a few hours of work a day in exchange for board and lodging. See **www.wwoof.org** for opportunities around the world or in the UK.

Contacts

www.tourismconcern.org.uk
www.greenglobe21.com
www.greenhotels.com
www.responsibletravel.com
www.ethicaltraveller.com
www.ecoturismolatino.com (for travel in South America)

Home

Using as little energy as possible in your home makes sense for the environment – and your pocket. There are loads of ways to save energy. For example:

- Keep the oven door closed to save energy (and avoid ruining your soufflé). Over 20 per cent of heat can be lost each time you open the oven door. Similarly, put lids on saucepans wherever your recipe allows it – water boils up to 6 per cent faster with a lid on the pan.

- Avoid tumble dryers – one of the most energy-hungry domestic appliances.

- Never put on half-full washing machine or dishwasher loads – even a half-load setting will use more than half the energy and water of a full setting.

- Consider double glazing: small chinks in windows can lead to up to 20 per cent of a home's heat loss. Fensa-accredited fitters (**www.fensa.co.uk**) have to meet the best thermal performance standards. The DIY version, putting purposely designed plastic sheeting on the inside of each pane, is much cheaper.

- Put aluminium foil, shiny side out, behind radiators to reflect heat inwards.

- Don't rely on the remote: it's estimated that 15 per cent of domestic electricity worldwide is wasted by people leaving appliances (TVs, PCs, DVD players and set-top boxes) on standby. Get up and turn them off properly.

- Find the most efficient boiler to suit you at **www.sedbuk.com**, and get it serviced every two years.

- Never, ever, shave or brush your teeth while the tap is running. If your water is metered this will save money over the year.

- Use energy-saving light bulbs and get a SavaPlug (**www.savawatt.com**) for your fridge – this can save up to 20 per cent of the fridge's energy costs by regulating its power use better.

- Find more tips at **www.actionenergy.org.uk**, **www.energyefficiency.org** and **www.thecarbontrust.co.uk/energy**.

Hot air

Air transport is currently contributing around 3.5 per cent to total human-caused global warming, but is forecast by the Intergovernmental Panel on Climate Change (IPCC) to rise to as much as 15 per cent by 2050. In the UK, air travel emissions are due to increase 350 per cent by 2030. The Tyndall Centre for Climate Change Research has recently said, 'If the UK government does not curb aviation growth, all other sectors of the economy will eventually be forced to become carbon-neutral' (**www.campaignstrategy.org**).

Ethical banks

For those looking to pop their money in a bank with principles without sacrificing convenience, the most ethical current accounts are those from the Co-op (**www.co-operative-bank.co.uk**) and its Internet arm, Smile (**www.smile.co.uk**). They offer all the usual rigmarole (chequebook, debit card and so forth) expected from a high street current account and give you a warm and cosy feeling inside.

Other ethical financial options worth checking out are the Ecology Building Society (**www.ecology.co.uk**), Shared Interest Society (**www.shared-interest.com**), Triodos Bank (**www.triodos.co.uk**) and Unity Trust Bank (**www.unity.uk.com**).

Ethical mortgages

There's not much to choose from in the mortgage market at the moment but lenders are constantly coming up with new mortgage ideas, so keep looking. Building societies and ethical banks (such as the Co-op) are the most likely to offer ethical or 'green' mortgages.

Energy-efficient homes have far cheaper running costs and a few mortgage companies offer 'green' mortgages for new homes with a standard assessment procedure (SAP) rating of 100 or more. The SAP rating refers to the energy efficiency of a building and you can find out more about this at **http://projects.bre.co.uk/sap2001/** and **www.odpm.gov.uk** (under Building Regulations).

To see which companies offer ethical mortgages look on comparison sites such as **www.charcolonline.co.uk**, **www.moneyfacts.co.uk** and the financial portal **www.find.co.uk**.

Ethical investing

Caring about where you invest your money is definitely something that's on the rise in Britain. Currently there are over forty ethical and environmental investment unit trusts. To be classed as 'ethical' funds must only invest in companies that pass an ethical test. This restriction has meant that ethical funds have had to eschew the big FTSE companies and look to the smaller ones for investment. Because these companies tend to be more volatile (though also, usually, more interesting), it has given ethical funds a reputation for poor performance and volatility.

However, as ethical investments have matured, some of the volatility has been smoothed out and more recent reports and surveys have found that, on the whole, ethical funds do no worse than others and sometimes do better. The White List, published each year by Principal Investment Management, which shows the top 12 income funds rated by overall merit, recently placed one of the ethical funds in second place. Also, the research company Datamonitor believes that ethical investment will increase in importance among high-net-worth individuals in the future. This means that these funds should grow in importance and, probably, in value, which should make them a good bet right now.

Increasing amounts of private and corporate money is being invested in specially branded unit trusts that shun shareholdings in companies trading in arms, alcohol or tobacco. Others go further and rule out holdings in companies that are considered to damage the environment or exploit their employees.

How to do it

There are various ways to make a difference (and make some money) with your investments.

- Buy shares in a company whose practices you disagree with and want to change. Admittedly, unless you are a major pension fund buying thousands of shares at a time, it will be hard to change the company's practices on your own. But, if you and many others buy shares in the company, the weight of your opinions will have some effect. At least you will have a voice in shareholders' meetings, which is often more potent than merely campaigning from the outside.

- Invest in ethical funds that include companies that adhere to most ethical guidelines set by the fund managers. This tends to mean a mixed bag and could include a few companies that do things you're not happy about but, overall, the fund would have better ethical standards than others.

- Invest in ethical funds that rigorously screen the companies they invest in. This means that companies are completely avoided if they deal in products or services that are deemed unethical. The organisation EIRIS (Ethical Investment Research Service – **www.eiris.org.uk**) looks into companies to determine their 'morals', and ethical investment funds use their findings when they decide what to invest in. Issues investigated will include codes of ethics, board practices, environmental and social risk management, history of pollution convictions, links to controversial industries such as pornography, tobacco, animal testing and arms, attitude to human rights, attitude to trade unions and even levels of staff training.

Of course, the usual warnings apply with ethical funds, as they do with all other managed investments. Past performance is no real guide to the future (although you don't really have much else to go by!). Also, some of the initial charges levied by ethical funds may seem unethically high, so keep those in mind. You can find out more about ethical investing and the funds that could meet your criteria by looking at **www.ethical investors.co.uk**, **www.uksif.org** and **www.eiris.org.uk**.

Invest direct

One problem with these funds is that they are managed and, as you saw in Chapter 9, 'Make Your Money Make Money', these tend to underperform. But worry not. There are alternatives. One possible way to go is to invest in individual companies that you have investigated yourself. When you invest in companies directly you will need to research them for some time before making a decision. Helpfully, EIRIS has done the ethical side of the investigations for you, but you should also do the usual research into the financial performance of the business yourself. Look at **www.fool.co.uk** for a mound of helpful information on how to read company reports, understand P/E ratios and so on.

Ethical trackers

The other, much easier way, is to invest in a tracker. There are now ethical trackers, thanks to FTSE4Good, a family of indices for socially responsible investment designed by FTSE, the index provider. FTSE4Good's marketing blurb says it 'aims to facilitate investment in companies which meet certain eligibility criteria in the area of corporate social responsibility'. You can find out about their trackers on their website at **www.FTSE4Good.com**.

Charitable giving

Don't think you need to be wealthy to give money to charity. In practice, it's those with the least who cough up the most. Around 70 per cent of people in the UK give regularly to charity, donating an average of 1 per cent of our monthly wage. However, the richest 20 per cent of us give around 0.7 per cent of household expenditure away, and the poorest 20 per cent give 3 per cent.

However much – or little – you want to give, it makes sense to make it go as far as possible. There are simple ways to maximise your contribution to charity without actually having to shell out more of your own cash.

- It's far better to give by direct debit or through your pay packet than to sling your cash about on an ad hoc basis. This is the best way of keeping charities' admin costs down and may prevent you getting a load of charity junk mail, as your details end up on more and more mailing lists.

- There's been a recent surge of interest in payroll giving in the UK, something that has long been popular on the other side of the Atlantic. Basically, it allows you to give money from your pay packet or pension straight to charity before tax is deducted – if you pay tax at 22 per cent and pledge a tenner, the real cost to you is only £7.80, bearing in mind the tax you would otherwise have paid on the money. The largest payroll-giving scheme in the UK is Give

As You Earn (**www.giveasyouearn.org**), which is operated by the Charities Aid Foundation (**www.cafonline.org.uk**). It's also worth asking your employer and checking with the taxman at **www.hmrc.gov.uk/payrollgiving**.

- Working on a similar principle, Gift Aid allows a charity to claim tax relief of 28p on every £1 that you give them. You have to fill in a Gift Aid form for each individual charity you give to – ask them directly or try the Inland Revenue's Gift Aid helpline (0151 472 6038).

- Be aware of where your money is going. There are good charity search facilities at **www.allaboutgiving.org**, **www.charitycommission.gov.uk** and **www.charitychoice.co.uk** (though be aware that some charities pay to be listed above others on this site). For general information, also try **www.fundraising.co.uk** and **www.alertnet.org.uk**.

- If you're interested in setting up a charitable trust, which allows trustees to set the aims for their trust and to set out how people apply for cash, contact the Association of Charitable Foundations (**www.acf.org.uk**, 020 7255 4499).

- You can't take it with you, so why not leave a little something for a charity in your will? A hundred and twenty-five charities have set up **www.rememberacharity.org.uk** (0808 180 2080) to help people do just that.

Christmas

Traditionally, this is one of the most expensive – and, not entirely coincidentally, the most stressful – times for British families. Don't feel you have to go too crazy – the environment will thank you for not splashing out on every decoration and trimming in sight.

If the endless round of present buying and the thought of struggling to get each and every relation something bigger and better than you did the previous year are taking their toll, earn some brownie points by spending the money instead on those in greater need of it. Try **www.goodgifts.org**, **www.presentaid.org**, **www.senda christmascow.org.uk** for gift ideas with a difference.

Living on nothing

- Try being a 'freegan' – the term describes people who eat free food otherwise destined for the rubbish heap. They raid supermarket bins, market stalls and bakery doorways for the (usually) perfectly edible foodstuffs that have reached their sell-by date. Currently, supermarkets waste about 5 per cent of their food each day because they're required by law to throw this stuff out. Altogether, though, it's estimated that total waste from the farm to the kitchen table is a staggering 70 per cent! The more freegans hoovering up wasted food, then, the better.

- Don't forget the food you can find for free – blackberries, elderflowers, shellfish, seaweed, nettles – are all there for the picking and eating. Find more ideas and recipes in Richard Mabey's book **Food for Free** (Collins Gem, £4.99).

- Give yourself a day off spending. Since its launch over a decade ago, National Buy Nothing Day (**www.buynothingday.co.uk** and **http://adbusters.org/metas/eco/bnd**) has grown into a worldwide celebration of consumer awareness and simple living. Observed about a month before Christmas, the West's busiest shopping period of the year, Buy Nothing Day has sparked debate and raised awareness of our consumerist culture.

Useful contacts

Best to Invest **www.best-to-invest.com**, 0800 542 4255
Ethical Investments – **www.ethicalinvestments.co.uk**, 0800 018 0881
Ethical Investment Association – **www.ethicalinvestment.org.uk**, 01242 539848
The Ethical Investment Co-operative – **www.ethicalmoney.org**, 0845 4583127
Ethical Investment Research Services – **www.eiris.org**, 020 7840 5700
Ethical Investors Group – **www.ethicalinvestors.co.uk**, 01242 539848
Ethical Money **www.ethicalmoneyonline.com**, 0870 871 6594
FTSE4Good Index **www.ftse4good.com**, 020 7448 1810
Investing Ethically **www.investing-ethically.co.uk**, 01603 661121
Profit with Principle **www.profitwithprinciple.co.uk**, 01772 733338

Book

A Good Life – Leo Hickman (Eden Project Books, £15.00)

17

Think Rich

'I don't like money, actually, but it quiets my nerves.'

– Joe Louis

It's all very well to go through the nuts and bolts of financial management but, as with everything else in life, our actual wealth depends very much on our thinking – far more than we realise. In life we may not get what we want but we do tend to get what we expect – whether consciously or unconsciously – so it's as well to expect good rather than bad and to expect success rather than failure. Why not?

Genuinely, thinking rich isn't really thinking about money. It's about expanding one's sense of life, of the possibilities of life and, in particular, the possibilities open to us in life. Merely thinking rich in money terms can actually narrow one's outlook and, therefore, one's life, so make sure you know what real richness is before you start thinking it!

How to think rich

There's a lot of nonsense written and said about 'thinking rich'. It's very popular to write books or do seminars on changing your thinking to attract riches to yourself. In fact, much of it is nothing more than self-hypnosis and general self-will. However, if you take the majority of it with a pinch of salt but keep an open mind you can pick up some very useful tips that *will* change your thinking and will, therefore, open up more opportunities for you, particularly if you combine them with actual work and practical steps.

For example, in his book *Secrets of the Millionaire Mind: Think Rich and Get Rich* (Piatkus, £9.99), the author, T Harv Eker, makes a few useful suggestions. He says, among other things, that:

- Rich people believe 'I create my life.' Poor people believe 'Life happens to me.' He then challenges readers not to complain out loud or even in their head for seven days (I can vouch that this is very difficult) and watch the results.

- Rich people think Big. Poor people think Small.

- Rich people admire other rich and successful people. Poor people resent rich and successful people.

- Rich people associate with positive, successful people. Poor people associate with negative or unsuccessful people.

- Rich people manage their money well. Poor people mismanage their money well.

- Rich people act in spite of fear. Poor people let fear stop them.

Actually, all these points could be made about 'happy' and 'sad' people or 'successful' and 'unsuccessful' people. They are universal (and practical) tips on protecting ourselves from thoughts, beliefs and attitudes that hold us back while developing more successful and happiness-making habits of thought.

Think of the people around you – do they think small, negative, poor? It's quite likely that you will take on their beliefs and have your own life limited in that way. Did your parents think that way? That thought pattern will be more deep-rooted, then, and might take more work to get it out. Take note of the kinds of things that more positive, successful people say and do. Try to spend more time with them – not necessarily wealthy people because many monied types are negative and limited in their thinking (in other words, they may have money but they don't have much of a life), but try to hang around more with people who have a more expansive and 'life-rich' attitude.

Consciously say 'yes' to life rather than 'no' all the time. It's amazing how much most of us don't do or don't have just because we think we can't have these things. If we say 'no' to ourselves at the very start of an idea, we don't even bother to try to work for it. So many people complain at the hand life has dealt them, not realising that much of the time they can make something good out of it. Start from a positive basis each day, even when times are hard, and you will find life and your money come a bit easier.

Think real riches

The problem with so many of these think-rich books and seminars is that they have such a narrow concept of what richness really is. In urging you (as they always do) to 'commit' yourself to getting rich above all things, they ignore all the other important aspects of life. For example, Eker tells his readers that, 'in my experience, getting rich takes focus, courage, knowledge, expertise, 100 per cent of your effort, a never-give-up attitude, and of course a rich mind set'. So no room for any real living then?

If we would be rich – really, substantially rich – it's worth considering what real riches are before going for them. A friend of mine who has a young teenage son recently described a family trip to the local swimming baths where he saw a number of fathers either disregarding or not even noticing the adoration of their children. 'What a huge collateral of love they're squandering,' he said. He has a point. Maybe some of those fathers had been on a think-rich seminar and believed they should focus totally on being rich. Meanwhile, they're missing out on the real riches poured into their laps.

Infinite possibilities

Contrary to popular belief, there isn't a finite amount of good in the world. There genuinely are infinite possibilities and an infinity of ideas, any one or more of which could do you good. Also, there isn't a finite amount of money. There really isn't. Money comes from all over the place and is constantly moving around, being created by different economies and, again, there's no reason why you shouldn't have more of it.

But don't limit yourself just to money for your supply. Supply comes in all sorts of forms and very often in a way we would never have expected. In practical terms, think of how many possible goods and services you can get for free (there are various tips in this book about this), how you can swap them, barter with friends and neighbours, gain grants or bursaries that you hadn't known about before, among other alternative sources of supply.

Being rich – really rich

> 'To need nothing is divine, and the less a man
> needs the nearer does he approach to divinity.'
> – **Socrates**

One sure-fire way of feeling rich without even increasing your income is to hang around with poor people, because we tend to rate our level of happiness and wealth by comparing ourselves with others. Billionaire American businessman Jim Clark recently said, 'I think that what Larry Ellison and Bill Gates have is phenomenal wealth. I'm just a two-bit billionaire.' One's heart bleeds.

But really, as Shakespeare said, 'comparisons are odorous', so work at not comparing yourself or your wealth level with others. This is also a very good way of getting out, and staying out, of debt. Many people get into debt simply by buying the things they think everyone else has but they themselves can't really afford. The unspoken need to keep up with the Joneses is a cruel disease that takes away our happiness, peace and, usually, money. Wake up to this kind of thinking – something that's very prevalent in our society – and start thinking your own thoughts.

If you want to be richer, cultivate a habit of gratitude. Sounds girlie and Pollyanna-ish but it's genuinely true that the more gratitude you actually feel, the richer you actually are. There's no objective measure of actual richness – it's entirely up to us whether we feel rich, poor or just about OK. You could have all the money in the country but still feel you needed more, so, to feel genuinely rich, make it a conscious habit to be grateful for what you have – not just the material goods but, more importantly, all the other things you have, such as friends, health, sunshine, your pets and so on. We do have to keep doing this because so much in life would seem to cancel it out or block it from our view. It takes work to keep the right state of thought.

Be practical

Thinking rich isn't the end of the story, of course. Together with the thinking there has to be some doing. As Thomas Jefferson put it, 'I find that the harder I work, the more luck I seem to have.'

For example:

- There's money for grants and special projects – government and corporate – so why shouldn't you have it?

- If you've had a yen to change job or even set up your own business, why not take steps to do this – work out what the first couple of steps would be and do those, then work out the next couple of steps and so on.

- Don't think of your salary as the only income. There are lots of other income streams and possibilities (see Chapter 6 for ideas). Don't be limited.

- Think laterally – what other routes could there be to getting what you want or need if the obvious way seems blocked?

- Consider bartering as one way of gaining what you need. Barter your skills with others.

- Who knows what's around us for free? Look in the hedgerows – there's food there; there are free offers all over the place (some of them genuine); some people manage to blag their way into celebrity parties or just put themselves in the way of freebies. Why not you?

- So you've failed at something; so you've lost some serious money. So? Everyone fails. It's the ones who pick themselves up, dust themselves down and go forward who succeed in the end. Pick yourself up, shake off the dust of that experience and go forward.

So, finally, some practical tips on thinking and being rich would include these ideas:

- Need less. Spend less. Enjoy a simple life.

- Acknowledge and be grateful for what you have – however little you might think it is to start with. Don't wait until it's taken away from you to realise what you had.

- Appreciate what's here for free. Use what's around – free air, sunshine, healthcare, free shows, free offers and so on.

- See how rich people think – those who are rich in money and rich in life – and copy them if you can.

- Expect good – why not? Change your habit of thought – why not?

- Hang around with upbeat, positive people – not offensively smiley all the time, self-satisfied types, but genuinely energetic, going-for-it people. It can rub off.

- Keep your feet on the ground and don't imagine that just 'thinking' it will create it. You've got to do some actual work, along with the positive frame of mind, to bring the good.

> *'He is rich or poor according to what he is, not according to what he has.'*
>
> **– Henry Ward Beecher**

18

Main Points

Let's now sum up the main points of what you've read in this book.

Chapter 1 – 'What Are You Living For?'

- Money isn't the be-all and end-all of our lives. It's only a *part* of life.

- However, it is one of the most important parts. It's essential for most of the things we need to do and for many of the things we want to do.

- Prioritise the different aspects of your life. Work out what is most important to you, and try to match your spending to your priorities.

- With a little understanding, you can manage your finances as well as any expert. No one cares more about your money than you do, so you're in the best position to get the most out of your cash.

- Many of the best things in life really are free: spending time with friends makes most people happier than spending money. But you can't be that happy if you can't afford to eat. It's all a question of balance.

Chapter 2 – 'Control Your Finances, Control Your Life'

- Knowledge is power! Become aware of your finances by scrutinising and then filing all your bank statements and bills.

- Don't be scared to budget – it's a way to control your finances, not a sentence to a life of penny pinching. Keep a spending diary and work out how much you have coming in and how much you can afford to have going out with the help of an online planner. Then, hopefully, you can pocket the difference.

- Learn how to get into the habit of saving up for nice things, rather than just whacking them on your credit card. Boring? Maybe, but it will make life a whole lot easier.

- If you're self-employed, be even more vigilant about what you spend and save.

- Keep spending as low as possible – check you are getting the cheapest deals possible.

Chapter 3 – Dump Your Debt, Live Cheaper, Make Money

- Face the demon now: the quicker you tackle the debt, the quicker, and cheaper, it will be to pay it off.

- Think long term: in order to get out of debt you need to spend less and, ideally, earn more. To stay out of debt and keep making money instead of constantly losing it you need to change the way you deal with money for good.

- Get debt management advice, preferably free.

- Squeeze your spending and look for new ways to make money. It's not as hard as it sounds.

- Deal with your creditors one by one – hiding from them

will only make things worse. Be aware of your rights – not everyone you owe money to has the right to send the bailiffs in, no matter how much they shout about it.

- Bankruptcy is not an easy way out. It should be used only as a last resort.

Chapter 4 – Saving and Borrowing

- Saving is different from investing, but essential nonetheless to be financially secure. As soon as you've killed any debts, start squirrelling money away into different savings pots on a regular basis.

- Work out the true cost of borrowing – an item can end up a whole lot more expensive once you've factored in the interest payments while you shift the balance from your credit card.

- Beware of exorbitant overdraft rates and bank charges.

- Shop around for the best interest rates – think high on savings and low on borrowing. And rates keep changing, so keep shopping around.

- Check your credit history, be aware of how it's judged, and do your best to keep it clean.

Chapter 5 – Financial One-upmanship Day to Day

- We waste about £500,000 during a lifetime on rip-off products and underperforming investments. It's high time to start spending smarter: shop around for everything, use price-comparison websites, consider buying second-hand goods, and never just assume that the most expensive thing will also be the best.

- The Internet is a veritable mine of cheap holiday deals,

auction sites and bargain books, CDs and household goods.

- Don't buy things you don't need, whether they be expensive insurance policies for unlikely eventualities that wouldn't matter anyway or extortionate Christmas gifts.

- Shops are designed to make us spend money, but this doesn't mean it's a good idea. Shop with a list or a thrifty friend and be strict with yourself to avoid coming home with a cartload of unnecessary and/or over-priced tat.

- Find out your rights as a consumer and learn to stand up for yourself if you're sold substandard products.

Chapter 6 – Making That Bit Extra

- Sell your unwanted junk, then sell yourself. No, not literally, but there are ways to use your talents, hobbies and interests to pull in a bit of extra money.

- Recover your forgotten funds, either in old bank accounts or investments, or just loose change down the back of the sofa.

- If you think you've got what it takes to set up your own business, then go for it. Be sure to think about your business plan, doing your accounts, marketing and publicity, insurance, and how to get paid on time.

- If that sounds a bit daunting, there are loads of other smaller ways to make a bit of extra money. Taking part in market research, mystery shopping, entering competitions, being a film/TV extra and volunteering for an ID parade can all bring in a few extra bucks.

Chapter 7 – Student Finances

- University is going to mean a lot of debt, but hopefully the student experience and the salary you'll eventually end up earning will make it worth it.

- As well as tuition fees, you need to find money to live on. Luckily, the government gives out loans (and sometimes grants) to cover the basics, so check what you're entitled to and get applying early.

- Look out for any bursaries and extra help you might be entitled to if, for example, you come from a poor family or have children to provide for yourself.

- Boost your income with a part-time and/or holiday job. You're unlikely to earn enough to pay tax, either, so long as you fill in the right forms.

- You can't rely on your parents to give you money, but get talking to them as early and as reasonably as possible about how much they can or can't afford to give you.

- Get the best-value bank account that you can, and try to avoid getting tangled up with the temptations of high interest credit cards if at all possible.

Chapter 8 – A House or a Home?

- Do your sums before you get tied up in bricks and mortar. Do you really want to buy a house? And can you really afford to?

- If you do, then get saving – preferably until you have a deposit of 5 per cent of the value of the property, plus at least another £4,000 to cover fees, taxes and the rest.

- There are a zillion different types of mortgage out there, offering different fixed and variable interest rates plus a bunch of add-ons and things in-between. There's no easy way of saying which type and from which company will best suit you, but the chances are it won't be the first, or even the second, or even the third one you look at, so leave no stone unturned.

- Don't overmortgage yourself – interest rates can rise, so check that your repayments won't be too scary after a 3 per cent or 4 per cent increase.

- Beware of mortgage payment-protection insurance (MPPI), higher lending charge (HLC) and special life-assurance policies. They're likely to benefit the lender or seller more than they do you.

- You may be able to make house buying more affordable by going in with a spouse or members of your family, by snapping up a bargain at auction, by buying from a housing association or, if you qualify, with help from the government's starter homes initiative, or even by building a house yourself.

- Getting a mortgage is only one part of the house-buying process – remember to set aside money (and time) to deal with legal paperwork, stamp duty, surveys and the rest.

- Buy-to-let property isn't necessarily an easy investment, but it can be a good one. Remember that it's a business decision – look for something that will be attractive to tenants on the rental market, which is not necessarily the same as a property in which you'd like to live.

- Property prices abroad can be cheaper than those in the UK, but the associated legal and buying costs can be far higher.

Chapter 9 – Make Your Money Make Money

- Think long term – invest in something that will, hopefully, make you money after a number of years.

- Investing isn't the same as saving: money in a savings

account doesn't have the same potential for growth as, say, money invested in shares.

- You can invest in just about anything – shares, bonds, property, collections of anything from wine to antiques that should increase in value.

- There's no right way to invest – everyone has different ideas of what constitutes a good risk and reward, so ultimately only you can make your own investment decisions.

- The two main things that make a difference to how your money grows are the rate of interest you're getting (high is good, low is bad) and the length of time it stays invested.

- It makes sense to minimise risk by spreading your cash over a few different types of investment.

- Go against the flow – don't just invest in something at a particular time because everyone else is.

Chapter 10 – Your Future

- Pensions may sound unglamorous, but they're really just another form of investment, and a very important one at that. You don't have to have a pension, but you do need to make some kind of provision for your later years.

- Start saving for your future as early as possible in order to keep the process as pain-free as possible.

- Ideally, you want to build a pension pot that's big enough to let you live off the interest when you retire. To get today's average salary of £20,000, that would mean having £400,000 squirrelled away.

- You get to take 25 per cent of your pension fund tax-free in cash when you retire. Depending on how much is in your pension pot you may have to use the rest to buy an annuity, which is a kind of insurance policy where a company agrees to give you an income every year until you die.

- You have to pay tax on this annuity, but all the money you pay into your pension fund will be tax-free.

- Currently, everyone is entitled to a state pension, but this is piddling and there's no guarantee it will be around for ever. Therefore, you also need to pay into another pension scheme.

- Company pension schemes are the ones where your employer contributes as well. Personal pensions are all down to you – stakeholder pensions and SIPPs (self-invested personal pensions) are the only ones worth bothering with.

Chapter 11 – Stop Them Taking Your Money!

- Don't believe banks are your friend. Scrutinise all your statements for unexpected charges and exorbitant interest rates, or simple mistakes. Vote with your feet if you're getting stung with the former, and raise the latter with the bank.

- Don't be conned into buying retail warranties or payment protection insurance for loans. You don't need them.

- Beware of dodgy lenders – loans secured on your home, cheque cashers, pawnbrokers and home-finance companies are all rip-off ways to get hold of cash.

- Always remember: 'If it sounds too good to be true, it probably is.' Gambling, the Lottery, chain letters, pyramid schemes and a load of other get-rich-quick schemes all fall into this category.

- New scams pop up all the time. Keep your eyes open for news on expensive SMS schemes, phishing (emails that try to get hold of your bank details) and card skimming.

- Identity fraud is on the rise – be extra careful about how you dispose of bank statements and letters containing your details, and check your credit rating regularly.

Chapter 12 – Being Together

- Sad, but true: money is the number-one cause of rows that lead to couples splitting up. You must talk to your beloved about your attitudes to spending money, and agree on practical stuff such as whether to have a joint account and who will pay which bills.

- Premarital agreements (where you set down how to divvy up your assets if it all goes wrong) have no legal force, but are often used as the basis for a divorce settlement. Worth considering, particularly if you're the wealthier partner or it's a second marriage.

- The average couple splurge around £18,000 on their wedding, but it's far from compulsory. You can tie the knot from as little as £100 with a little thought.

- Contrary to popular belief, there is no such thing as a common-law marriage. It's very important to be aware of this – even if you've lived together for a decade and have three children, you have no automatic right to each other's pension or other assets if you split up or one of you dies.

- There are ways to safeguard yourself, however, including drawing up a cohabitation agreement, looking at different ways of buying property together, and naming your partner as a beneficiary in your will.

- Set up a joint account for all the expenses you've agreed to cover jointly, but keep your personal accounts to give yourself a bit of privacy, freedom and independence.

- Things are all going to change once children come along – agree a fair system between you to make sure there's adequate money for the non-working, childcaring partner, too.

- A civil partnership gives a gay couple the same entitlement to each other's assets and financial protection as a marriage.

- In theory, divorce settlements split your joint assets 50–50, but other factors can be taken into account, such as which parent will have to care for any children. The process can be dragged through the courts or, ideally, resolved amicably between you, which saves oodles of money in legal fees.

- Above all, communicate, communicate, communicate!

Chapter 13 – Family Matters

- There are no two ways about it: having kids costs money. Just how much you spend on them is up to you, but you still need to start saving as soon, and as much, as possible.

- The usual principles still apply as well – you should look for bargains and good second-hand items for your children just as you would for yourself.

- Assuming one of the parents doesn't stay at home all the time to wipe noses and change nappies, childcare will be a big expense. There are, however, a range of more and less expensive options out there, and you may be able to get vouchers from your employer to make it a little bit more affordable.

- Think of the worst-case scenario – life insurance and a will are essential once you have a family to provide for.

- There are, thankfully, a range of benefits available for people with children. You should be eligible for at least some of maternity/paternity pay, tax credits and child benefit. Find out from the government, and get claiming.

- Get investing for your kiddies ASAP – even a little money will have a lot of time to grow. New babies get money from the Child Trust Fund, which kicks off with some free money from the government. You can top this up with extra cash, or look at other investments available.

- There's no point just flinging money at your children if you don't teach them the value of money, and how to save it. There's no shame in letting them know you're not made of money – it will give them a healthier attitude to the paper stuff in the long term.

Chapter 14 – Taxation

- Don't pay any more tax than you need to: billions of pounds are wasted every year in this country through people paying too much tax.

- 'A fine is a tax for doing wrong. A tax is a fine for doing well.' As well as income tax and National Insurance, there's capital gains tax and inheritance tax to think about.

- There are, however, lots of ways to minimise the amount of tax you have to pay, including maximising your and your partner's tax-free allowances and making the most of tax-free savings incentives such as ISAs.

- Luckily, there's lots of tax advice available from the relevant government departments and websites. And, if your tax situation is complicated, hiring an accountant could save you money in the long term.

- Tax returns are very boring, but very necessary. Not filling in yours on time could cost you in overpaid tax and fines and penalties.

Chapter 15 – Finances for the Mature Type – That'll Be You, Then

- Ideally, you will have started saving and investing for your retirement as early as possible. But, even if you're nearing retirement age, it's not too late to start – there are still ways to get some money together for your treasure years.

- If you do have plenty of cash stocked away, consider income drawdown or phased retirement to delay buying an annuity and allow your investments to keep growing for longer.

- A few factors affect the size of your annuity, including how old you are and what kind of shape you're in. However, whatever your circumstances, it's important to shop around in order to get the best deal.

- You can consider equity release if you're asset-rich and cash-poor (that is, you own most or all of your house, but have little money on which to live). However, this is rarely as good as it sounds – seek independent advice before doing anything rash.

- You may be eligible for government help in the form of pension credits if your income is particularly low.

- An increasing number of people are retiring abroad – usually to warmer and cheaper countries. However, about a fifth of these live to regret it, perhaps because of homesickness or because things don't turn out the way they'd hoped.

- If you are going to go abroad, research UK and foreign taxes, residency rules, the property markets, healthcare and your entitlement to your pension thoroughly before taking the plunge. These things are pretty complicated and confusing, and vary according to where you're looking to go.

- Planning your long-term care and even paying for your funeral in advance may sound morbid, but it makes financial sense and will be a weight off the mind of those around you.

- You're expected to pay for your own long-term care if you

have savings above a certain amount. There are other ways of paying for your care and safeguarding your estate, such as through an insurance policy or annuity. This is something you need to organise before you become seriously ill.

Chapter 16 – Ethical Money

- Ethical living makes financial sense. Consuming is bad for the Earth's resources – and for your pocket.

- Running a car is bad for the environment and expensive. Look at cheaper, and greener, transport alternatives.

- Cut down your household bills by making your home as energy-efficient as possible.

- Putting your money into ethical investments often makes sound financial sense, as well as making you feel good about how your cash is being used.

- Help charities get the most out of your donations through schemes such as Gift Aid.

- Don't splurge on things you don't need – put your Christmas money to a good cause by sponsoring a charitable gift scheme.

Chapter 17 – Think Rich

- To be rich, you have to think rich.

- But this doesn't just mean thinking in terms of money. It's more about keeping yourself open to life's possibilities.

- Consciously say 'yes' to life rather than 'no' all the time. Hang around with positive, upbeat people – you may find it's infectious.

- There's no reason why you can't have more money: there isn't a finite amount of money in the world any more than there is a finite amount of good or a finite amount of ideas.

- Appreciate all the things that make your life richer, no matter how much or how little they cost. Some of the best things – such as the love of your children – really are free.

- Try not to compare yourself with others. The unspoken need to keep up with the Joneses takes away our happiness, peace and, usually, money.

- Keep your feet on the ground and don't imagine that just 'thinking' it will create it. You've got to do some actual work, along with the positive frame of mind, to bring the good.

19

Glossary

'Accept no one's definition of your life; define yourself.'

– Harvey Fierstein

Accountant: Professional number cruncher. Traditionally much maligned for having about as much charisma as a dial tone, but, come tax-return time, they can be your best friend, taking the headache out of your financial form filling and saving you serious amounts of money.

Additional voluntary contribution (AVCs): Extra payments you can choose to make into your pension, on top of what your employer asks you to pay.

Annual equivalent rate: The amount of interest your money will earn in a savings account if you leave it alone for a year.

Annual percentage rate: A common way of expressing how much borrowing money will cost. It's the amount of interest you will be paying, over a year, on a sum you have borrowed.

Annuity: An income you're paid after you retire, until you die. You buy the annuity from a company, which then agrees to give you a fixed sum every year. Worth putting off pushing up the daisies for as long as possible or you'll lose out.

Bankruptcy: A way of dealing with debts you can't pay. Usually to be avoided. You can voluntarily declare yourself bankrupt, or you can be forced to by a creditor to whom you owe more than £750. You're then bankrupt for a certain amount of time (normally a couple of years, though this can vary), during which you lose control of your assets and are stopped from doing lots of things such as getting much credit or acting as a company director.

Bond: Nothing to do with James. More like an IOU: lenders hand over their money to a business or the government and expect to get it back, plus interest, in the future. There are many different kinds of bond – they may be short term or long term and interest may be paid at a fixed or variable rate.

Broker: Quite often if you use one of the posh ones with expensive offices, you are. Broker, that is! A broker is basically a middleman who brings together two parties for a financial transaction – by selling customers insurance policies or shares, for instance.

Capital: A load of money! Or the value of your assets.

Capital gain: The profit you make when you sell an asset – for example, the proceeds you get from selling shares, minus the cost of the shares. You have to pay capital gains tax on this profit if it goes above a certain threshold.

Compound interest: *See also* Interest. Compound interest is a bigger version, since it is calculated both on the sum, and on the interest that has accrued on the sum in previous periods. Basically a get-rich-slow scheme.

Defined-benefit scheme: An occupational pension scheme with no surprises. Rules specify what you'll get when you retire, which will depend on, for instance, what your salary is and how many years you've worked there.

Defined-contribution scheme: An occupational pension scheme with surprises. Your contributions are fixed, but the amount of pension you finally receive will depend on things such as the size of the fund that you've built up.

Dividend: Money that companies give out to shareholders. British companies usually fork out a couple of dividends a year, one larger and one smaller. You usually get an amount for each share; the company can decide how much cash to share out and how much to keep in the business.

Dividend yield: The dividend expressed as a percentage of the share value.

Endowment: A combination of life-insurance policy and investment – you or your dependants are guaranteed a payout either on your death or on a fixed date, whichever is sooner. Generally expensive and poorly performing and a better money maker for the person who sold it to you than for you.

Equity: A word for a plain old share in a company. Can also mean the proportion of your house that you own (the value of the property minus any mortgage you still have to pay on it).

Exchange-traded funds (ETFs): A relatively new kind of investment fund that can be bought through most stockbrokers. They are similar to tracker funds, because, effectively, they track the stock market. A cheap way to get into the stock market, since admin charges tend to be very low.

Final-salary scheme: A rather nice little pension scheme, where you get an annual payout of a percentage of whatever your salary was when you retired. Expensive for employers to run, and consequently disappearing fast.

Financial Services Authority (FSA): Not to be confused with the similarly abbreviated Food Standards Agency. This one is the independent, non-governmental body that regulates the finance industry, including mortgages.

Friendly society: The place to go when you're feeling lonely? No, not really. A friendly society is a non-profit-making, mutual organisation whose funds (after running costs are deducted) are owned by its policyholders. They've been kicking around for hundreds of years – the idea is to give members life assurance and help them out during times of illness or unemployment. Now that's what friends are for. However, as a place to put your money, they lag behind various other organisations, because their charges tend to be high and performance low.

Front-end loading: Nothing to do with washing machines, or any kind of domestic appliance for that matter. A front-end load is the initial admin and/or commission charge made when you invest in a unit trust, life-assurance company, or any other kind of investment fund.

FTSE All-share Index: Includes around 700 of the top companies in the country.

FTSE 100 Index: (pronounced Footsie): A share index of the 100 biggest companies listed on the London Stock Exchange (LSE). The FTSE 250 tracks the big firms ranked at 101 to 350.

Gilts: A bond (see above) where you lend money to the government, rather than to a company. Should be a low-risk investment – governments rarely go bust.

HM Revenue and Customs: Quite possibly the most exciting government department in the world. It has responsibility for all sorts of taxes, VAT, customs and excise, National Insurance, tax credits, child benefit and child trust funds, among other things. Find out more at **www.hmrc.gov.uk**.

Independent financial adviser (IFA): Someone with a posh Merc and a second home in Marbella. IFAs are licensed to advise you on financial products offered by a range of different companies. Some earn commission for selling particular products, which might lead you to question just how independent they really are.

Index tracker: An index is, quite simply, a way of measuring how well a stock market is performing by comparing the performance of shares in a group of different companies. A tracker fund is basically a baby microcosm of the index – shares in the same companies and in the same proportions they are found in the index. The idea is that the tracker will emulate the performance of the index, and hopefully get bigger as the market goes up.

Individual savings account (ISA): A way of saving money without having to pay tax on it. You can pop up to £3,000 in cash or up to £7,000 in shares into ISAs each year.

Inflation: The tendency of prices to rise over time. This means the value of your money can drop if you don't keep up – by investing, for instance.

Inland Revenue: *See* HM Revenue and Customs.

Investment club: A group of individuals who have got together to invest their cash collectively. This way they can invest in a range of different stuff, making it a bit less risky than going it alone.

Investment trust: It's up to you whether or not you trust them. A company that invests its shareholders' funds in the shares of other companies. This might sound a bit Kafkaesque, but it means people without a lot of money can invest in a wide range of companies without incurring massive trading fees.

Life assurance: The stuff of a million murder-mystery motives, this started off as a way to cover your funeral expenses, but these days can be a way of getting some tax breaks on your savings. A type of policy where you pay a premium in order to get a lump sum paid out in the event of your death.

Life insurance: The term is often used interchangeably with life assurance, although, technically, insurance protects holders from events that might happen.

Mutual society: A mutual is a company that has no issued stocks or shares. Instead, it is owned by its investors.

Negative equity: A nasty little thing that can happen when house prices crash. If the value of your house falls below the value of your mortgage, you are said to have negative equity.

Occupational pension scheme: A pension scheme for employees of a particular company, or possibly a trade.

Open-ended investment company (OEIC): A US idea that came over to the UK in 1997. A bit of a hybrid between a unit trust and an investment trust, OEICs sell shares in themselves, then use that cash to invest in other companies. They usually operate as umbrella funds, often having a few different, smaller funds. They're known as open-ended because, if demand for their shares rises, they simply issue more. Unlike in a unit trust, OEICs tend to have just one share price, whether you're buying or selling.

Personal pension plan (PPP): A pension scheme for those without occupational pensions – for instance, the self-employed and people whose employers don't have a group pension scheme. An employer can contribute to your PPP, but there's nothing to say they have to. You can take a PPP with you when you change jobs. PPP contributions get tax relief, and you can buy life assurance, which may also be eligible for tax relief. Apart from stakeholder pensions, though, PPPs tend to be expensive, opaque and badly performing.

Self-invested personal pension (SIPP): A kind of DIY personal pension for people who know a bit about the stock market themselves. Rather than let an insurance company decide where to invest your cash, you can choose what to invest in – including shares. Fees and charges for a SIPP usually work out at about 2 per cent a year, though (they're capped at 1 per cent in a stakeholder pension), so they're best reserved for those with lots of money to invest.

Share: If you buy a share, then you own a part of a company. Usually, of course, you'd buy lots of shares in the hope that they'll go up and up in value – one on its own is unlikely to be much of an investment. Roughly speaking, a company's share price is determined by market forces: if a lot of people want to buy shares, their value will go up; if a lot of people want to sell shares, their value will fall. So, in theory, there's a lot of money to be made, but it's always a risk, and, if a company goes bust, shareholders are last in line to get any of the cash.

Shareholder: As the name suggests, anyone who holds shares in a company. Shareholders are also entitled, among other things, to receive the company's accounts and vote at its annual general meeting. Most companies pay regular dividends to their shareholders.

Stakeholder pension: A fairly new type of low-cost, flexible pension. Even if you're not earning you can pay in a limited amount each year, and get tax relief on this. Anyone in a company pension scheme earning less than a certain amount a year (set by the HMRC) can pay into a stakeholder pension as well, and employers with five or more employees must give them access to a stakeholder scheme if the company doesn't have any other kind of pension fund set up.

Stamp duty: Another way the government punishes us for doing well. It's a fixed tax you pay when you buy shares (0.5 per cent) or property (1 per cent to 4 per cent, depending on the value of the property).

Stock: The basis of many a good soup. What Americans call shares. And, in the UK, a fixed-interest financial asset such as a government bond. There is usually a redemption date and, in the meantime, they are traded on stock exchanges.

Stock exchange: A market on which securities are traded, such as the London Stock Exchange. The other big ones are in Tokyo and New York.

Stockbroker: An agent who does the trading on the stock exchange – usually far from broke.

Tax: Money you have to pay to the government. There are many different kinds: income tax, for example, comes out of your pay packet and VAT is charged on many goods that you buy.

Tax credit: A well-intentioned but rather bureaucratic system of extra tax-free allowances. A tax credit is an amount taken off the tax bill of certain groups of people, such as some couples with children under 16, so the lucky souls don't have to pay as much.

Tax relief: A system whereby someone doesn't have to pay tax on part of their income. Always worth snapping up, if you qualify.

Yield: The annual income you get from an investment, expressed as a percentage of the value of that investment. The interest rate on a savings account, for example or the value of dividends from any shares you own.

Help and Information

Here, you will find websites, phone numbers, books and so on, which you can use for a wealth of information, advice and help in the various financial areas.

Useful official information:
Department for Work and Pensions – **www.dwp.gov.uk**
Directgov – **www.direct.gov.uk**
HM Revenue and Customs – **www.hmrc.gov.uk**
IFA Association – **www.unbiased.co.uk** (for local financial advisers and lots of tax-saving ideas)
Inland Revenue – **www.inlandrevenue.gov.uk**

Books:
A Girl's Best Friend Is Her Money – Jasmine Birtles and Jane Mack (Boxtree, £12.99)
Extraordinary Popular Delusions and the Madness of Crowds – Charles Mackay (Harriman House, £11)
The Money Diet – Martin Lewis (Vermilion, £7.99)
Winning the Loser's Game – Charles Ellis (McGraw-Hill, £16.99)
Your Money or Your Life – Alvin Hall (Coronet, £6.99)

Cheaper everything:
www.fool.co.uk
www.moneyextra.co.uk
www.moneysavingexpert.com
www.moneysupermarket.com
www.onecompare.com
www.switchwithwhich.co.uk

Cheaper mortgages:
www.charcolonline.co.uk
www.easyquote.co.uk
www.moneyfacts.co.uk
www.moneynet.co.uk
www.moneysupermarket.com

Cheaper insurance:
www.find.co.uk
www.insuresupermarket.com
www.kwik-fit.co.uk
www.moneyfacts.co.uk
www.the-aa.com

Cheaper utilities:
www.buy.com
www.moneysavingexpert.com
www.uswitch.com

Cheaper phone and Internet:
www.adslguide.org.uk
www.broadbandchecker.co.uk
www.moneysavingexpert.com
www.switchwithwhich.co.uk

Shopping around:

To switch your gas, electricity, phone, mobile phone, Internet package, insurances and bank accounts, look at websites such as:

www.buy.com

www.find.com

www.fool.co.uk

www.insuresupermarket.com

www.moneyextra.co.uk

www.moneysupermarket.com

www.switchwithwhich.com

www.uswitch.com

For getting the best prices, see comparison sites such as:

www.123pricecheck.co.uk

www.checkaprice.com

www.froogle.co.uk (part of Google)

www.kelkoo.co.uk

www.pricerunner.co.uk

http://uk.shopping.com (part of eBay)

And you can find product reviews at:

www.reviewcentre.com

General good advice

BBC website – **www.bbc.co.uk/money**

Economy.com – **www.economy.com**

Financial Services Authority budget planner – look it up at **www.fsa.gov.uk**

Financial Times – **www.ft.com**

Guardian – **www.guardian.co.uk**

Independent – **www.independent.co.uk**

Moneyfacts – **www.moneyfacts.co.uk**

Moneysavingexpert – **www.moneysavingexpert.com**

Motley Fool – **www.fool.co.uk**

Personal Finance Education Group – **www.pfeg.org**
Telegraph – **www.telegraph.co.uk**
Mail – **www.thisismoney.com**

Keeping your spending down

Cars

www.autotrader.co.uk
www.dixonmotors.co.uk
www.drivethedeal.com
www.jamjar.com

Travel and holidays

www.cheapflights.co.uk
www.ebookers.com
www.expedia.com
www.lastminute.com
www.opodo.com
www.teletextholidays.com
www.travelocity.com

Get cheaper holidays through a house swap:
www.digsville.com
www.echangeimmo.com
www.holswop.com
www.homeexchange.com

Or do it by being an air courier:
www.aircourier.co.uk
www.azfreight.com
www.courier.org

Books, CDs and DVDs

Books:
www.abebooks.co.uk and www.bookbutler.co.uk
www.amazon.co.uk
www.bookbrain.co.uk
CDs and DVDs:
www.cdwow.com
www.dvdbrain.co.uk
www.dvdpricecheck.co.uk
www.find-dvd.co.uk
www.play.com

Shopping villages and outlet stores

www.shoppingvillages.com

Clothes

www.bbclothing.co.uk
www.designerdiscount.co.uk
www.designersalesdirect.com
www.swerve.co.uk

Cashback

www.bighair.co.uk
www.greasypalm.co.uk
www.mutualpoints.com
www.rpoints.com

Groceries

www.tesco.com
www.sainsbury.co.uk
www.ocado.com

Fraud, scams and consumer rights

For information on online scams:
www.crimes-of-persuasion.com
www.scambusters.org

Callcredit – **www.mycallcredit.com**
Equifax – **www.equifax.co.uk**
Experian – **www.experian.co.uk**
Office of Fair Trading – **www.oft.gov.uk**
Serious Fraud Office – **www.sfo.gov.uk**
UK's Fraud Identity Service (CIFAS) – **www.cifas.org.uk**

Stand up for your consumer rights:
www.complaindomain.com
www.financevictims.co.uk
www.fsa.gov.uk
www.getmethemanager.co.uk
www.howtocomplain.com
www.tradingstandards.gov.uk
www.bankchargeshell.com

Be aware of how shops manipulate you:
Influence – Science and Practice – Robert B Cialdini (Allyn and Bacon, $21.99)
Advertising Standards Authority, **www.asa.org.uk**

Avoid junk mail and annoying telesales calls:
Emails: **www.dmaconsumers.org**
Faxes **.fpsonline.co.uk**
Post: **www.mpsonline.org.uk**, 0845 703 4599
Phone: **www.tpsonline.org.uk**, 0845 070 0707

Tax

Association of Chartered Certified Accountants – **www.acca.org.uk**
Association of Taxation Technicians – **www.att.org.uk**
Chartered Institute of Taxation – **www.tax.org.uk**
HM Revenue and Customs – **www.hmrc.gov.uk**
Inland Revenue Self Assessment Helpline: 0845 900444
Low Incomes Tax Reform Group – **www.litrg.org.uk**
Tax Aid – **www.taxaid.org.uk**
Tax credit helpline – **www.hmrc.gov.uktaxcredits**, 0845 300 3900
Tax credits – **www.entitledto.co.uk**
www.janevass.net/tax (author of *The Daily Mail Tax Guide*)

The Daily Mail Tax Guide – Jane Vass (Profile, £9.99)
The Daily Telegraph Tax Guide – David B Genders (Pan, £9.99)

Saving and investing

National Savings and Investments – **www.nsandi.com**

Banks:
British Bankers Association – **www.bankfacts.org.uk**
Building Societies Association – **www.bsa.org.uk**

Find extra money:
Unclaimed Assets Register (UAR) – **www.uar.co.uk**
Lottery ticket checker: **www.national-lottery.co.uk/player/p/results/winCheck/winChecker-Start.do**

Investing:
Investopedia.com – **www.investopedia.com**
Global Investor – **www.global-investor.com**

Association of Friendly Societies – www.afs.org.uk
Venture Capital Trusts – www.trustnet.com/vct

Tracker funds:
Legal and General – www.landg.com, 0800 0920092
M&G – www.mandg.com, 0800 390390
Scottish Widows – www.scottishwidows.com, 08457 678910
Virgin – www.virginmoney.com, 08456 101020
Fidelity – www.fidelity.co.uk, 0800 414161
Gartmore – www.gartmore.co.uk, 0800 289336

Managed funds:
There are hundreds to choose from but you can start with:
Association of Investment Trust Companies – www.aitc.co.uk
IFA Association – www.unbiased.co.uk
Investment Management Association – www.investment
uk.org
www.find.co.uk

Common Stocks and Uncommon Profits – Philip Fisher (Wiley)
The Intelligent Investor – Benjamin Graham (Harper Business,
£12.99)
The Motley Fool UK Investment Handbook – David Berger and
James Carlisle (Boxtree, £12.99)

Collecting

BBC Antiques – www.bbc.co.uk/antiques
Bonhams – www.bonhams.com
Christies – www.christies.com
Random paraphernalia – www.ebay.co.uk
Sotheby's – www.sothebys.com

Antiques Magazine – www.antiquesmagazine.com
Superhobby Investing – Peter Temple (Harriman House, £14.99)

Earning extra money

Be a B&B: British Tourist Authority, **www.visitbritain.com**, 020 8846 9000

Be an extra: *Contacts* (£10.99, Spotlight Publications); Casting Collective – **www.castingcollective.co.uk**, 020 8962 0099

Clinical trials: Biotrax – **www.biotrax.co.uk**, 0161 736 7312

Hot Recruit: **www.hotrecruit.com**

House sitting: **www.safehandssitters.co.uk**

Market research: Saros Research – **www.sarosresearch.com**

Cosmetic research: **www.cosmeticresearchonline.co.uk**

Mystery shopping: Retaileyes – **www.retaileyes.co.uk**; TNS – **www.tns-global.co.uk**; IMS – **www.ukims.co.uk**; Cinecheck – **www.cinecheck.com**, 0800 5870520; Field Facts Worldwide – **www.fieldfacts.com**, 020 7908 6600

Sell your hair: Wigsuk.com – (also known as Banbury Postiche) **www.wigsuk.com**, 01295 750606

Win stuff! **www.competitions.com**

A Bit on the Side: 500 Ways to Boost Your Income – Jasmine Birtles (Piatkus, £7.99)

Setting up your own business

Business Link – **www.businesslink.gov.uk**

Small Business Service – **www.sbs.gov.uk**

Federation of Small Businesses – **www.fsb.org.uk**

Small business advice – **www.smallbusinessadvice.org.uk**

www.success4business.com

www.businessbricks.co.uk

www.entrepreneur.com/business-plan

www.startups.co.uk

Accounting software: Quickbooks – **www.quickbooks.com**; Sage – **www.sage.co.uk**; **www.accounting-software.qck.com**

The Which? Guide to Starting Your Own Business (Which Guides, £10.99)

Working for Yourself – Godfrey Golzen and Jonathan Reuvid (Kogan Page, £12.99) – a bestselling guide for people going it alone

Insurance

Car insurance: try insurance broking sites such as **www.the-aa.com**, **www.kwik-fit.com**, **www.confused.com** and **www.insuresupermarket.com**.

Buildings and contents insurance: have a look at **www.find.co.uk** for all kinds of insurance companies; also brokers such as **www.kwik-fit.com**, **www.insuresupermarket.com**
Life assurance: critical-illness cover and so forth: **www.lifesearch.com**
Students: **www.endsleigh.co.uk**

Students

For students in England:
Department for Education and Skills – **www.dfes.gov.uk**
Student Loans Company – **www.slc.co.uk**
Student Finance Direct – **www.studentfinancedirect.co.uk**
Aim Higher – **www.aimhigher.gov.uk**

For students in Wales:
Education and Learning Wales – **www.elwa.org.uk**
Student Finance Wales – **www.studentfinancewales.co.uk**

For students in Scotland:
Student Awards Agency for Scotland – **www.student-support-saas.gov.uk**

For students in Northern Ireland:
Department for Employment and Learning Northern Ireland: **www.delni.gov.uk**

NUS in Ireland: **www.nistudents.org**

Course information – **www.hotcourses.com**
Directory of Social Change – **www.dsc.org.uk**
Education Guardian – **www.educationguardian.co.uk**
Educational Grants Advisory Service – **www.egas-online.org**
Funding advice – **www.support4learning.org.uk**
Higher Education Funding Agency for England –
www.hefce.ac.uk
Higher Education Statistics Agency – **www.hesa.ac.uk**
Mature Students Union: **www.msu.org.uk**
National Bureau for Students with disabilities:
www.skill.org.uk
National Union of Students – **www.nusonline.co.uk**
Office for Fair Access – **www.offa.org.uk**
Prospects – **www.prospects.ac.uk**
Push – **www.push.co.uk**
Research Councils UK – **www.rcuk.ac.uk**
Scholarship Search – **www.scholarship-search.org.uk**
Student 123 – **www.student123.com**
Student money – **www.studentmoney.org**
Student Money Net – **www.studentmoneynet.co.uk**
Student UK – **www.studentuk.com**
Study placements abroad – **www.erasmus.ac.uk**
Teacher training – **www.tda.gov.uk**
Times Higher Education Supplement – **www.thes.co.uk**
Universities and Colleges Admissions Service – **www.ucas.com**
Universities UK – **www.universitiesuk.ac.uk**

The Grants Register (£165, Palgrave Macmillan – look at it in the library!)

Borrowing and debt

Credit ratings: Experian – 0870 241 6212,
www.uk.experian.com
Equifax – 0870 010 2091, **www.equifax.co.uk**

Credit unions: Association of British Credit Unions Limited – **www.abcul.org**
Credit Unions Online – **www.creditunionsonline.com**
Zopa – **www.zopa.com**

Work and careers

More than Work – **www.morethanwork.net**
National Association of Student Employment Staff – **www.nases.org.uk**
Shell Technology Enterprise programme – **www.step.org.uk**
Student jobs – **www.justjobs4students.co.uk**
Summer jobs – **www.summerjobs.co.uk**
The TUC's workSMART – **www.worksmart.org.uk**
Work experience – **www.work-experience.org**

Mortgage and house buying

First Rung Now: **www.firstrungnow.com**
Magazines: *What House, What Mortgage, Mortgage Advisor, Your Mortgage, BBC Good Homes*

Auctions:
www.propertyauctionnews.co.uk
www.propertyauctions.com
www.ukauctionlist.com
www.eigroup.com

Council for Licensed Conveyancers – **www.theclc.gov.uk**
Royal Institution of Chartered Surveyors – **www.rics.org.uk**
Solicitors: **www.lawsociety.org.uk**

Housing co-ops: **www.housingcorp.gov.uk**, 020 7292 4400
Housing for key workers: **www.housing.dtlr.gov.uk**, **http://society.guardian.co.uk/keyworkers**

Build your own:

www.channel4.com/homes
www.ebuild.co.uk
www.homebuilding.co.uk
www.selfbuild.co.uk

Finding property:
www.findaproperty.com
www.gumtree.com
www.hotproperty.co.uk
www.loot.com
www.propertytoday.co.uk

For a free guide, 'How to Buy a Home' or 'How to Buy a Home in Scotland', phone the Council of Mortgage Lenders on 020 7437 0075 or 020 7434 3791 or go to **www.cml.org.uk**
Land registry: **www.landreg.gov.uk**

Mortgages:
www.charcolonline.co.uk
www.fool.co.uk
www.moneyextra.co.uk
www.moneyfacts.co.uk
www.moneysupermarket.com

Buy-to-let:
Association of Residential Letting Agents (ARLA) –
www.arla.co.uk, 0845 3455752

Renting Out Your Property for Dummies – Melanie Bien (Wiley, £14.99)

Buying abroad:
Advice on moving abroad: **www.direct.gov.uk/ BritonsLivingAbroad/fs/en**
Federation of Overseas Developers, Agents and Consultants – **www.fopdac.com**
Buying Property Abroad, Liz Hodgkinson (Kogan Page, £12.99)

Pensions

Age Concern – **www.ageconcern.org.uk**
Age Positive – **www.agepositive.gov.uk**
Association of British Insurers – **www.abi.org.uk**
Department of Work and Pensions – **www.dwp.gov.uk**
Direct Gov – **www.direct.gov.uk**
Government Actuary's Department – **www.gad.gov.uk**
Hargreaves Lansdowne – **www.hargreaveslansdown.co.uk**
Help the Aged – **www.helptheaged.org.uk**
Occupational Pensions Regulatory Authority (OPRA) –
www.opra.org
Pensions Protection Fund –
(www.pensionsprotectionfund.org.uk)
Pensions Service – **www.thepensionservice.gov.uk**
Stakeholder pensions – **www.stakeholderpensions.gov.uk**
Treasury – **www.hm-treasury.gov.uk**

Equity release – **www.cml.org.uk/servlet/dycon/zt-
cml/cml/live/en/cml/pdf_pub_misc_Equityrelease.pdf**
Safe Home Income Plans (SHIP) – **www.ship-ltd.org**

Retiring abroad:
Pensions abroad: International Pensions Centre, Tyneview
Park, Newcastle upon Tyne, NE98 1BA, 0191 218 7777, or
medical benefits unit: 0191 218 7547, or **www.directgov.uk**

To find lost pensions:
AMP Pension Find Service, 0800 068 5456
Pension Schemes Registry, 0191 225 6393
Unclaimed Assets Register – **www.unclaimedassets.com**,
0870 241 1713

Couples

Tying the knot: **www.confetti.co.uk**
National Trust (properties available for weddings):
www.nationaltrust.org.uk, 0870 609 5380

If it all goes wrong:

Child Support Agency – **www.csa.gov.uk**, 0845 7133133

Children and Family Court Advisory Service – **www.cafcass.gov.uk**

Equal Parenting Council – **www.equalparenting.org**

Families Need Fathers – **www.fnf.org.uk**

Family Mediation Scotland – **www.familymediationscotland.org.uk**

Family Mediators' Association – 0117 946 7062

Gingerbread – **www.gingerbread.org.uk**, advice line – 0800 018 4318

National Council for One-Parent Families – **www.oneparent-families.org.uk**, advice line – 0800 018 5026

National Family Mediation – **www.nfm.u-net.com**

Relate – **www.relate.org.uk**

Solicitors Family Law Association – **www.sfla.org.uk**

www.divorce.co.uk

www.divorce-resource.org

www.lone-parents.org.uk

www.single-living.com

www.singleparents.org.uk

www.soyouvebeendumped.com

Gay finance:

Gay Business Association – **www.gba.org.uk**

Official information on civil partnerships – **www.womenand-equalityunit.gov.uk/civilpartnership.htm**

www.fresh-finance.co.uk

www.gayfinance.info

www.gaytimes.co.uk

www.pinkfinance.com

www.pinkmortgage.co.uk

Solicitors and legal stuff:

www.lawsociety.org.uk, **www.lawsoc-ni.org** (the Law Society of Northern Ireland)

www.solicitors-online.com
www.lawscot.org.uk

Families

Parenting advice:
Babycentre – **www.babycentre.co.uk**
Babyworld – **www.babyworld.co.uk**
BBC Parenting – **www.bbc.co.uk/parenting**
Better Homes and Gardens – **www.bhg.com**
Families Online – **www.familiesonline.co.uk**
Handbag.com – **www.handbag.com**
iCircle – **www.icircle.co.uk**
iVillage – **www.ivillage.co.uk**
Mumsnet – **www.mumsnet.com**
Parents Centre – **www.parentscentre.gov.uk**
Parents.com – **www.parents.com**
Raising Kids – **www.raisingkids.co.uk**
Thinkbaby – **www.thinkbaby.co.uk**
UK Parents – **www.ukparents.co.uk**

Mr Thrifty – Jane Furnival (Michael O'Mara, £4.99)
Miserly Moms – Jonni McCoy (Bethany House, $12.99)

Childcare:
National Childminders Association – **www.ncma.org.uk**
National Daycare Trust –
www.daycaretrust.org.uk,www.ndna.org.uk,
www.everychildmatters.gov.uk,www.bbc.co.uk/
parenting/childcare
www.nannytax.co.uk
www.childcarevouchers.co.uk

The Good Nanny Guide – Charlotte Breese and Hilaire Gomer
(Vermilion, £14.99)

Ethical money

Transport:
British Association for Bio Fuels and Oils –
www.biodiesel.co.uk
Car sharing – **www.carclubs.org.uk; www.liftshare.com;
www.nationalcarshare.co.uk**
Electric Vehicles – **www.plugitin.co.uk**
Electric Vehicles UK – **www.evuk.co.uk**
LP Gas Association – **www.lpga.co.uk**
Transport Energy (part of the Energy Saving Trust) –
www.transportenergy.org.uk
UK National Cyclists' Association – **www.ctc.org.uk**, 0870
873 0060

Holidays:
Association of Independent Tour Operators – **www.aito.co.uk**
ATG Oxford – **www.atg-oxford.co.uk**
Ethical Traveller – **www.ethicaltraveller.com**
Green Globe 21 – **www.greenglobe21.com**
Green Hotels Association – **www.greenhotels.com**
The Man in Seat Sixty-One – **www.seat61.com**
Responsible Travel – **www.responsibletravel.com**
Tourism Concern – **www.tourismconcern.org.uk**
Willing Workers on Organic Farms – **www.wwoof.org**

Retiring abroad

Pensions abroad: International Pensions Centre, Tyneview
Park, Newcastle upon Tyne, NE98 1BA, 0191 218 7777, or
medical benefits unit: 0191 218 7547, or **www.directgov.uk**.

Tax abroad: Inland Revenue, International Branch, Benton
Park View, Newcastle upon Tyne NE98 1BA. Tel: 0845
9154811; abroad +00 44(0) 191 225 4811,
www.hmrc.gov.uk/international/index.htm

UK income tax while abroad: Inland Revenue, Centre for Non-Residents, St John's House, Merton Road, Bootle, Merseyside, L69 9BB, UK: 0845 0700040; abroad: +00 44(0) 151 210 2222

Expat Investor: **www.expatinvestor.com**
Foreign and Commonwealth Office, King Charles St, London, SW1A 2AH, **www.fco.gov.uk**; general enquiries: 020 7270 1500; service for Britons overseas: 020 7008 0117
Government advice: **www.direct.gov.uk/Britons LivingAbroad/fs/en**
Retirement matters: **www.retirement-matters.co.uk/gparchive/livingabroad.htm**
See **www.ageconcern.org.uk** for Age Concern's 'Retiring Abroad' help sheet

The Daily Telegraph Guide to Living Abroad – Michael Furnell and Philip Jones (Kogan Page, £9.99).
The Good Non Retirement Guide – Rosemary Brown (Enterprise Dynamics, £15.99)

Long-term care

Care Funding Bureau – **www.carefundingbureau.co.uk**
Pensions Annuity Friendly Society – **www.friendlysocieties.co.uk/pensionannuity**
Sharing Pensions – **www.sharingpensions.co.uk**

Wills

DIY versions:
www.lawpack.co.uk
www.tenminutewill.co.uk

Find a qualified will writer: **www.searchwill.co.uk**
Society of Trust and Estate Practitioners (STEP) – **www.step.org**, 020 7838 48850

Wills, Probate and Inheritance Tax for Dummies – Julian Knight
(Wiley, £12.99)

Funerals

If I Should Die: **www.ifishoulddie.co.uk**
Heavens Above Fireworks:
www.heavensabovefireworks.com
Humanist funerals: **www.humanism.org.uk**
The Natural Death Centre: **www.naturaldeath.org.uk**

Index